THE HOME UNIVERSITY LIBRARY
OF MODERN KNOWLEDGE

243

ETHICS SINCE 1900

EDITOR OF

The Home University Library
of Modern Knowledge

SIR GEORGE CLARK, D.LITT., F.B.A.

Ethics Since 1900

MARY WARNOCK

LONDON
OXFORD UNIVERSITY PRESS
NEW YORK   TORONTO
1960

Oxford University Press, Amen House, London E.C.4

GLASGOW NEW YORK TORONTO MELBOURNE WELLINGTON
BOMBAY CALCUTTA MADRAS KARACHI KUALA LUMPUR
CAPE TOWN IBADAN NAIROBI ACCRA

© Oxford University Press 1960

Printed in Great Britain by
Butler & Tanner Ltd., Frome and London

PREFACE

In a book of this kind the accident of where and when the author was educated is bound to make a difference, both to the selection and the treatment of the material. I am aware of numbers of omissions; and doubtless prejudice appears on every page. I have not been able to discuss all the philosophers who have contributed towards the different kinds of moral philosophy current in the last sixty years. Some of the omissions are made good in the bibliography, but this is, I realize, no substitute for a full treatment of their arguments.

It may be thought that in some cases too long has been spent on the details of a rather trivial argument, at the expense of a wider view of the whole subject. My defence would be that in a subject such as Ethics, the details of the arguments are all-important. Conclusions are valueless and positively misleading without some at least of the reasoning which led up to them being set out.

I have not, I hope, had any preconceived idea of what Ethics is. I have discussed what seem to me the most important contributions to philosophy which have been made roughly under that heading; there could, of course, be very different selections. I have purposely left out all political philosophy, although aware that it is sometimes very closely connected with ethics.

Finally, it hardly needs saying that no problems are settled in this book; but I should like to think that perhaps some questions, though they are not raised for the first time, are at least re-opened. It is agreeable to reflect that there is a great deal of moral philosophy still to be written.

CONTENTS

Chapter One

METAPHYSICAL ETHICS:
F. H. BRADLEY

AT the beginning of the twentieth century ethics was predominantly metaphysical. The most important writers on moral philosophy explicitly linked their discussions of morals with views about the nature of the universe as a whole, and man's place in the universe. A *system* of ethics was what such philosophers aimed to set out, and this meant a total explanation of the way things are, which contained as part of itself an explanation of the demands and the requirements of ethical behaviour. In thus basing ethics upon metaphysics, English writers, at least, were defending the subject against the blows they thought had been dealt to it by Hume, Bentham, Mill, and the utilitarians. For instance, in 1925 A. E. Taylor, himself a metaphysician, wrote an essay entitled 'The Freedom of Man'.[1] In it he listed the most important of his immediate predecessors in the subject: T. H. Green, the Cairds, Nettleship, William Wallace, Adamson, Bosanquet, Bradley; and he said: 'The chief part of their united work was to continue the age-long war of believers in genuine morality and real obligation against every kind of naturalistic substitute.' Naturalism was supposed to explain away ethics altogether by associating ethical

[1] *Contemporary British Philosophy*, 2nd Series. Edited by J. H. Muirhead. Allen and Unwin, 1925.

concepts such as goodness or duty with non-ethical concepts such as pleasure or utility or the desire that society should be preserved. It was believed that metaphysical ethics could reinstate the subject by demonstrating the necessary uniqueness and irreducibility of these ethical concepts.

Of these metaphysical philosophers by far the most powerful was F. H. Bradley. His *Ethical Studies* was first published in 1876, but his views did not radically alter thereafter. In 1893 he explicitly referred to the book and said that it still, for the most part, represented his views; and in 1924 he started to revise, though not to re-write it. The second edition was published after his death, in 1927. It is fair, therefore, to count this as a book belonging to the twentieth century.

The second essay in *Ethical Studies* is entitled 'Why Should I be Moral?' In this Bradley states in outline his solution to what he thinks are the problems of ethics, the problems, that is, of the nature of the end for man, and of the supreme good. His solution is that the good is self-realization, and that this is the end or the purpose of the moral man's life. At first he seeks to establish this by an appeal to moral consciousness. He takes for granted that there is a certain set of facts with which everyone is acquainted, such as the fact that we often feel ourselves to be under some obligation, or that we often feel that morally we have failed in some way. To these facts, or rather our knowledge of them, he refers as moral consciousness. He raises no question about the scope of morality, or the application of moral concepts. These things are accepted as the data on which the moral philosopher has to work. This unquestioning attitude to the supposed facts of our moral life, and the appeal to such arbiters as 'pleasure', 'duty', 'moral consciousness', all absolutely in general, makes Bradley's writing seem at times fantastically abstract and difficult to connect with any single particular phenomenon. But in this generality also lies its power, since if his account seems explanatory at all, it seems explanatory of every aspect of life.

It is worth considering in a little more detail what he says in this second essay.[1] The question why I should be moral is, he says, illegitimate; for to ask it would suggest that there was some ulterior purpose behind the exercise of virtue, or the performance of duty. 'To take virtue as a mere means to an ulterior end is in direct antagonism to the voice of moral consciousness.' But in spite of this, later, in a footnote, Bradley does himself offer an answer to the question.[2] 'A man is moral because he likes being moral; and he likes it partly because he was brought up to the habit of liking it, and partly because he finds it gives him what he wants while its opposite does not do so.' This last statement looks practically tautological, but it does lead to Bradley's main solution to the problem of what is the end for human life. The most general expression for the end in itself is, he says, *self-realization*. It is to the amplification of this solution that the rest of the book is mainly devoted. His first attempt to prove the truth of the general statement comes in this same essay.[3]

[1] *Ethical Studies*, p. 58.   [2] Footnote to p. 62 *op. cit.*
[3] *op. cit.* p. 65 *sqq.*

Once again he appeals to moral consciousness to 'see what it tells us about its end'. And he asks the ordinary reader to reflect whether we do not all aim not only at the realization of self, but of self as a whole. At first glance, it must be admitted, these words are not particularly lucid or revealing.

It is not clear what is meant by 'realizing' the self, let alone realizing it 'as a whole'. But though it is easy either to be put off by the unclarities, or to stop trying to understand, and simply to drift along with the style as one reads, it is all the same possible to detect in Bradley's theory something which is important and is very often at the back of people's minds when they talk about morality. Bradley thinks of people's wills, as opposed to their chance or random desires, as being directed over a period of time to a way of life, a system of interconnected actions. Everybody makes his own system, in the sense that no one else can exercise his will for him. His actions are necessarily his own and no one else's. Moreover, in the case of acts which would naturally be thought of as the concern of morality, not only is there something to be done, but the whole point, for the agent, is that it should be done *by him* and no one else. Thus a morally good or a morally bad act is a kind of self-assertion or self-expression. It is, in fact, not merely a tautology that a man's acts are his own; for when we judge a man's acts from a moral point of view it is as *his* acts, part of his whole system of actions, that we judge them. Our judgement might have been different if someone else had done the same thing, or brought about the same consequences.

Bradley takes this to be a difference between moral action and acts of artistic production. In producing a work of art someone might believe that there was something which had to be done, a certain aesthetic result to be achieved. In morality an action has to be done, too, but not as a means to a result. The doing of it *by me*, he says, can actually be considered as the end. He does not, in this essay, do more than suggest this contrast between the aesthetic and the moral, and I do not think that it would bear much looking into, at any rate as a criterion for distinguishing them. But it does throw light, perhaps, on the kind of thing that is meant by self-realization. Furthermore it serves to direct our attention to what was for Bradley the most important feature of morality . . . its essential dynamism. The moral world is a world of active agents, choosing things and doing things, and projecting themselves upon their environment. He says:

For morality, the end implies the act, and the act implies self-realization. This if it were doubtful, would be shown . . . by the feeling of pleasure which attends the putting forth of the act. For if pleasure be the feeling of self, and accompany the act, this indicates that the putting forth of the act is also the putting forth of the self.

So far, the concept of self-realization seems to be connected first with the concept of dynamism as the essential element in the moral life, and, secondly, with the concept of character. To be truly moral or immoral, our actions must in some sense be consistent. They must arise, that is, out of a consistent character, and manifest that character. This is in fact a very important part of morality and enters more than is often allowed into our moral judgement of others. Moreover, as so far stated, the self-realization theory has another great advantage. Many people, especially those who are temperamentally puritanical, or who are used to setting very high standards for themselves, feel strongly that some kinds of behaviour, though utterly harmless to other people, should nevertheless be avoided for their own sakes, and that this is a moral matter. They may feel, for instance, that to indulge in some kinds of pleasurable activities such as reading novels in the mornings, is wrong, not only because they have been brought up to think this, but because they feel that to indulge in them would be to start some kind of downward trend, some degeneration which it is their duty to avoid. The feeling that, consequences apart, one should do better, is a strong and familiar moral feeling and one which is, again, unduly neglected by writers about morals. Self-realization is not so far from self-improvement, and it is, among other things, in its power to account for this range of moral concepts that the attraction of Bradley's theory lies.

But Bradley, as I have said already, claims that the aim of morality is not only realization of the self, but of the self *as a whole*. This part of his doctrine is both less clear, and less attractive, if I understand it. In the essay we are now considering, he makes two serious attempts to elucidate the concept of the self as a whole. The first is by means of an analysis of a choice between two incompatible alternative actions.[1] He says that in

[1] p. 71 *op. cit.*

choosing between A and B not only must a man be aware of the nature of the acts between which he is choosing, but he must also be aware of himself set above these two actions and deliberating between them. This self-awareness he denominates the universal element in volition, the particular element being the agent's awareness of each of the individual possibilities. The volition *as a whole* is the identification of the self willing with one or other of the possible actions; and this resulting unity, that is, the volition completed in an action, he calls the individual whole, or the concrete universal. It is at achieving such a whole that the moral action aims, and this is what is meant by saying that the end is self-realization *as a whole*. I cannot pretend, however, that the necessity of talking about the whole is made any more apparent by this obscure Hegelian reasoning, nor, in particular, that the relation between the whole volition and the whole self is obvious.

The second attempted elucidation, also purely Hegelian, is by means of an analogy with understanding.[1] In matters of theory our aim, he says, is to understand an object, to 'get at the truth of it'. As long as the object seems odd or unfamiliar we say that we have not reached the truth about it. We go on until we can see the consistency and the necessity of some explanatory theory of the object. 'There we rest, because then we have found the nature of our own mind and the truth of facts in one.' If ever our knowledge of anything were complete, the distinction between the knowing mind and the object known would disappear. It is towards

[1] *op. cit.* p. 73.

this identification of subject with object that Bradley thinks we strive, in trying to understand anything. There is an analogous striving, he claims, in the case of action. 'Here our aim is not, leaving the given as it is, to find the truth of it; but here we want to force the sensuous fact to correspond to the truth of ourselves.' The distinction at removing which we aim in practice is the distinction between ourselves and the alien world of other people and external events. 'My nature tells me that the world is mine'; and therefore I try to alter the facts, till I express myself in *them* as well as in what first seemed distinct from them. The aim is to find in the facts 'nothing but myself carried out'. I possess the world when my will is expressed in the world.

The idea that knowing implies some kind of identification between the person who knows and the known object has of course a long and serious metaphysical history. Aristotle thought that there existed a kinship between the objects of intellectual comprehension and the intellect. Spinoza held that if one understood nature completely one would thereby become identical with nature, that is identical with God. Bradley regarded the unitary nature of reality as both the most important and the least dubitable part of his whole metaphysical account of the universe; and he meant his statement that reality was one, to carry the implication, among others, that anything less than unity, such as the distinction between a person and the object of his thought, is necessarily unreal or illusory. To aim, therefore, at identifying oneself, whether with the object of one's thought or with the world in which one is living and acting is to do no more than to aim to remove illusion, and to exist in reality. In this context, self-realization takes on a more literal sense than at first it seemed to have. It means now not only satisfying oneself, but actually making oneself exist. It means making oneself real instead of illusory. Furthermore, the notion that the self must be realized *as a whole* becomes a necessary part of its being realized at all, since if there is more than one thing, or rather if there is less than total identification between myself and the world around me, then the realization is not complete; if it is complete, then myself and the world form one whole. Thus moral action will not only remove the *sense* of isolation or separateness which each one of us may have, but it will, on this theory, actually bring such separateness to an end.

So, by restating his moral theory in the context of the idealist theory of knowledge, Bradley attempts to elucidate his utterance, that the aim of moral action is self-realization. At the end of this same essay he adds the qualification that not only must the self be realized as a whole, but as an infinite whole.[1] This too, presumably, follows from the proposition that reality is one; it follows, at least, on the hypothesis that reality is infinite, which Bradley doubtless accepted. But it is impossible not to feel, at this stage of the argument, that any application of the theory to what are normally thought of as the peculiar problems of moral philosophy has been left rather alarmingly far behind. In this

[1] p. 74 *op. cit.*

B

essay, Bradley only hints at any such application, at the
very end:[1]

> The difficulty is: being limited and so not a whole,
> how extend myself so as to be a whole? The answer is,
> be a member in a whole. Here your private self, your
> finitude, ceases as such to exist; it becomes the function
> of an organism. You must be, not a mere piece of, but a
> member in, a whole; and as this, must know and will
> yourself.

This, though still vague as a guide to the nature of
what is morally good, has at least a slightly sinister note.
There is the suggestion that the end for man, self-
realization, may turn out after all to be the destruction
of the individual.

The next two essays in *Ethical Studies* are critical
considerations of other people's views of the nature of
the end. First Bradley considers and rejects the suggestion that the end is pleasure, and then that it is duty
for duty's sake. In each case he aims to show that the
suggestion is actually contradictory. These essays,
especially the second of them, are both subtle and
forcible. No doubt in Duty for Duty's sake, he is not
entirely fair to Kant, but all the same this seems to me
one of the very best things ever written about Kant's
moral philosophy. In the fifth essay, 'My Station and
its Duties',[2] he returns to his own theory, and to the
task of illustrating the concept of self-realization in a
more concrete form. The good for man is now definitely
stated to be 'the realization of ourselves as the will
which is above ourselves'. This will is identical with a

---

[1] p. 79 *op. cit.*   [2] *op. cit.* p. 160 *sqq.*

'moral organism'. It is referred to as a concrete universal which cannot exist except in and through its members. The individual, Bradley says, must necessarily be thought of as having relations with other people. He is not born into a vacuum, but has a definite place in society and in history. Whatever he does must be done in relation to the circumstances into which he was born, and it is with this external world that he tries to identify himself, by altering the facts until they express himself. This view, the belief in the necessary dependence of people upon one another and upon their circumstances, is set out in explicit opposition in the first place to individualism, that is to utilitarianism interpreted as a kind of egoistic hedonism, and secondly to the Kantian and abstract formulae of Duty for Duty's sake. The theory of self-realization as a part of a moral organism, the theory which Bradley actually refers to by the name of 'My Station and its Duties', is said to have three great advantages. First, the universal end for man which is proposed by it is concrete. The theory takes into account actual facts and is therefore prepared to allow that duty will not be the same at every time or place. In this Bradley thinks it is superior to both hedonism and the abstract view. But though the end proposed is concrete, he claims that it is not given by mere caprice, 'for although within certain limits I may choose my station according to my own liking, yet I and everyone else must have some station with duties pertaining to it, and those duties do not depend on our opinion or liking'. Secondly, the end is objective, and this is one of the demands which the moral consciousness makes upon anything that could qualify to be an end. The reasons which Bradley gives to support this claim of objectivity are, it must be confessed, less than clear. The justification appears to be that the objective, systematized moral organism, which is not something each of us just thinks up for himself, is the medium through which the individual man must realize the end.[1]

My private choice, so far as I am moral, is the mere form of bestowing myself on, and identifying myself with, the will of the moral organism, which realizes in its process both itself and myself. . . . What I have to do, I have not to force upon a recalcitrant world; I have to fill my place—the place that waits for me to fill it.

The third advantage of 'My Station and its Duties' is said to be that the end which it proposes leaves nothing of us outside it. It gets rid of the contradiction which Bradley found in the Kantian theory of pure duty, the contradiction, that is, between duty and the empirical self of desires, inclination, character and circumstances. All these, as we have seen, are included in the end, on Bradley's theory, since duty now becomes the duty to make all these empirical elements part of the wider external world.

The concept of 'My Station and its Duties' is the core of Bradley's moral theory. The last two essays in *Ethical Studies* are devoted to further elaboration of this notion of the end, to a consideration of the bad will, the opposite of self-realization, and to a discussion of the relation between religion and morality. The

[1] p. 180 *op. cit.*

respects in which the theory is essentially metaphysical are perhaps now clear. More specifically, it is essentially an idealist moral philosophy, deriving from the idealist view of the unitary and coherent nature of reality. In *Appearance and Reality*[1] Bradley returns to the question of The Good. Here the connexion between the concept of goodness and that of reality as a whole is most clearly stated, and ethics is seen as a small part of metaphysics. Evil and good, he says, are not illusions but they are appearances, 'they are one sided aspects, each over-ruled and transmuted in the whole'.[2] The opposition between good and bad is not supposed to be absolute, any more than, on the idealist theory, is the opposition between true and false absolute. 'The interval which exists between, and which separates, the lower and the higher, is measured by the idea of perfect Reality. The lower is that which, to be made complete, would have to undergo a more total transformation of its nature.' If, in general, then, the more good anything is the more reality it has, it follows that in the sphere of action, the better an action is, the more reality will it bestow upon the agent. Self-realization is only one aspect of the general superior reality of things as they approach closer and closer to *absolute* reality (in so far, that is, as they improve). Moreover, the good man will necessarily realize himself in a wide context; his actions will necessarily take their place in a whole system of morality, because what he is aiming at in exercising

---

[1] *Appearance and Reality.* London: Sonnenschein, 1st edition, 1893.
[2] *op. cit.* p. 401 *sqq.*

his good will, is, in some sense, to comprehend and identify himself with everything that exists.

Bradley was not, of course, the only metaphysical moral philosopher of this period. Nor was he even interested in all the problems which seemed important to his contemporaries. For instance he was comparatively uninterested in the problem of human freedom. It seems probable that this lack of interest was due to the fact that there was really no place for freedom in his system, which, like Spinoza's, must entail that the more we know, the more we realize that our actions are a necessary part of the total system of the universe. Just as good and bad are not opposed except as appearances, so voluntary and necessitated would only *appear* to our ignorance to be opposed. Any believer in an idealist theory of truth almost has to hold that ultimately everything is necessary. There were other metaphysical philosophers, however, such as A. E. Taylor, who conceived of the problem of freedom as the central ethical problem, and who attacked Bradley for overlooking it. Again, Joseph, in *Some Problems of Ethics* (1931), starts with a chapter called 'Metaphysical Preliminaries', which is entirely devoted to the question whether or not we may say that any human actions are voluntary. All the same, it was Bradley's Hegelian idealist ethical theory which dominated the beginning of the century, and it is against this background that the later developments must be seen. In ethics, as in philosophy in general, the greatest blow to be struck in the twentieth century against idealism was struck by G. E. Moore. And though in *Principia Ethica*, which will be the subject of the next chapter, he had other targets as well as Bradley and the idealists, it was his arguments against them and therefore, it seemed, against metaphysical ethics in general, which were most novel, and which perhaps have had the greatest influence on twentieth-century ethics as a whole.

Chapter Two

G. E. MOORE

G. E. MOORE's *Principia Ethica* was first published in 1903.[1] It has become the custom to regard it as the source from which the subsequent moral philosophy of the century has flowed, or at least as the most powerful influence upon this moral philosophy. There is no doubt that it is a very remarkable book. But I am not sure that some later writers have not submitted to the temptation of seeing in it only what they would themselves subscribe to, and of leaving out of account altogether those features of the book which are idiosyncratic and eccentric. This is a pity; Moore has, no doubt, exercised a great influence on other philosophers. But it is almost as if some of these philosophers, especially some in Oxford, had read only the first one or two chapters of the book; if they had read on, they might have been more cautious about ranging themselves under Moore's supposed banner.

In the Preface to *Principia Ethica*, Moore states what his main intention was in writing the book. 'I have tried', he says, 'to distinguish clearly two kinds of question, which moral philosophers have always professed to answer, but which ... they have almost always confused both with one another and with other questions.' These two questions are 'What kind of things ought to exist for their own sake?' and 'What

[1] *Principia Ethica*. Cambridge University Press, 1903.

kind of actions ought we to perform?' From knowing the answers to these two different questions, Moore says, we shall be able to go on to find out with what kind of evidence, if any, it is proper to support moral judgements; we shall know what kinds of ethical proposition are, and what kinds are not, susceptible of proof. In general, Moore's answer to his questions is this: (1) The things which ought to exist for their own sake are things which we call intrinsically good. It is impossible to define 'good', since it is the name of a simple unanalysable characteristic of things. But this does not entail that we cannot recognize when we see them those things which intrinsically possess this unanalysable characteristic. Moore's contention is that we can, if we think about it hard enough, certainly recognize intrinsically good things, and at the end of the book he lists some of the things which he thinks are intrinsically good. But it is a matter simply of recognition. No evidence can be adduced to show that something is intrinsically good; it is just a matter of seeing that it is so. Nothing could *prove* that if something is said to be intrinsically good, it really is so. 'We can guard against error only by taking care, that, when we try to answer a question of this kind, we have before our minds that question only and not some other or others' (p. viii). (2) Answers to the second question, what kinds of action ought we to perform, are capable of proof or disproof, of an empirical sort. For we ought always to do that action which will cause most good to exist. So the kind of evidence necessary to show that some proposed course of action is right will be causal

evidence that the course of action will bring about such
and such results or consequences. In addition, it will
be necessary to know that the consequences are
intrinsically good. It is necessary, therefore, on Moore's
view, first to know what kinds of things are intrinsically
good, that is what kinds of thing ought in general to
exist, before it is possible to embark on any demonstration that a certain course of action ought to be undertaken, since the evidence brought up to support this
last contention must contain some statement of the
former kind.

This, then, is what Moore took to be the main
purpose of his book, namely to distinguish those ethical
judgements which were susceptible of proof by reference to evidence from those which were not. The first
step in establishing this distinction was to consider the
concept of goodness, in order to show that 'good' was
simple and indefinable, and to this consideration the
first chapter of the book is devoted. In this chapter
Moore expounds his famous theory that it is fallacious
to attempt to define 'good' in any way, and, particularly,
fallacious to attempt to define it in terms of a natural
object. Moore calls the attempt to define 'good', which
is indefinable, The Naturalistic Fallacy. But it is important to notice that the fallaciousness consists in the
attempting of a definition at all, rather than specifically
in defining a so-called non-natural object in terms of a
natural object. Moore says (p. 13) that if anyone confused two natural objects together, and defined one in
terms of the other, this would be to commit the very
same fallacy as that contained in the attempt to define

good, only in this case there would be no reason to call
the fallacy 'naturalistic'. The appropriateness of that
name does come from mixing the two classes, natural
and non-natural; but even if 'good' were a natural
object 'that would not alter the nature of the fallacy,
nor diminish its importance one whit'. It is clear, then,
that first and foremost it is supposed to be fallacious to
define 'good' and secondly it is fallacious to define a
non-natural in terms of a natural object. I have laboured
this point, not without reason. For people often talk
not only as if Moore were interested in nothing except
exposing a logical fallacy for its own sake, but also as
if the nature of this fallacy were simply to confuse
a natural with a non-natural object, to define the latter
in terms of the former. And it must be admitted that
the name 'Naturalistic Fallacy' does carry this suggestion. But Moore does not care much for the name.
'It does not matter what we call it provided we recognize it when we meet it.' The true fallacy is the attempt
to define the indefinable.

There are several obscure points in this doctrine as
so far expounded. Some of them, it must be admitted,
must remain obscure but I will try to set out Moore's
argument as clearly as I can.

Moore distinguishes three possible meanings of the
question 'What is good?' First, it may require a
particular answer. Obviously in this sense the question
would not in fact be put in this general form, but would
be of the form, for instance, of 'Which is a good
restaurant?' or 'What would be a good way to begin a
speech?' So I think we may dismiss this supposed

meaning of the question. The second meaning is that in which the question requires a general answer in the form of a statement that some kind of thing is good—such as that charitable actions are good or pleasure is good. Moore, at the end of the book, proposes answers to this version of the question. Thirdly, the question 'What is good?' may be the demand for a *definition*. In this form, Moore says that the question is absolutely central to ethics, and belongs to ethics alone. But by 'definition' it should be noticed that Moore here means 'analysis'. He dismisses the suggestion that he could reach the kind of definition demanded in the question 'What is good?' by observing how people in fact use the word 'good'. This kind of definition he regards as trivial, and a matter of mere lexicography. But, taking for granted that he is discussing the word 'good' in the way that it *is* usually used, he is interested in the object or idea which he says it is usually used to stand for. A definition, then, in the interesting sense, would be an analysis of this idea. It is this which he claims is impossible, in the case of the object denoted by 'good'. Moore's view of definition is very obscure, and his examples do not help to make it clearer. He contrasts the case of 'good' with the case of 'Horse' (p. 8). The definition of 'Horse' is said to be 'hooved quadruped of the genus equus'. This may be either (1) an arbitrary verbal definition telling you only how I propose to use the word, or (2) a statement about how English people do or should use the word 'horse', or (3) we may, Moore says, 'mean something much more important'. We may mean that a certain object familiar to all of us is composed in a certain manner. 'That it has four legs, a head, a heart, a liver etc. all of them arranged in definite relations to one another.' It is in this sense of definition that Moore denies that 'good' is definable. But it is difficult to see how the quoted definition of 'horse'—that it is a hooved quadruped of the genus equus—could ever be taken as *meaning* that the horse had a heart, liver etc. arranged in a certain order. No doubt one could list the parts of the horse, and even state their relation one to another, but to do this would not be to say 'Hooved quadruped etc.', with a special meaning; nor would it normally be taken to be defining 'horse' at all. However, I do not think one should waste very much time on Moore's eccentric treatment of the word 'definition'. For one thing, the concept of definition is itself very vague, and it is not clear that anything very important would come of laying down the different ways in which things may or may not be defined. Furthermore, if we drop the word 'definition', and drop the confusing analogy of the horse, nothing much will be lost. For Moore makes it perfectly clear that what he thinks you cannot legitimately do to 'good' is to analyse it. It is impossible to name its parts because it has no parts. Like Descartes and Leibniz, Moore takes it as absolutely self-evident that if some things are complex and therefore capable of analysis, then there must be some things into which the complex things are analysed which are themselves simple, and without parts. This is a very widespread and natural belief. Moore thinks that the quality of goodness, which he talks of, confusingly, as 'good' either with or without inverted commas, is one of these simple natures which can enter into the composition of complexes, but are non-complex themselves. He compares goodness with yellowness in this respect (p. 10): 'Yellow and good, we say, are not complex: they are notions of that simple kind out of which definitions are composed and with which the power of further defining ceases.' 'Good' and 'bad', he says, are the only simple notions which are peculiar to ethics. The indefinability of 'good' is, he thinks, one of the most important facts, if not the most important fact, with which ethics has to deal. Again I quote:

If I am asked 'what is good?' my answer is that good is good and that is the end of the matter. Or if I am asked 'How is good to be defined?' my answer is that it cannot be defined, and that is all I have to say about it. But disappointing as these answers may appear, they are of the very last importance.

Having set out his contention that goodness, like yellowness, is unanalysable, Moore goes on to use the analogy between 'good' and 'yellow' to establish two further points. The first point is that though it is impossible to define colour words, it is possible to state the physical concomitants of the colours. We may state what light vibrations must strike the normal eye in order that the colour may be perceived. But, Moore says, these light vibrations are not what we mean when we talk about the colour. In this he is perfectly right. The colour word is the name of a property perceptible to the normal eye, not the name of something which it needs scientific measurement to discover. Similarly,

Moore argues, with 'good', it may be possible to state what else besides being good all good things are; for instance it might turn out that if ever anything was good it was also pleasant, or the object of approval. But this would not entail that when we talked of a thing's being good we *meant* that it was pleasant or the object of approval. In fact, if it were not possible independently to distinguish things which were good from those which were not, it would never be possible to find out that all the good things were also pleasant. To identify the light waves with the colour or the pleasantness with the goodness is to commit the fallacy of trying to define what is simple and indefinable. This argument, it will be seen, rests entirely on the assumption that 'good' is indeed like 'yellow', the name of a discernible property of things.

The second point which the analogy with colour is used to make is this: nobody thinks that because 'yellow' is indefinable, therefore it is impossible to say what things have the property of being yellow. Nor does anybody think that there can be only one thing which is yellow, nor that all the other properties which the yellow thing has are identical with the property of yellowness. We know perfectly well that primroses are yellow, that other things besides primroses are yellow, and that primroses are sweet-smelling as well as yellow, and that their sweet smell is different from their yellowness. Yet, Moore thinks, people have failed to see all these points when they have thought about the goodness of things. Saying that goodness is indefinable does not prevent one from saying that, for example, pleasure is good, that other things besides pleasure are good, and that pleasure may have other properties, such as being the object of desire, which are distinct from its goodness. This point is very important for Moore's argument, since his interest in ethics is by no means confined to the supposed logical point about the simplicity of certain concepts; he is interested in actually stating what things have the property of intrinsic goodness; in giving examples, that is, of his first, unprovable, kind of ethical proposition. This he plainly could not do unless he could show that it was possible to pick things out as possessors of the indefinable property of goodness.

So far Moore has given no arguments to show that 'good' is indefinable; there has been nothing except an analogy. He next attempts an actual proof, by means of a dilemma (p. 15). Either 'good' is indefinable, or, if it is not, it must be either a complex, about the correct analysis of which there could be disagreement, or the word must mean nothing at all. There is a certain amount of confusion here and elsewhere in the discussion, about whether we are supposed to be discussing a word or some object denoted by a word, such as a property; but this confusion is not very important, and Moore's dilemma can easily be presented in a way which avoids the difficulty. We must accept either that the word 'good' denotes a simple unanalysable property, or that it denotes a complex analysable property, or that it denotes nothing at all. This, Moore thinks, exhausts the possibilities. He then aims to show that each of the last alternatives is impossible, and that therefore we must necessarily accept the first. (1) 'The hypothesis that disagreement about the meaning of good is disagreement with regard to the correct analysis of a given whole, may be most plainly seen to be incorrect by consideration of the fact that, whatever definition be offered, it may be always asked, with significance, of the complex so defined whether it is itself good.' Thus, if I try to define good as, let us say, self-realization, Moore's objection is that it is still significant to ask whether self-realization is good; and since this is significant, it cannot be the same as asking whether self-realization is self-realization, which it would have to be if the original definition had been correct. One cannot doubt that self-realization is the same as self-realization; but we can and may well doubt whether self-realization is good, and the mere fact that we understand very well what is meant by doubting it, shows clearly that we have two different notions before our mind. This argument begs the question. For it already assumes what it is supposed to prove, namely, that goodness is simple and unanalysable. If goodness were allowed to be a complex notion, then not only might one perhaps be able to analyse it, but it would naturally be significant to convert the proposition and inquire whether that into which one had analysed it was good. This might well be a way of testing out the correctness of the analysis. An analysis of a complex notion never sets out to give an identity, nor is the statement in which the analysis is given an identity statement. Therefore the converse of the proposition in which the analysis is set out will not be trivial. It is only because

c

Moore is already convinced that 'good' is the name of a simple property that he thinks the possibility of significant conversion is fatal to the definition's being correct. This is clearly shown by the sentence quoted above. 'We have two different notions before our mind.' If the definition were correct, he thinks, we would have only one, as I might be said to have only one notion before my mind when I say that 'good' is '*bon*'. But if I can succeed in giving a correct analysis of a complex notion, then it cannot plausibly be said that I have only one notion before my mind; I must necessarily have at least two, and probably more. It is doubtful whether the method of counting the notions before the mind is a good or even possible method in fact. But if Moore requires that we use it, then for what it is worth, it must be admitted that it fails to prove what he wants it to. Moore seems to have been misled here by his own eccentric concept of definition. If he had used the word 'analysis', and had aimed to show that it is analysis of the concept of goodness which is impossible, then the argument from the possibility of converting any proposition of the form 'good is so and so' would not have seemed so formidable.

(2) The same considerations, Moore says, serve to show that 'good' is not totally meaningless. When anyone says that anything is good, Moore says, they are not saying nothing about it, nor are they saying something which can be paraphrased by another word. If, that is, I say that pleasure is good, I am not merely stating that pleasure is pleasure (a trivial proposition which would be saying nothing), nor am I saying some-

thing which could just as well be expressed by saying pleasure is, for instance, desired, or approved.

Everyone does in fact understand the question 'Is this good?' When he thinks of it, his state of mind is different from what it would be, were he asked 'Is this pleasant, or desired, or approved?' It has a distinct meaning for him, even though he may not recognize in what respect it is distinct. Whenever he thinks of intrinsic value or 'intrinsic worth' or says that a thing ought to exist, he has before his mind the unique object—the unique property of things—which I mean by 'good'.

This looks much more like a restatement of the position than an argument.

Both alternative possibilities having been thus ruled out, Moore is in a position to assert the truth of the first proposition, namely that good is simple and indefinable. The next step in the argument of the book is to illustrate the mistakes into which moral philosophers have been led by overlooking this, and thereby committing the naturalistic fallacy. Rather confusingly, Moore divides those theories of the nature of good which commit the fallacy into two groups, the naturalistic and the metaphysical. Both types of theory suggest that there is some definition or analysis of good to be found, but the first kind seeks to define good in terms of some natural object, the second in terms of a metaphysical object. This is the distinction Moore makes. Unfortunately it is not only obscure in itself, but it is also additionally confusing in the light of the fact that the fallacy which both types of theory equally are supposed to commit is the *naturalistic* fallacy. However, once again, if Moore's terminology is less than perfect, this need not unduly alarm us.

The first kind of theory Moore considers is naturalism proper, and he takes as his examples first the evolutionary theory of Spencer, according to which 'good' means 'more evolved'; and secondly the hedonistic utilitarianism of, among others, John Stuart Mill. It will be enough to examine his criticism of the last of these, to get more light on what exactly is supposed by Moore to be so bad about naturalism.

Introducing his criticism, Moore says (p. 59)

. . . that pleasure has been so generally held to be the sole good, is almost entirely due to the fact that it has seemed to be somehow involved in the *definition* of good . . . to be pointed out by the very meaning of the word. If this is so, then the prevalence of Hedonism has been mainly due to what I have called the naturalistic fallacy—the failure to distinguish clearly that unique and indefinable quality which we mean by good.

Moore quotes Mill's words in order to establish, in the first place, that he uses the expressions 'good as an end' and 'desirable as an end' as absolutely equivalent expressions. He then suggests that Mill tries to prove that pleasure is the only thing desirable as an end by appeal to the fact that people do actually desire it and it alone as an end. This attempted proof is, he says, a glaring example of the naturalistic fallacy. Mill's proof consists in arguing that 'desirable' is like 'visible'; and just as you could establish what things were visible by finding out what things people actually saw, so you could find out what things were desirable by discovering what people actually desired. What they do desire, Mill says, is pleasure, and therefore pleasure is desirable and therefore it is good; and since pleasure is *all* that people desire, it can be said not only to be good, but to be *the* good. Moore's criticism of Mill's argument here has had a considerable effect upon the subsequent history of ethics, and therefore it is worth considering both what Mill's argument was in fact meant to show, and what precisely it was of which Moore accused him.

Mill started by saying that it is impossible to prove the truth of statements about ultimate ends. 'Whatever can be proved to be good, must be so by being shown to be a means to something admitted to be good without proof.' With this of course Moore does not disagree; for Mill is simply making the distinction which it is the purpose of Moore's book to establish, between the type of ethical statement for which evidence is required and the type for which there can be no evidence. But Mill goes on, just as Moore does, to attempt to show what things are as a matter of fact good as ends. His argument here, as we have seen, falls into two parts: first he argues that pleasure or happiness is good as an end, and secondly, more dubiously, that it is the only thing which is good as an end. Now though Moore admits that he agrees with Mill's initial distinction between propositions which are and those which are not susceptible of proof, he does not, I think, realize that his approval of Mill ought to go further. When Mill uses the argument from the analogy between 'visible' and 'desirable' he is attempting to establish what things are good, and this, Moore constantly assures us, is a perfectly legitimate undertaking. Mill is not, that is to say, going back on his contention that it is impossible to *prove* what is good as an end. He is saying rather that if people did not already regard some things as ends, and therefore desire them, it would be impossible to prove to them that these things really were ends. 'How is it possible to prove', he asks, 'that health is good?' The answer is that it is *not* possible to prove it; but the fact is that everybody knows that it is good, and shows this by desiring it. When he says 'the sole evidence it is possible to produce that anything is desirable, is that people actually do desire it' he is repeating the same point. 'The sole evidence' is not evidence in the sense of *proof* that something is good, but it is evidence simply that people already know, without waiting for proof, that it is good. In the very next sentence, Mill makes this clear: 'If the end which the utilitarian doctrine proposes to itself were not, in theory and practice, acknowledged to be an end, nothing could ever convince any person that it was so.' The question of proving what is an ultimate end does not arise; but you can find out what people recognize as ultimate ends by finding out what they desire. What they desire, Mill goes on to say, is happiness. I cannot see anything wrong or fallacious about this. But Moore's criticism of this first part of Mill's argument has become part of the accepted dogma of moral philosophy. This has been due partly to misunderstanding Mill, in the way that Moore taught us to, but partly also to misunderstanding Moore. That Moore did misunderstand

mis. Mill.

Mill is fairly clear. Mill, he said, committed the naturalistic fallacy because he defined 'good' which is indefinable; and he committed it in its strongest form,
because he identified good, which is non-natural, with a
natural thing, namely 'what is desired'. Moore does
not object to Mill's identification of 'good' with
'desirable'. This is at first sight surprising, for we have
come to expect that the identification of good with anything would count as a commission of the fallacy. But
the reason is that, according to Moore, 'desirable' means
'worthy to be desired'; and 'worthy to be desired' must
mean 'good'; therefore the identification of 'good' with
'desirable' does not matter, in the sense that it is actually
tautological. Moore does not actually say this in so
many words, but it is assumed in his argument. His
attack is levelled against the passage from the concept
of desirability to that of being desired. 'The fallacy', he
says (p. 67), 'in this step is so obvious that it is quite
wonderful how Mill failed to see it.' There is, after all,
he claims, no analogy between 'visible' and 'desirable'.
'Visible' means 'able to be seen', but 'desirable' does
not mean 'able to be desired' but 'fit to be desired'. The
analogy is rather to be sought between 'desirable' and
'damnable', which does not mean what *is* damned, but
what should be damned. It is this part of Moore's
argument which appears to have fascinated moral
philosophers and from which they have drawn such
inspiration that it has sometimes seemed as if there
were no other virtue in a moral philosopher except that
he should avoid the naturalistic fallacy. But, in the first
place, as an argument against Mill it is misconceived.

Moral
and
J. Mill

If Mill had first defined 'good' as 'desirable' and had
then gone on to define 'desirable' as 'desired', he would
no doubt have been open to criticism. But it was no
part of his interest to define 'good' or 'desirable' at all.
Indeed, if anything, his remarks about the impossibility
of proving propositions concerned with ultimate ends
would suggest that he agreed with Moore that 'good'
was indefinable, though it need not mean this. The fact
is that the question of definition was never raised by
him at all. He was interested in discovering the under-
lying principles of ethical conduct, and not in defining
ethical terms. His introduction of the concept of 'what
is desired' was, as I hope I have shown, due to the very
fact that you cannot prove what is or is not good. All
that you have to go on is what people think is good,
what, that is, they have always thought worth desiring.
What they have always thought worth desiring is what
they have in fact desired. Mill's procedure here is like
Hume's, who argues that the qualities which we have
come to regard as virtuous are those which we in fact
find are desired for the sake of the general well-being
of society; and it is not so very unlike Moore's own
procedure when, in the last chapter of *Principia Ethica*,
he turns to consider the question what things are
intrinsically good. In each case the question at issue is:
What is it that people value most highly? Mill's perhaps
unduly simple answer is, happiness. Mill cannot, therefore, be rightly accused of trying to define 'good'; and
this accusation must be at least part of what Moore
meant by his statement that the naturalistic fallacy had
been committed, since we have been told over and over

again that the naturalistic fallacy consists in just this. But, even if Mill had been trying to define 'good', and had therefore offered 'What is desired' as a definition of 'desirable', which he did not, I think that Moore would have been unduly hard on him. If the argument comes down to a discussion of the meanings of words, then, though the analogy between the meanings of 'desirable' and 'visible' is not close, still the distinction between 'desired' and 'desirable' is not so clear and sharp as Moore suggests. When house agents speak of houses as desirable they do not mean that these houses are such that we ought to desire them. Very often 'desirable' means something like 'What any sane person would desire', and if this is what it means, then the relevance of the consideration of what sane people do in fact desire is at once obvious. But this defence of Mill should not be taken very seriously, for I hope I have said enough to show why I do not believe that for Mill the question was one of the meanings of words at all.

I said just now that not only Mill but Moore also was misrepresented by those moral philosophers who attached great importance to the breakdown of the analogy between 'visible' and 'desirable'. I do not mean to suggest that Moore himself did not think it important. I am sure that he did; and in this particular chapter of *Principia Ethica* there is no doubt that the major fault of the utilitarians is taken to be that they defined 'good', which is a non-natural property, in terms of pleasure or desire, which are natural objects. For instance, twice in this chapter Moore sums up his arguments against the first part of Mill's contention,

namely the contention that pleasure or happiness is
desirable. The first summary is as follows (p. 73):

> In this argument, the naturalistic fallacy is plainly
> involved. That fallacy, I explained, consists in the con-
> tention that good means nothing but some simple or
> complex notion, that can be defined in terms of natural
> qualities. In Mill's case, good is thus supposed to *mean*
> simply what is desired; and what is desired is something
> which can thus be defined in natural terms. Mill tells us
> that we ought to desire something (an ethical proposi-
> tion) because we actually do desire it; but if his conten-
> tion that 'I ought to desire' means nothing but 'I do
> desire' were true, then he is only entitled to say, 'we do
> desire so and so because we do desire it'; and that is not
> an ethical proposition at all; it is a mere tautology.

It is to be noticed that in this summary he uses the
argument against defining 'good' which he used in the
first chapter, namely that if you do define it, you are
landed with a tautology; and this has nothing specially
to do with the naturalism or otherwise of the terms of
the definition. There is here, in fact, the very same
ambiguity which was to be found in the first chapter,
where Moore called his fallacy 'naturalistic' but went
on to say that the metaphysical philosophers who
defined 'good' in terms of non-natural objects committed the fallacy just as much as the naturalists did.
Once again, he is first and foremost accusing Mill of
attempting to define good, and secondarily accusing
him of naturalism, in the ordinary sense . . . that is of
reducing non-natural to natural concepts. Moore's
second summary (p. 108) at the very end of the chapter
is shorter. There he simply states that his refutation of

utilitarianism consists, in the first part, in pointing out
that Mill commits the naturalistic fallacy 'in identifying "desirable" with "desired"'. Now it is very easy
to read this as meaning that the whole of the fallacy
consists in passing from the non-natural concept
'desirable' to the natural concept 'desired'. And this is
how later philosophers have been inclined to regard it,
though they have usually substituted the more specific
and understandable expression 'ethical' for 'non-
natural', and 'non-ethical' for 'natural'. But even here
it is important to remember that at least part of what
Moore was attacking was the identifying of 'desirable'
with anything at all, on the grounds that 'desirable'
was somehow identical with 'good'. Even if, in this
particular chapter, Moore was chiefly concerned with
naturalism properly so called, nevertheless, regarding
the book as a whole, it must be admitted that the
simplicity and unanalysability of the quality of goodness was his major concern, and it was as overlooking
this that his fallacy was chiefly supposed to be fallacious.

In connexion with this same argument of Mill's,
there is a further difficulty in Moore's treatment, which
may perhaps be thought to be fundamental, and that is
the difficulty of understanding exactly what Moore
meant by 'natural' and 'non-natural'. It might be held
with some plausibility that if this point is not clear,
then no part of the argument which is concerned with
the naturalistic fallacy can be clear either. But in fact I
do not think this would be fair, for two reasons. The
first I have laboured enough already, and that is that
I do not believe the distinction between natural and

non-natural was as important for Moore's purposes as
the title of his fallacy would suggest. The second reason
is that it is fairly clear from the examples that he gives
what *kinds* of thing he means to characterize as natural
and non-natural objects, (although it is obscure why he
talks of *objects*; and he also fails actually to provide any
satisfactory definition, in *Principia Ethica* itself.) Later,
he was apparently willing to accept a criterion for 'non-
natural' which suggested that a non-natural property
was one which could not be discerned by the senses.[1]
This, in its turn, is exceedingly obscure; but this and
Moore's own use suggest that at any rate metaphysical
concepts such as 'more real' and ethical concepts such
as 'good' would be non-natural because non-sensory;
while yellowness or pleasantness would be natural,
because detected by the senses. But I think that those
philosophers who have attempted to state the doctrine
of *Principia Ethica* in terms merely of ethical as contrasted with non-ethical terms, have misrepresented
Moore. They have somehow put the cart before the
horse. Moore, when he laid down that non-natural
properties could not be defined in terms of natural
properties, conceived himself to be making a perfectly
general point, from which, in conjunction with the
premise that 'good' was the name of a simple property,
it could be inferred that 'good' could not be analysed at

[1] See *The Philosophy of G. E. Moore*: The Library of
Living Philosophers, editor Paul Arthur Schilpp (North-
western University, 1942), p. 43; C. D. Broad, 'Certain
Features in Moore's Ethical Doctrines'; and 'Reply to my
Critics', p. 581 *sqq*.

ll. If 'non-natural' simply meant 'ethical', then one part
of this inference would go. For since nobody would
dispute that 'good' was, or could be, an ethical term,
to say 'good' is non-natural and therefore cannot be
defined in natural terms would, on this interpretation,
be to state only that 'good' cannot be defined in non-
ethical terms, not to *derive* this from any more general
prohibition. This would reduce the interest, though
perhaps it would not affect the truth of Moore's
position.

So far I have discussed only Moore's treatment of
the first part of the utilitarian argument and this is by
far the most important part of his criticism. But Mill
had not only to establish that pleasure or happiness was
desirable in itself, but also that it was the *only* thing
desirable in itself. Mill admits that whether or not this
second proposition is true is a psychological matter,
and therefore his answer is supposed to be based on
empirical evidence. But he concludes by saying that 'to
desire anything except in proportion as the idea of it is
pleasant, is a physical and metaphysical impossibility'.
This is rather mysterious. 'Metaphysical impossibility'
suggests that it is supposed to be necessarily true that
we desire only pleasure. But if this is so, it is hard to see
how the question whether we do or not could be said
to be one of psychology. The trouble arises largely, it
seems to me, because of the extreme difficulty of using
expressions such as 'pleasure' or 'for the sake of
pleasure' intelligibly. There is in fact no contradiction between saying that we desire something for its
own sake and that we desire it for the sake of pleasure,

in at least one possible meaning of that expression.
Moore is very savage with Mill for saying just this.

> Pray consider a moment [he says (p. 72)] what this
> contemptible nonsense really means. 'Money', says Mill,
> 'is only desired as a means to happiness'. Perhaps so,
> but what then? 'Why,' says Mill, 'money is undoubtedly
> desired for its own sake.' 'Yes, go on,' say we. 'Well,'
> says Mill, 'if money is desired for its own sake, it must
> be desirable as an end-in-itself: I have said so myself.'
> 'Oh,' say we, 'but you also just now said that it was only
> desirable as a means.' 'I own I did,' says Mill, 'but I will
> try to patch up matters, by saying that what is only a
> means to an end is the same thing as a part of that end.
> I daresay the public won't notice.' And the public
> haven't noticed.

Once again, I feel inclined to defend Mill. The language
of means and ends would doubtless be better dropped,
since it does suggest just the incompatibility which
Moore finds. But there is no need to employ it. If
Mill had instead talked about doing things 'for the
sake of pleasure or happiness' and 'for their own sake'
then I should find nothing ludicrous in his remarks.
This, then, is one part of Moore's criticism of Mill's
argument to show that only pleasure is desired. He
argues that Mill confuses what is a means to an end
with what is part of an end. I do not think this criticism
is well founded. On the other hand, it is because one can
speak of pleasure in these ways that it can be made to
look plausible to say we desire nothing except pleasure.
For whatever end anybody suggests as a possible object
of desire it is always open to Mill to say that pleasure is
part of that end, though the end *is* desired for its own

sake. And because it is open to him in every case whatever to do this, he is really landed with an uninteresting
tautology. Pleasure turns out to be 'whatever we desire',
and therefore, necessarily, whatever we desire turns
out to be pleasure. This necessity, whi n is the necessity of tautology, is, I suspect, what M l was referring
to, confusingly, as the *metaphysical* npossibility of
desiring anything but pleasure.

The second part of Moore's criticism is borrowed
from Bradley. Mill confuses, says Moore (p. 74), 'a
pleasant thought' with 'the thought of a pleasure'. It
is only where the thought of a pleasure is present that
the pleasure can be said to be the object of desire or the
motive to action. Where there is only, for instance, the
pleasant thought that I will have a drink, I do not have
the drink for the sake of the pleasure, but for the sake
of the drink. The pleasant thought is here, Moore says,
the cause of my action, but not the motive, and therefore pleasure is not the object of my desire. This
objection is ingenious, and there is no doubt a distinction here to be made. But even this is not enough to
prevent Mill using the word pleasure if he chooses to
do so, as 'the object of all desire'.

I am aware that this discussion of pleasure is highly
unsatisfactory. I do not think that either Mill or Moore
was entirely clear what sort of a problem they had
before them. The only excuse for treating it so cursorily
is that Moore's criticism of this second part of Mill's
argument is of comparatively little importance whether
regarded as a part of Moore's own ethical theory, or as
a factor in the subsequent history of the subject. On

the other hand his criticism of the first part, his allega-
tion that Mill has committed the naturalistic fallacy, is,
as I have said, of very great importance, and to later
philosophers' interpretations of this we shall have cause
to return.

Having sho how Spencer and the utilitarians committed the nat alistic fallacy by attempting to define
'good' in empi al terms, Moore in the next chapter
goes on to show how the same fallacy was committed by
those philosophers who tried to explain the nature of
goodness in a quite different way, namely by reference
to metaphysics. We have seen how these metaphysical
philosophers thought that they were reinstating ethics
by divorcing it from naturalism. Moore thought, on
the other hand, that their treatment of the subject was
no less fatal and destructive than that of the empiricists.
He gave them credit, it is true, for realizing the possibility of the existence of properties other than natural
properties; or rather for recognizing, as he says, that
there may be objects of knowledge which do not exist in
time, and which we do not perceive. But he criticized
them for supposing that these possible objects of knowledge were actually existing, though super-sensible
objects. At this point it is very difficult to be clear
exactly what the difference between Moore and the
metaphysicians was. For Moore himself, in the first
chapter of *Principia Ethica*, insisted, as he insists
throughout the book, that 'good' is the name of a super-
sensible property of things. What he apparently does
not want to say is that goodness *exists*. He maintains
that metaphysical philosophers have been led on to the

absurdity of saying that goodness exists by a false analogy between ordinary empirical propositions, such as that I am writing, and propositions of the form 'This is good' (p. 111 *sqq.*). Empirical propositions, Moore says, do assert a relation between two or more *existent* things, and metaphysicians are unable to believe that you can ever assert a proposition without asserting that something or other exists. Moore thinks that, to take a non-ethical example, when you assert that $2 + 2 = 4$, what you mean is 'merely what you say' and you do not mean that 2 and 4 exist, nor that anything else exists at all. 'Every truth, they [the metaphysicians] think, must mean somehow that something exists; and since, unlike the empiricists, they recognize some truths which do not mean that anything exists here and now, these they think must mean that something exists *not* here and now.' So far this is intelligible enough. But when Moore goes on to apply this to the particular case of ethics it is less easy to see what he means.

On the same principle, since 'good' is a predicate which neither does nor can exist, they are bound to suppose either that to be good means to be related to some other particular thing which can exist and does exist in reality; or else that it means merely 'to belong to the real world'—that goodness is transcended or absorbed in reality.

The oddity is to find Moore saying that goodness is a predicate which cannot exist. But what he means is that when you say that something is good, as when you say that $2 + 2 = 4$, you mean merely 'what you say'.

D

No analysis or elucidation of it is possible. No *other* actual or possible object needs to be brought in to explain what it is you are asserting. If asked what you mean, all you could do would be to repeat that you meant the thing was good. Moore does not mean to suggest that there is no such predicate as good, nor that 'good' is not the name of an actual property which things have; only that *what property it is* cannot be explained in terms of a super-sensible 'reality' over and above what we see, any more than it can be explained in terms of what we do see. His use of 'existing' is perhaps muddling. He appears to use it to mean existing in either of two ways, namely 'in time', which is how empirical objects exist, or 'not in time', which is how the supposed total and unified reality of the metaphysicians is held to exist. Since he does not want to say that the property of goodness exists in either of these ways, he suggests that it does not exist at all; and this, on the ordinary interpretation of 'exists', is contrary to his own stated views.

Moore maintains that it is mistaken to suppose any connexion between metaphysics and ethics. The main question in ethics being, as he said in the first chapter, the nature of goodness, no investigations of the general features of reality can possibly throw any light on this. To hope that one could explain goodness in terms of reality in general, must be to commit the naturalistic fallacy, for it must imply that goodness is *not*, as in fact it is, unanalysable in terms of anything else. The simple nature of goodness is not to be explained by any account of the universe as a whole. Moore concedes that it is possible that metaphysics might have some relevance to the question of what we ought to do, though it can have none to the question of what is good. For what we ought to do is determined by some practical and causal questions about the consequences of our acts. Metaphysics, Moore suggests (p. 117), might throw light on what the consequences of our acts will in fact be, though it cannot settle whether or not these consequences will be good. There is a good deal of irony in this apparent concession to the metaphysicians. First, it is not likely that they would happily accept the role of mere practical guides; secondly the only two examples Moore gives of the way in which metaphysicians could help are not very encouraging. He suggests, in the first place, that if they could definitely prove that there was a system of rewards and punishments after death, this would affect our actions; or alternatively, if they could prove what they do in fact maintain, namely that there is an absolutely unchanging, timelessly real system of which we are part, that time and change are mere illusions, then it would follow that there was no point in action at all (for if reality is unchanging what difference can it make if we act?). This could be said to affect our actions, by showing that all actions were either impossible or unnecessary. The concession, then, that metaphysics could, even in this sense, be relevant to ethics is more apparent than real.

The beliefs of metaphysical philosophers, once they have committed the initial mistake of supposing that their general theories will explain ethics as well, are divided by Moore according to whether they rest on logical or epistemological errors. In the first class he places all those philosophers who hold that moral judgements are like natural laws, and state a necessary connexion between subject and predicate. He associates this mistake with the mistake of supposing that goodness can be explained in terms of a super-sensible reality. For he says such philosophers think of the proposition 'this is good' as stating a relation between two existent entities, but because the predicate is peculiar in being part of unchanging reality, therefore it is connected with its subject in a particularly unchanging way. The metaphysicians and the naturalists proper misconceive the nature of the predicate 'good' in basically the same way. Moore's own manner of talking about predicates and properties is exceedingly surprising (p. 124).

It is immediately obvious that when we see a thing to be good, its goodness is not a property which we can take up in our hands.
But I would challenge anyone to name a property which we *could* take up in our hands, precisely,
or separate from it even by the most delicate scientific instruments, and transfer to something else. . . . But philosophers suppose that the reason why we cannot take goodness up and move it about is not that it is a different *kind* of object from any which can be moved about, but only that it *necessarily* exists together with anything with which it does exist. They explain the type of ethical truths by supposing it identical with the type of scientific law. It is only when they have done this that the naturalistic philosophers proper—those who are empiricists—and those whom I have called metaphysical part company.

The metaphysicians think that there is some absolute
necessity in the laws, derivable from the nature of the
universe, while the naturalists do not. A variation of this
logical error is to hold that the proposition 'this is good'
is not a natural law, but some kind of absolute natural
command.

The metaphysical philosophers who, in Moore's view,
base their theories on epistemological rather than
logical errors are those, headed by Kant, who hold that
a thing is good if it is willed in a certain way. Besides
Kant, the post-Hegelian English metaphysicians are
here the target. Moore calls attention to the analogy,
which, as we saw, was explicitly drawn by Bradley,
between knowing something and bringing it about in
practice. It is equally false, Moore says, to say that if
you understand something in some particular way,
then you have understood something true, as it is to
say that if you will something in a particular way, then
you have willed something good. That a proposition is
true is distinct from the fact that anyone thinks it true,
and that an action is good is distinct from the fact that
anybody wills it, or brings it about. For Bradley, as for
Spinoza, the concept of truth was dependent upon the
concept of understanding. The truth about the universe
was identical with what was understood about the
universe. In the same way, there could be no concept
of morally good actions if there were not already the
concept of persons realizing themselves in action. Truth
and goodness are, on this view, both of them relative.
It is only that some acts of will realize the self more
successfully than others. Once again Moore accuses

philosophers such as Bradley of failure to see that goodness is a simple property of things; at the very most, he
says, that an action should have been willed in a certain
way could be a test or criterion of its goodness. It could
never be what its goodness actually consisted in, any
more than the truth of a statement could actually
consist in its being consistent with other statements,
though this might be a test of its truth.

Metaphysical philosophers, then, stand convicted of
the naturalistic fallacy. So far are they from reinstating
ethics, after the ravages upon it of the utilitarians, that
they actually make matters worse, for the non-naturalism of their version of the fallacy might deceive people
into thinking that no fallacy had been committed.
Moore's treatment of the metaphysical moral philosophers is a particularly good example of the extreme
and marvellous literalness of his mind. He represents
metaphysicians as just asserting that a number of extraordinary objects, such as the true self, or the real will,
exist; and as simply asserting that goodness is to be
analysed in terms of such objects. Of course they do
assert these things, but not perhaps quite in the manner
which Moore suggests. If anyone started to expound a
metaphysical system in Moore's language, or Moore's
tone of voice, he would not, it is true, win much acceptance for his theory. But what Moore in no way allows
for, and it may be thought rightly, is the very different
tone of voice of these philosophers themselves. Moore
makes no concessions to the satisfaction which is to be
gained from the contemplation of a highly general
theory, from which truths about human conduct are to

be deduced, as a mere part of the whole. This is the kind of satisfaction which is to be got from reading Spinoza, in whose system human passions and human behaviour are fitted into the general scheme, and propositions about them are supposedly deduced with the rigour of Euclid from propositions about the nature of substance. It would be useless, as a means of giving this particular kind of pleasure, to invent a system, the point of which was exclusively to account for human obligations and which, in order to do this, considered nothing but human nature. The metaphysical pleasure precisely consists in *not* being the centre of the universe, but in seeing familiar problems, such as the problem of how it is right to behave, somehow reduced, and also answered, by being shown to be part of a total scheme of things. This kind of pleasure may be partially aesthetic; it certainly has very little to do with how many of the propositions contained in the sytem are actually true statements. Moore, judging other philosophers by his own standards, tends to speak of the metaphysicians as though they had intended to set out a series of true statements of fact—that this, that or the other object existed; because of this his discussions of their writings seem sometimes rather odd, and unlike what they actually wrote. But he is surely right in saying that they, all of them, attempted to derive ethics from something non-ethical. If this is the naturalistic fallacy, then they committed it; and their committing it is the secret both of their charm and of their power.

We are now at last in a position to consider Moore's own positive contribution to ethics. This is to be found mainly in the last two chapters of *Principia Ethica*. These two chapters have had very little influence indeed upon the subsequent course of moral philosophy; it is, however, worth remarking that Moore has perhaps been more frequently misrepresented than most other moral philosophers, and this is largely due to the neglect of these two chapters. Chapter Five of *Principia Ethica* is entitled 'Ethics in relation to Conduct'. At the beginning of it, Moore summarizes the course of the argument so far (p. 142). He has first, he says, tried to show what the adjective 'good' means; he has then discussed various proposed self-evident principles of ethics. The conclusion of this second step was negative, namely that neither pleasure nor any non-natural object was the sole good. The final step in the argument of the book is to deal positively with the question, What things are good? But this final step is postponed till the last chapter. In the present chapter he declares his intention of dealing with a quite separate question, namely What ought we to do? It will be seen, therefore, that on Moore's own admission, this chapter is outside the main course of the argument, and it is fairly clear that he is far less interested in this question about conduct than in the more general question about what is good. His theory of conduct is extremely simple. There is no such thing as a moral obligation which is not an obligation to produce the greatest amount of good. 'Our "duty", therefore, can only be defined as that action which will cause more good to exist in the universe than any possible alternative.' What we ought to do is always, he thinks, to be determined by a calculation of the consequences of our act, and an assessment of the goodness or badness of these. Thus, on the question of conduct, Moore is in far closer agreement with the utilitarians than with any other moral philosophers. The utilitarians held that an act was to be regarded as a duty if its consequences were such as to produce greater total happiness than misery. Moore held that an act was a duty if it produced more good than harm. They differ only about the question of how to assess the value of the consequences. On the question of general moral rules, too, Moore is in close agreement with Hume, Austin, and Mill. The utilitarians, on the whole, held that established moral rules, such as the rule not to commit murder, must be regarded as universally binding for two reasons: first because the wisdom of past generations has discovered that the consequences of murder are in fact conducive to misery rather than happiness; secondly because even in the case of an apparent exception, where the murder might seem certain to have good consequences, still the rule should be kept, because in general it is right, and one breach of it has, among other things, the consequence of weakening the authority of the rule, which we wish to see generally observed. But Mill does not deny the possibility that sometimes these general moral principles may conflict with each other, or may seem inadequate to the complexities of the situation, and in this case a direct consideration of the particular contemplated action, without reference to general principles, may be necessary, and an attempt must be made to assess the consequences of this individual act. In general, Moore is in complete agreement with this view. But he states more clearly than any utilitarian that there can be no certainty attaching to moral rules. Since moral rules lay down duties, and since duties are determined by consequences, they can never be more than probably right, since certainty about the consequences of actions is impossible. But in the case of fairly broad *types* of action, such as lying, stealing, or murder, the probability that the consequences will be harmful are fairly high, and Moore would subscribe to the two reasons given by the utilitarians for not breaking these general, well-worn moral rules. But he is far more explicit than Mill in allowing that there may be a great number of cases in which the only moral rule which would apply would be a new or revolutionary rule, or where, owing to the complexity and particularity of the circumstances, no rule can be formulated at all. In such cases, Moore says, 'The individual should rather guide his choice by a direct consideration of the intrinsic value or vileness of the effects which his action may produce.' Such considerations as this can, he says, lead to definite and certain conclusions. That is, you may be able positively to assert that if you do a certain action, and if the consequences which will probably follow from it do in fact follow from it, then you will have produced good rather than harm. In this case you must perform the act, if you wish to do what is right. There is still an element of probability in your assertion, namely the probability that the consequences will be as you predict; but there is also, Moore says, the certainty, if you give your mind to discovering it, of the intrinsic worth of the consequences. Moral rules, then, are basically predictions about what will happen. They may therefore always be falsified. Sometimes where there is no stock moral rule to help us, we have to make our own predictions and assessments, and in these cases we do not and cannot attempt to generalize. Each case is decided on its own facts. This theory seems to me to have extreme beauty and economy, and to fit many of the facts of moral life. It succeeds as few other moral theories, except Hume's, do, in allowing for the difference between those cases where the possession of a principle, the avoidance of breaking a rule, is the paramount consideration (as, for instance, where we feel we must keep a promise, because there is a principle against breaking promises); and those cases where we feel it would be immoral to be bound by any ready-made principle, since none would be adequate to the situation. We may not share Moore's confidence that it is possible to see, if we attend to the matter, what has the property of goodness and what has not; but that we try to work out in some such way what it is right to do seems to me beyond question.

Finally, in the last chapter, Moore addresses himself to the question what things in fact possess intrinsic goodness. The method which must be employed, he says, to decide what things have intrinsic value and in what degree, is to consider what things are such that if they existed by themselves in absolute isolation we should yet judge their existence to be good; and to settle the question of degrees of value we must compare these isolated things. This, so far, might not seem to give us much help; and we feel obstinately inclined to ask how we could know when we had come across something with intrinsic value, let alone how we should know if we had carried out the comparison rightly. For Moore, however, there suddenly seem to be no difficulties left (p. 188).

Once the meaning of the question is clearly understood, the answer to it, in its main outlines, appears to be so obvious, that it runs the risk of seeming to be a platitude. By far the most valuable things, which we know or can imagine, are certain states of consciousness which may be roughly described as the pleasures of human intercourse and the enjoyment of beautiful objects. No one probably, who has asked himself the question, has ever doubted that personal affection and the appreciation of what is beautiful in Art or Nature, are good in themselves; nor if we consider strictly what things are worth having *purely for their own sakes*, does it appear probable that any one will think anything else has *nearly* so great a value as the things which are included under these two heads.

The rest of the chapter is devoted to a further analysis of these intrinsically good things, and a discussion of what things are intrinsically bad. The great evils are three in kind: the love of what is ugly or bad; the hatred of what is beautiful or good; and the consciousness of pain. Moore is aware that his conclusions in this chapter may *seem* arbitrary; but since they seem to him obviously true, there is no serious sense in which he can agree that they are arbitrary. He does, however, agree that they are not particularly systematic or unified. But this, he thinks, is just the nature of the case.

To search for 'unity' and 'system' at the expense of truth is not, I take it, the proper business of philosophy, however universally it may have been the practice of philosophers. And that all truths about the universe possess to one another all the various relations which may be meant by 'unity' can only be legitimately asserted when we have carefully distinguished those various relations and discovered what those truths are.

The only two questions which should be asked, he concludes, of any object of ethical inquiry, are first, Has it intrinsic value? and second, Is it a means to the best possible? The results of his attempt to reduce the legitimate questions of ethics to these two will, he says, surprise philosophers but he hopes that they will be acceptable to common sense.

Brief quotation from this final chapter of *Principia Ethica* cannot convey the impression of force and passion which strikes one as one reads it. But if philosophers were, as Moore predicted, surprised by it, they hid their surprise in total silence—perhaps the silence of embarrassment. Moore has frequently been spoken of as the philosopher who concentrated our attention upon the meaning of the word 'good'; and who exposed most fully the nature of the naturalistic fallacy in ethics. This second feat was a matter, it is generally agreed, of great importance, although it is also agreed that the fallacy itself, and arguments against it, had occupied the attention of English moral philosophers from the seventeenth century. I do not of course want to dispute either of these claims to fame. But I think that Moore's concentration on the meaning of the word 'good' should be considered side by side

with his insistence that the point of ethics was to state
what things are good; and his exposure of the naturalistic fallacy should be considered in the context of his
claim that 'good' is the name of a simple unanalysable
quality of things. Moore was not primarily concerned
to discuss the nature of moral words, nor to analyse
what does and does not constitute, in general, an
ethical argument. His concern was simply to find out
what things were good and what were bad. Not sur-
prisingly, therefore, though the final chapter of his
book was neglected by philosophers, it had a powerful
effect upon people actually interested in answering
these questions. This effect was, it must be admitted,
partly produced, not so much by Moore's actual arguments, as by his personality; but I think there is no
passage in all his writing which conveys so powerful an
impression of personality as this. Keynes, in his
memoir 'My Early Beliefs',[1] has much that is extremely
sympathetic and extremely funny to say about the
effect which Moore had upon himself and his contemporaries at Cambridge. He quotes from the last
chapter of *Principia Ethica*, the chapter which he considered contained Moore's religion; and he wrote of it
as follows:

The New Testament is a handbook for politicians
compared with the unworldliness of Moore's chapter on
the Ideal. I know no equal to it in literature since Plato.
And it is better than Plato because it is quite free from
fancy. It conveys the beauty of the literalness of Moore's

[1] J. M. Keynes, *Two Memoirs*, p. 94; Rupert Hart-Davis,
London, 1949.

mind, the pure and passionate intensity of his vision, *un*-fanciful and *un*dressed up. Moore had a nightmare once in which he could not distinguish propositions from tables. But even when awake, he could not distinguish love and beauty and truth from the furniture. They took on the same definition of outline, the same stable, solid objective qualities and common sense reality. I see no reason [Keynes goes on] to shift from the fundamental intuitions of *Principia Ethica*; though they are much too few and too narrow to fit actual experience. That they furnish a justification of experience wholly independent of outside events has become an added comfort, even though one cannot live today secure in the undisturbed individualism which was the extraordinary achievement of the early Edwardian days.

Chapter Three

INTUITIONISM

AFTER the publication of *Principia Ethica*, the climate, in England, was on the whole unfavourable to metaphysical speculation in ethics. It was not so much Moore's actual arguments against the metaphysicians as his whole method of writing, on this and other subjects, which seemed to demand that in future philosophy must be written carefully, and attention must be paid to the actual literal meaning of what was said. I propose to consider next a group of writers, who, like Moore, were, broadly speaking, intuitionists, and who, like him, renounced all claim to deduce an ethical theory from any wide explanatory theory of the nature of reality at large. Typical of this group were the Oxford philosophers Carritt, Prichard, Ross, and Joseph, and in Cambridge, C. D. Broad. I cannot discuss all their theories in detail, but by considering the work of two of them, Prichard and Ross, I hope to be able to show what kinds of methods were used, and conclusions reached. Prichard's publications on moral philosophy were in the form of various articles and lectures, which have now been collected and published together in a book entitled *Moral Obligation*.[1] In his writings, intuitionism can be seen in perhaps its most extreme form and since his appeal in making his points is seldom to reason but usually to 'what will seem obvious if the

[1] *Moral Obligation*. H. A. Prichard. Oxford, 1949.

reader thinks clearly for a moment'; since, that is, we are required to follow arguments less often than to make admissions of what we are supposed really to think, to summarize his views is a matter of some difficulty. The result will inevitably seem somewhat random.

Perhaps the most famous of Prichard's articles was one published in *Mind* in 1912, entitled 'Does Moral Philosophy Rest on a Mistake?'[1] The main purpose of this article was to suggest that arguments are out of place in trying to settle the question of what obligations we are under; and therefore that moral philosophy as hitherto conceived is a non-existent subject. This is of course an exaggeration; but it does appear that Prichard thought of himself as pioneering to introduce a new version of the subject, with new clarity of method and new accuracy. One of the most surprising things about the opening paragraphs of this article is his apparent unawareness of the existence of similar arguments both in Bradley and in Moore. 'Personally', he says, 'I have been led by growing dissatisfaction . . . to wonder whether the subject . . . consists in an attempt to answer an improper question.' The improper question is supposed to be the demand for reasons why something which has the characteristic of being obligatory, has this characteristic. All demands, he says, for proof that something is a duty are mistaken. This view is related to Bradley's. For Bradley explicitly stated that in his opinion the question Why should I be moral? was nonsensical both in general, and in particular cases.

[1] *Moral Obligation*, p. 1.

E

But the likeness to Moore is of course far greater. For Moore's main purpose was, as we have seen, precisely to distinguish those statements in morals for which proof could be given from those for which it could not. And though he, in *Principia Ethica* at least, confined his attention to the characteristic of goodness, and said that statements which ascribed goodness to anything were such that proof was impossible, while Prichard's main concern is with the obligatory, still the likeness is considerable; and indeed in his later book, *Ethics*,[1] Moore also was inclined to treat 'obligatoriness' as another intuitable property. Neither Prichard nor Ross seemed to notice any particular debt to Moore. There are few references to him in Prichard's book, and nearly all that there are are derogatory. He came off a little better at the hands of Ross, who is very careful and fair in his discussions of other philosophers. But neither showed any awareness of the closeness, in many essentials, of their own work to his. But perhaps it is naïve to be surprised at this. Even when considering books written less than half a century ago, it is absurdly easy to regard them as forming a continuous stream of publication, in which the later works somehow flow out of those which came before. We tend to regard Moore as the source, because of the historical accident that *Principia Ethica* was published at the beginning of the century, and because of the powerful impression that he makes upon us. It is difficult not to think, not only of the later as flowing from the earlier, but of the lesser as at least influenced by the greater. But perhaps even 'influence'

[1] *Ethics*. G. E. Moore. Home University Library, 1912.

is too strong a word to use. In any case, if we were to pursue the sources of intuitionism, we should have to go back at least as far as Sidgwick, which would be beyond the scope of this book. The impression remains, however, that Prichard's article was not quite so revolutionary as its title suggests.

I return now to the article itself. Answers to the question 'why should we do our duty?' take, he says, one of two forms. Either they say that doing it would be for our happiness, or alternatively that doing it realizes some good. In the strongest cases these two views are combined, and it is suggested that happiness is the good to be realized. But, Prichard says, there is a gap between the concept of 'good' and the concept of 'what I ought to bring about'. It is always possible, when you have accepted somebody's argument that a thing is good, to go on to ask 'but why should I bring it about?' Prichard considers only briefly, in order to reject it, the view that 'good' and 'what I should bring about' mean the same, or are to be defined one in terms of the other. In any case that would make no serious difference to his case. His point is that ultimately the gap between the apprehension that a thing has any characteristic whatever and the apprehension that it is a duty has to remain unclosed. The apprehension that something is a duty is always a further step. Moore had defined duty in terms of good, and then said that the apprehension of goodness was always a further step, beyond the apprehension of the other qualities of a thing. In his later book, *Ethics*, he regarded the apprehension that something was a duty as separate from the apprehension that it was good, and equally irreducible. Prichard, at least in this article, is inclined to think that the ultimate quality, which cannot be analysed, is that of *being a duty*. If goodness is a rather mysterious quality, obligatoriness seems to me even more so; but I shall return in a moment to the curious difficulties into which Prichard gets, through regarding it as a property of actions. For the moment let us return to this first article. While Bradley appealed to moral consciousness for confirmation of his views, Prichard seems to appeal to something more like common sense. He does not try to show that there is a logical fallacy in identifying obligatoriness with something else; he simply maintains that we do not really do it.

Suppose we ask ourselves whether our sense that we ought to pay our debts or to tell the truth arises from our recognition that in doing so we should be originating something good, e.g. material comfort in A or true belief in B, i.e. suppose we ask ourselves whether it is this aspect of the action which leads to our recognition that we ought to do it. We at once and without hesitation answer 'no'.[1]

Common sense apparently tells us that when we say that something is a duty, or should be done, we are reporting what we simply see to be so.

This apprehension is immediate, in precisely the same sense in which a mathematical apprehension is immediate, e.g. the apprehension that this three-sided figure, in virtue of its being three-sided, must have three angles. Both apprehensions are immediate in the sense that in both, insight into the nature of the subject directly leads

[1] *Moral Obligation*, p. 4.

us to recognize its possession of the predicate; and it is only stating this fact from the other side to say that in both cases the fact apprehended is self-evident.[1]

It is not clear exactly what is meant by 'self-evident', but the mathematical example seems to show that Prichard regards moral truths as necessary. He certainly regards them as indubitable. There has been, he thinks, a parallel in the history of epistemology to the mistake he is calling attention to in the history of morals, namely an insistence on asking for proofs where none is available. (Like Bradley, he just states the analogy between the theory of knowledge and that of morals; but it is perhaps his nearest approach to an argument.) In epistemology, philosophers such as Descartes have been led, by noticing that we all of us sometimes make mistakes, to raise the question whether there can be a proof that, in some cases at least, we are *not* mistaken. Since in any given case, they argue, it is possible to make a mistake, we can never be certain unless we have proof, that in the particular case before us we are not mistaken. Therefore, Prichard says, these philosophers embarked upon a hopeless quest for proof that what we take to be knowledge really is knowledge. But, he says, they have overlooked the fact of the matter, which is that scepticism is impossible. For since when you know something you always and necessarily know also *that* you know it, you cannot be mistaken when you come across something that you know. Genuine knowledge carries with it a kind of trade mark such that it is impossible to mistake it for anything else. If you know, you can't be

[1] *op. cit.* p. 8.

wrong. Descartes had just failed to notice the trade mark which knowledge carries. In moral theory, then, the same mistake is supposed to occur. The demand for proof of the truth of ultimate moral intuitions is as nonsensical as the demand for proof in the case of genuine knowledge. Once you have got a moral intuition, it is impossible to doubt what it is that you have; and anything in terms of which you tried to prove its truth would be necessarily less certain than the intuition itself. Of course it is sometimes possible to suffer momentary doubts in matters of behaviour; but these, Prichard says, can be easily set at rest by merely thinking of the matter more carefully.

Suppose we come genuinely to doubt whether we ought to pay our debts, owing to a genuine doubt whether our previous conviction that we ought to do so is true, a doubt which can, in fact, only arise if we fail to remember the real nature of what we now call our past conviction. The only remedy lies in actually getting into a situation which occasions the obligation, or if our imagination be strong enough in imagining ourselves in that situation, and then letting our moral capacities of thinking do their work.[1]

Prichard elaborates these views about moral obligation in a long essay of this title, which appears in the book, and which was apparently designed to form part of a complete book on the subject.[2] In it, he goes into more detail about the relation between obligation and the happiness of the agent, on the one hand, and on the other hand the relation between obligatoriness and the

---

[1] *op. cit.* p. 16.   [2] *op. cit.* p. 87 *sqq.*

production of good. The essay contains discussion of
the views of other moral philosophers, including Plato,
Butler, Mill, and Kant. My interest in it is solely to call
attention to a curious refinement of his own view about
obligation which is to be found in it. He says that the
main question to be answered is the question 'What is
being under an obligation to do some action?' There
are, he says, two possible answers to this. (1) We may
say that if X is under an obligation, for instance, to
educate Y, then the statement, that he *is* under this
obligation, is the ascribing of a predicate to the true
subject of the proposition, which is the name of an
action, viz. educating Y. On this view, then, the true
analysis of the proposition 'X ought to educate Y'
would be 'educating Y is obligatory-upon-X'. Alternatively (2) we may hold that the predicate is really to be
attached not to the name of the action, but to the name
of the agent. Thus the analysis would be 'X is obliged-
to-educate-Y'. In the earlier essay, I think that
Prichard would have accepted the first of these analyses.
But now he sees a difficulty. For he thinks that 'being
obligatory-upon-X' cannot really be the name of a
quality which is possessed by the education of Y. But
'ought to exist' can be the name of a quality, and so he
thinks 'obligatory-upon-X' must be said to mean the
same as 'ought to exist'. But, he says, where we say that
something ought to be done, we imply that it has not
yet been done; thus in this case we imply that the
education of Y has not yet been undertaken, and therefore does not exist. But 'we can no more either think
or assert of something which we think does not exist

that it ought to exist than we can think or assert anything else about it. Of what we think does not exist, we
can think and assert nothing at all.' Therefore the first
analysis would have to become 'educating Y would be
something which ought to exist, if it existed', which is
to make the original statement hypothetical instead of
categorical. Therefore the first interpretation must be
rejected. This seems to be one of Prichard's odder
intuitions. But he repeats it at the end of the essay:

> If this idea were true, there could be no such thing as
> an obligation to do some action until the act is already
> done, whereas from its very nature there can only be an
> obligation to do an action as long as it is not done. This
> must be so, because though it may at first escape our
> notice, only something which *is* can be something which
> ought or ought not to exist.

This difficulty is generated by the insistence that
being obligatory would, if it were a property, be a
property like yellowness. For Prichard could hold with
some plausibility that if you say of some non-existent
object that it is yellow you must be understood to mean
either that it was yellow when it did exist, or that it
would be yellow if it did exist. But perhaps, equally, the
difficulty is caused by thinking of actions as objects
which have properties, and do or do not *exist*. In any
case, Prichard is forced by these considerations to adopt
the second analysis of the proposition that X is under
an obligation to educate Y, namely that 'being-under-
an-obligation' is a quality of X.

It would be possible to find many more examples of
Prichard's technique applied to problems of moral

philosophy, but one more will be enough. It turns on the very same problem his solution of which we have just noticed. In an essay entitled 'Duty and Ignorance of Fact', which was delivered as a lecture to the British Academy in 1932,[1] Prichard considers the following problem, 'If a man has an obligation, i.e. a duty, to do some action, does the obligation depend on certain characteristics of the situation in which he is, or on certain characteristics of his thought about the situation?' This second solution, that the obligation depends on his thought, Prichard calls the subjective view, and it is upon this that he finally decides. His progress towards this conclusion is typical not merely of his technique, but of the method of intuitionism as a whole. The first thing to be done, he says, is to ascertain which of the two possible views better corresponds with the thought of our ordinary life. He then suggests with considerable plausibility that both the views correspond to at least part of our ordinary thought about moral situations. We often think without question that the *facts* of the situation are 'what render us bound to do the act' . . . for instance to administer a drug which we know would cure a man who is ill. On the other hand we often think we ought, for instance, to slow down as we approach a main road in our car, not because there is traffic on the main road, but because we think there is, or at least may be, traffic. It does not turn out not to have been our duty just because there happens to be nothing coming this time. Prichard will not allow that, in such cases as this, what renders us bound to do

[1] *op. cit.* p. 18 *sqq.*

the act is a probability. Probabilities, he says, are not facts. To speak of a probability is just a short-hand way of speaking about our *thought* about the situation. If this is agreed, it is fairly easy to see that the subjective view will win. And so it does; but at first there seem to be grave objections to it. One objection raised is that on the subjective view what is my duty in a given situation may not be your duty in the same situation, because our thoughts may be different. Another is that, supposing we were omniscient, then on this view, if we are bound to do something (to shout to revive a fainting man is Prichard's rather surprising example), then what renders us bound to shout is not the fact that shouting would revive him, but our knowledge that it would. Thus knowledge is not knowledge *of* the ground of the obligation, but is itself the ground of the obligation. Knowledge of the ground of the obligation would, if it existed, consist of knowledge that we knew that shouting would cure the man. Prichard then sets about to get over these objections to the subjective view. At first he tries reformulating, in general, all statements about obligations. He considers what is meant by 'acting', and he says that 'we have in the end to allow' that we mean by 'acting' 'bringing about the existence of some new state of affairs'. This we may do either directly or indirectly. 'We think that in moving our head we bring about a change of place of our head directly, whereas in giving a friend the family news we bring about his receipt of the news indirectly, i.e. by bringing about directly certain other changes which in turn cause it.' Confining his attention to those cases of actions which are 'bringing about directly', even here he thinks that there is a further distinction which we all of us make:

In no case whatever, where we think of ourselves as having brought about something directly, do we think that our activity was that of bringing about that something. On the contrary we think of the activity as having been of another sort, and mean by saying that we brought about directly what we did, that this activity of another sort had the change in question as a direct effect.

This activity which we *really* think that we performed is the activity of 'setting ourselves' to bring about the change we did bring about. Similarly, if we claim that we *can* do something in the future, what we mean is that we can set ourselves to do that thing; and if now we say we are obliged to do something, what we mean is not that we are obliged to *do* it, but that we are obliged to *set ourselves* to do it. This, Prichard admits, is contrary to the implication of ordinary language; but in this case ordinary language apparently fails to do justice to what we think. If we reformulate the original question about obligation in terms of obligation to set ourselves to bring things about, then Prichard thinks that the objective view, according to which the grounds of the obligation are facts, is rendered less plausible. For since it is acknowledged that setting ourself to do something may not have any effect at all (we may become paralysed quite suddenly), it is less plausible to think that our obligation must rest on the fact that what we are obliged to do will have some particular effect. It can only rest on the fact that we think it will probably have some effect. But the difficulties in the subjective view remain.

For an obligation to do an action seems, he says, to be a characteristic of the action, and therefore *cannot* depend on whether we think it likely that the action has the characteristic; it must depend on its actually having it. And it makes no difference to this difficulty whether we are to characterize doing something or setting ourselves to do something as obligatory.

Finally, he resolves the difficulty in the way we have considered already. He decides that it is a mistake after all to consider obligatoriness as a characteristic of actions. Rather we should think of being-under-an-obligation as a characteristic of people. If this is right, and being under an obligation is a characteristic of ourselves, there is nothing to prevent the presence of this characteristic in us being dependent on some thoughts we may have about the situation we are in. 'Indeed', Prichard says, 'its existence *must* depend on some fact about ourselves.' Thus the fundamental difficulty which seemed to stand in the way of accepting the subjective view has suddenly been dissolved. It remains only, Prichard says, to take some actual case, to consider what we ought to do, and then to ask ourselves whether in fact, in that particular case, the subjective or the objective view was true. Did we, that is, make our decision on the facts of the case, or on what we thought about the facts? Here Prichard engagingly tells us that there is little that need be said,[1] 'For we have only to carry out this procedure to find not that we are *inclined to think*, or even that we are of the opinion that, but that we are *certain*, i.e. *know* that the answer turns not on

[1] *op. cit.* p. 38.

the nature of the situation but on that of our thought
about it.'

So the problem posed at the beginning of the essay
is solved. We may be inclined to ask why, if this simple
introspective method was to be so successful in the end,
it could not be applied at the beginning. But the
problem has first to be defined clearly. Next we have to
consider what we would ordinarily think about its solution. If difficulties seem, as they did here, to be
generated by what we would ordinarily think, we have
to think further what we really mean when we use
certain of the expressions involved. At this stage in the
argument, Prichard is not merely consulting ordinary
use, nor what the plain man would say. He is prepared
to legislate; we ought to think of being obliged as a
characteristic of people, and not of obligatoriness as a
characteristic of actions, even if we do not think this at
first. The reason is that problems are resolved by the
proper way of thinking, or rather they need never arise.
In order to bring out the proper way of looking at the
matter he suggests that it is better to use the form of
words 'I ought to do X' rather than the form 'X is
right'. Then, once these confusions have been cleared
out of the way, simple inspection of the facts will
indeed be sufficient to solve the original problem. We
have not exactly progressed. It is rather that the object
we started by looking at has been stripped of its
obscuring and confusing covers so that now one quick
look will be enough to tell us its true nature. But all the
same, doubts may remain; and for two reasons. First
we may doubt whether the object we were required to

look at was really worth it. Do we, or can we, care very much about the solution to Prichard's problems? Secondly, we may doubt whether we are really seeing so clearly in the end. Prichard pushes us through the argument with a great deal of energy. But it is doubtful whether we want to admit all the things he says we must admit, or whether we really do think all the things he tells us we think. It is here that the appalling weakness of Prichard's position lies. If a problem is supposed to be solved by the consideration of common sense and what people ordinarily think, then not only has the problem to be one which people would be ordinarily prepared to think about, but what they would ordinarily say and think must be truly stated. It is not in fact so easy, as Prichard seems to think, to say *what* our moral vocabulary means or *what* our moral concepts are. It is all very well to ride roughshod over ordinary language; this may often be necessary and desirable for philosophers. But it is in the highest degree undesirable to do this in the name of ordinary language itself.

With Prichard, then, the intuitive clarity of his conclusions turns out to be a fake clarity; and there is a good deal of bluster in the assurance with which he finally states the conclusions themselves.

If we turn now to Ross, the tone is very different. I shall discuss, very briefly, Ross's book *The Foundations of Ethics*. This was published in 1939, and is based on the Gifford Lectures, delivered in 1935.[1] Ross says of his book that it is to be a critical study 'of the moral

[1] *The Foundations of Ethics.* Sir W. David Ross. Oxford, 1939.

consciousness and of the main moral theories'. In fact the ground it covers is not quite so wide as this description might make us hope. But the topics which he selected to discuss were those which seemed central to the whole of this group of intuitionist philosophers. The task of moral philosophers, Ross held, is to resolve the difficulties into which plain men might fall if they considered, not this or that particular moral problem, but the status of those moral principles which they would use to settle *any* moral problem. People may become confused by the fact that their principles, none of which perhaps they want to give up, may conflict in some cases; they may find, for instance, that they cannot tell the truth without endangering someone's life, or they cannot keep a promise without telling a lie. Another source of confusion may be that they see that principles change at different times, and are different in different societies. It is to the solution of such general difficulties as these that moral philosophers should address themselves.

As regards the first problem, that of the conflict of principles, Ross holds that principles cannot survive if they are taken to be absolute.

The only way to save the authority of such rules is to recognize them not as rules guaranteeing the rightness of any act that falls under them, but as rules guaranteeing that any act which falls under them tends so far as that aspect of its nature goes, to be right, and can be rendered wrong only if in virtue of another aspect of its nature it comes under another rule by reason of which it tends more decidedly to be wrong.

Kant, Ross says, overshot the mark in saying that

principles could be absolute. But the trouble is that it would be hard not to overshoot the mark which Ross has set before us. If you shoot at all you are sure to go too far. Intuitionism has here lost all its dash; we are to be so cautious in stating moral principles that they will scarcely serve us as guides at all. The second puzzle, that of the relativity of moral principles, is to be dealt with by grading principles in order of self-evidence. There are some which appear, according to Ross, to be completely self-evident, and can never be given up. Such, for instance, is the principle that we should produce as much good as we can. Ross does not, I think, mean to suggest that even this principle can *never* conflict with any other, for later he says that it might conflict with the principle of keeping promises. It is only that no consideration of the morals of another age or society would ever make us doubt whether this is a moral principle at all. No doubt this is correct; at least it is very natural to regard it as true by definition that it is a moral duty to produce as much good as possible. This at any rate was Moore's view (though admittedly not Ross's). But just because of the tautological nature of this rule, it is not very likely that we shall find any disputes centring upon it. The top grade of principles therefore, even if there are more of them than this one, is not likely to be very helpful. The second grade is made up of those principles which can be derived from the first by reference to general truths about human nature; the third grade is of principles derived from the first by reference to the particular circumstances which obtain in any given period or place; the fourth and last grade is of principles wrongly derived from the first by reference to false opinions about human nature.

In order to help non-philosophers in these and perhaps other ways, Ross says that it is further necessary for philosophers to consider moral words, and moral characteristics. Moral words should be considered in their actual use; but this study, Ross suggests, is more properly lexicography than philosophy. It is, as we should by now expect, to the study of moral characteristics that the philosopher is really supposed to devote himself. If you take any moral characteristic, there seem to be three questions which, Ross says, we should answer with regard to it. The first question is whether or not it exists at all; the second is what is its nature; and the third is what objects are possessed of it. Ross himself attempts to answer these questions first about the characteristic 'rightness' and then about 'goodness'. To take 'rightness' first; we are told that it is self-evident that rightness exists since it is self-evident that there are many situations in which there would be one right thing to do. We see in a moral situation a number of prima facie duties, that is, things which at first glance seem right, because they fall under some moral principle. And because these prima facie duties exist, 'we see that there must be some action which would have a higher degree of resultant suitability than any of the other actions that could be done in the circumstances, though we may have no certainty as to which action would have this characteristic'. Regarding a moral situation that is, is enough to assure us that there is *something* which is right, though not to assure

F

us *what* is right. As a matter of fact it is not obvious *either* that we always suppose that there is something which it would be right to do, *or* that we therefore think of rightness as a characteristic of anything. Ross assumes that we do both these things, and so the next step is to reflect on the nature of this characteristic. Ross examines a number of attempts to define 'right' doing for it rather what Moore does for 'good', and concludes that rightness is indefinable; and even if it can be put into some more general category such as 'suitability', its differentia cannot be stated, 'just as while red is a species of colour, what distinguishes it from other colours can be indicated only by saying that it is the colour that is red'. As to what things have this indefinable characteristic, Ross allows that a number of things may be said to possess it, but that *properly* only actions, acts of self-exertion, are right. Like Prichard Ross is inclined to be cautious about saying that a whole overt action can be right, since he, like Prichard, thinks that the whole complete action contains some element for which we are not responsible, or rather that there are some aspects of an action which it is not in our power to bring about. Once again, the spectre of paralysis is made to haunt us. It cannot be that moving my arm is what is right, since suddenly I may not be able to do so much, and still I may have done right. What is right is exerting myself or setting myself to move my arm. This is the general nature of the thing which may qualify to have the characteristic of rightness. But Ross goes on to ask *how* they qualify. This is surprising, since we have already been told that right ness is indefinable. And, as one would expect, the answer to the question is negative. It is not only, and not always, the fact that they lead to the production of good that makes right actions right; what it is that makes them right has to be grasped intuitively, from a general consideration of the circumstances. Once again we are offered the analogy with mathematics: 'We see the predicate, though not included in the definition of the subject, to belong necessarily to anything which satisfies that definition.' But Ross suggests that, if anything, we can be *more* certain of the truths of ethics than of the truths of mathematics, since, whereas in mathematics we have to make do with diagrams which are less than perfect representations of true circles or squares, in ethics we can find actual examples of cruelty, generosity, promise-keeping and the other subjects of ethical propositions.

From 'right' Ross moves on to 'good'. 'Good', he says, is used in two main senses, 'good as means' and 'good as an end' or 'good in itself'. Ruling out the first sense as of no interest to ethics, Ross sub-divides the second sense into 'good' meaning 'worthy of interest' and 'good' meaning 'worthy of admiration'. In both these sense 'goodness' is the name of a quality; but in the sense of 'worthy of interest' it is a quality which can be recognized only by reference to rightness, for a thing is good in this sense if and only if it is such that interest in it would, if it existed, be 'right or morally suitable'. The primary quality of goodness, however, that is, the quality of being *worthy of admiration*, is recognizable only by a separate intuition. Finally Ross tries to throw light on the question what things have this characteristic of goodness. The answer is that various interests, motives, and desires are the things which possess the characteristic. Kant was wrong to say that only the disinterested desire to do one's duty was good; Ross suggests instead that it is the best of all motives or desires, but may be made better still by the addition of some other good motive, such as the desire to give pleasure to others, or the desire to improve our own characters.

In the whole book, the only arguments we find are those directed to the refutation of the views of other philosophers; for Ross, like Prichard and Moore, could not consistently argue for views which were supposed either to be self-evidently true, or at least certain, if one thought about the matter clearly. But Ross does not speak with the passion of Moore nor with the frenetic emphasis of Prichard. His is a cool voice simply making statements, dividing, sub-dividing, and categorizing. He says that we know the truths of ethics as we know the truths of mathematics, even perhaps better; but what we know suddenly seems to be rather boring: we know that we should do good; we know that we should keep promises, at least as long as nothing very important stands in the way of keeping them; we know that we should take an interest in the pleasures of others, but not in our own pleasures; we know that we should try to improve ourselves. Rightness and goodness are the two moral properties with which Ross is concerned. Both of these have to be intuitively grasped when they are present in a thing. But we can of course, with long experience, come to make inductive generalizations

about moral matters. For instance, if we have frequently observed cases of lying and noticed that among
their other qualities they have the quality of moral
wrongness, then we can generalize and say 'lying is
wrong'. This, then, becomes a moral rule, if we convert
it to the legitimate form 'we ought not to lie', and this
moral rule binds us, though not absolutely. We have a
prima facie duty to obey it. If we wish not to, the onus
is on us to show why not. For of course moral generalizations, like any generalization, are fallible and may not
apply exactly in every case. So we may have to apply
our intuitive faculty again to the individual case before
us, to see whether perhaps, in this case, we can detect
moral rightness instead of moral wrongness in the lie.
Ross is not even *certain* that rightness is indefinable. He
thinks that it is, but he is at least prepared for us, if we
choose, to use a synonym, namely 'moral fittingness, or
moral suitability'. These permitted synonyms seem to
me to be revealing. The intuitive powers which are
ascribed to us by Ross are very small powers; and they
will work only in well-worn fields. The concept of the
fitting or the suitable is a concept properly applied in
cases where we know our way around pretty well. They
suggest a set of conventions, any breach of which will
be immediately detected by us. They suggest, just as
Bradley suggested before, that we each of us have our
place and our position, to which some behaviour is
proper, some is not. But suppose all these conventions
and systems break up? Shall we still know what is
fitting? I do not see how we could be expected to. I do
not know what is fitting behaviour in a prison camp or

in an occupied country, even though I may know what is fitting in my role of housewife or college tutor. It is not accidental that in both Prichard and Ross we notice the examples grow more and more trivial and absurd. It is difficult to imagine feeling very greatly exercised about whether to shout to revive a fainting man, whether to slow down as we approach the main road in our car, or whether to return the book that we have borrowed. It is no comfort in cases like these to be told that we need only set ourselves to do them, and that we shall not be blamed if we do not thereafter succeed. We do not want comfort in these cases. Perhaps if Bradley had said that it was enough to set ourselves to possess the whole universe, we should have been grateful that we did not have to succeed. But when it comes to returning what we have borrowed, if not only is this a fair example of our duties, but if we need not actually succeed in doing even so much, then we begin to feel that the intuitionists' moral philosophy is a cheat. It does not really deal with the subject we had been led to expect. There may always be a step to be taken between saying that an action has any characteristic at all and saying that we should do it; and we may need intuition to help us to take the step. But if the actions are so obvious or so farcical, the intuition cannot be much of a thing either. If moral philosophy had always been based on a mistake, perhaps the best course would have been to stop doing it. It is certainly difficult to see that much more of it could profitably have been undertaken in this particular way.

Chapter Four

THE EMOTIVE THEORY

IN 1936, three years before the publication of *The Foundations of Ethics*, *Language, Truth and Logic* was published.[1] No book has more clearly called for metaphorical description. It was obviously a bombshell. Ayer made no particular claims to originality. In the preface to the first edition he said: 'The views which are put forward in this treatise derive from the doctrines of Bertrand Russell and Wittgenstein, which are themselves the logical outcome of the empiricism of Berkeley and David Hume.' And it is true that the book is firmly in the empiricist tradition. But he goes on himself to say that the philosophers with whom he was in closest agreement were the logical positivists; and the tremendous impact of the book was largely due to its being the first, and most brilliant, exposition of their views to be published in England.

The book contains one chapter on ethics, which is entitled 'Critique of Ethics and Theology'.[2] It is superbly short, less than twenty pages. Ayer's general contention is, briefly, that any statement which has meaning must fall into one of two categories. Either it must be analytic, that is necessarily true but not concerned with empirical matters of fact; or it must be empirical. If it

[1] *Language, Truth and Logic*. A. J. Ayer. Victor Gollancz, 1936.
[2] *op. cit.* chapter 6.

is empirical, it can never be more than probable; it is, in fact, a hypothesis. Both the meaning and the probability of the hypothesis are established by empirical verification. That is to say, if a statement is to qualify for the second category, it must be capable of verification by sense-experience. According to this theory, then, no statement can be said to have any meaning which is not either analytic, or verifiable by observation of the world. The propositions of logic and mathematics, and all definitions of symbols, fall into the first category; the propositions of science and of ordinary life, in so far as these simply state matters of fact, fall into the second category. There are no other categories. It can be seen at once that this creates a problem for ethics. Ethical propositions, such as that theft is wrong, or that generosity is to be encouraged, do not come under either of the possible headings. No one would wish to say that such statements were analytic; they do not, in Ayer's words, 'simply record our determination to use symbols in a certain fashion'. But it would be equally implausible to suggest that they were capable of verification by ordinary sense-experience. Even the most enthusiastic intuitionist would never maintain that one literally saw or heard the goodness of an action or motive. In Chapter 6 of *Language, Truth and Logic* Ayer sets out to deal with this problem. 'It is our business', he says, 'to give an account of "judgements of value" which is both satisfactory in itself and consistent with our general empiricist principles.'

Ayer first considers the suggestion that, while ethical propositions cannot be directly verified by appeal to sense-experience, yet they can be translated without loss into propositions which can be so verified. If this suggestion were accepted, value judgements would be saved, since they could fit ultimately, though not immediately, into the second class of meaningful statements. Ayer considers two versions of this view, which he calls respectively, subjectivism and utilitarianism. Subjectivists hold that to say a thing is right is to say that it is generally approved of, or alternatively that it is approved of by the speaker. Ayer rejects this view, on the grounds that it cannot *mean the same* to say the one as to say the other, since it is possible without contradiction to say of something that it is both generally approved of and wrong. And even if the extreme subjectivist view is taken, still it is not actually contradictory to say 'I approve of this and it is wrong'. Ayer therefore rejects the contention that ethical predicates such as 'right' or 'good' can be translated into the empirical predicates 'approved of by everybody' or 'approved of by me'. On exactly the same grounds he rejects utilitarianism. Since it is not actually a contradiction to say that it is sometimes wrong to perform the action which would cause the greatest happiness, 'right action' and 'action causing the greatest happiness' cannot mean the same. For it *would* be contradictory to say 'It is sometimes wrong to perform the right action'. It is therefore shown, Ayer thinks, that no translation of ethical terms into empirical terms is possible.

It looks at first as though the only alternative to the naturalism thus rejected is what Ayer calls 'Absolutism'. 'The view that statements of value are not controlled by observation as ordinary empirical propositions are, but only by a mysterious "intellectual intuition".' But to accept this would obviously be incompatible with the general theory that the only significant non-analytic propositions are those which are empirically verifiable. Therefore Ayer rejects absolutism too and adopts a third theory. Ethical concepts are agreed to be unanalysable but this is because they are not real concepts at all. They are 'pseudo-concepts'. The predicates used in value judgements are not proper predicates; they do not stand for qualities of things which can be picked out by the senses.

The presence [Ayer says] of an ethical symbol in a proposition adds nothing to its factual content. . . . If I say to someone 'you acted wrongly in stealing that money', I am not stating anything more than if I had simply said 'you stole that money'. In adding that this action is wrong I am simply evincing my moral disapproval of it.

And so, if nothing is stated in any given proposition except that something is wrong it follows that nothing is stated in it at all. If for instance I say not 'you were wrong to steal the money' where at least 'you stole the money' purports to be true, but 'stealing money is wrong', then what I have said 'expresses no proposition which can be either true or false'. I have done *nothing* but evince my moral disapproval, and the question of truth or falsehood does not arise. It follows from this, in accordance with the general verification theory, that a pure value judgement does not qualify as a meaningful statement at all. It plainly is not analytic; nor does it come into the second class of meaningful statements for the good reason that it is not a statement, and therefore cannot, naturally, be verified. 'If a sentence makes no statement at all, there is obviously no sense in asking whether what it says is true or false.' It follows further, on Ayer's view, that it is impossible for two people to contradict each other on points of morals (or indeed of aesthetics either, for all value judgements are analysed in the same way). Nor am I contradicting myself if I say first that something is right and then that it is wrong. All I am doing by using the words 'right' and 'wrong' is expressing my ethical feelings. I am not stating that I have certain feelings, for if I were, I could contradict myself in saying that I had them and that I did not have them at the same time. But expressions of feeling are not assertions, and though they may suggest a contradiction (as laughing and crying together might be thought to), they cannot actually contradict each other. It is not possible, therefore, to argue about questions of value; the most we can do is continue to express ourselves, and give vent to our emotions.

This, then, is the bald statement of Ayer's view, which he offers as an alternative to both absolutism and naturalism. In passing, Ayer adds a further refinement, which turns out, in the later development of the theory, to be very important. 'It is worth mentioning', he says, 'that ethical terms do not serve only to express feeling. They are calculated also to arouse feeling, and so to stimulate action. Indeed some of them are used in such a way as to give the sentences in which they occur the effect of commands.' He goes on to distinguish ethical terms one from another by the forcefulness of the command contained in the meaning of each. Thus 'duty' contains an emphatic command, 'ought' a less emphatic one, and 'good' contains scarcely any element of command at all.

It is obvious that what we have in *Language, Truth and Logic* is a sketch of an ethical theory, rather than a complete theory. In the years that followed there was a considerable number of articles by various philosophers, all of them filling in the gaps, and elaborating the details of this kind of theory. But, though I shall say something about some of these in the second half of this chapter, I want to stop for a moment to consider the theory as it was presented by Ayer. It is not unfair to him, I think, to regard this chapter, not so much as an argument, as a statement of a view, and a view which could properly be said to be that of a school of philosophy. It is part of the measure of the importance of his book that no sooner was it published than it seemed that emotivists in ethics were everywhere. They had not been converted by the book; it was their creed already. For instance in the same year as *Language, Truth and Logic* came out, Ogden and Richards published their famous book, *The Meaning of Meaning*.[1] They first introduced the word 'emotive' and used it in just the way that Ayer did. And their ethical theory, being derived from the same sources, and the outcome of the very same influences, is, even verbally, very close to his. One quotation will be enough to show this:

'Good' is alleged to stand for a unique, unanalysable

[1] *The Meaning of Meaning.* C. K. Ogden and I. A. Richards. Kegan Paul, 1936.

concept ... (which) is the subject matter of ethics. When so used the word stands for nothing whatever, and has no symbolic function. Thus when we use it in the sentence 'This is good' we merely refer to *this* and the addition of 'is good' makes no difference whatever to our reference. When, on the other hand we say 'this is red', the addition of 'is red' to '*this*' does symbolize an extension of our reference, namely to some other red thing. But 'is good' has no comparable *symbolic* function: it serves only as an emotive sign expressing our attitude to *this* and perhaps evoking similar attitudes in other persons, or inciting them to actions of one kind or another.[1]

The extreme simplicity of Ayer's remarks about ethics (which he himself called attention to in the preface to the 1947 edition of the book), as well as their brevity, made them peculiarly suitable as dogma, and this is what emotivism, in one form or another, became.

Two preliminary points should be made. First, there is no purpose in discussing the almost hysterical fury with which the doctrines of *Language, Truth and Logic* were greeted in some quarters. On the whole, the rage was in inverse proportion to the intelligence of the attack. Logical positivists were accused not so much of being mistaken as of being wicked. They were held actually responsible for the greatest evils of the twentieth century. It is easy to see why. The verification principle entailed the total dismissal of metaphysics; and with metaphysics had to go the propositions of religion. Even ethical and aesthetic propositions were, as we have seen, said to be literally meaningless. It is

[1] *op. cit.* p. 125.

not surprising that people felt called upon to defend
their most deeply held convictions. Moreover, the
whole point of the book was polemical. No doubt Ayer
aimed to upset people, and he admirably succeeded.
But by now we can distinguish this temporary and
therapeutic aim from the question of the actual truth
or falsity of the doctrines. We can try to interpret the
language of 'pseudo-concepts' and 'nonsense' soberly
and without emotion. No doubt the verification
principle, as a theory of meaning, was grotesquely
narrow and limited in its applicability. But our concern
here is not with this general question but with the
emotive theory of ethics itself. And this leads to my
second preliminary point. In the chapter on 'Ethics'
Ayer, perhaps unwisely, presents his case for emotivism
as though it rested primarily on a desire to find an
ethical theory which would not conflict with the general
verification doctrine. He wrote almost as if any theory
would do, so long as it was consistent with the rest of
the book. In particular, he appears to reject what he
calls absolutism on the grounds that to accept it 'would
undermine the whole of our main argument'. Criticisms
of the emotive theory have therefore sometimes taken
the form simply of criticisms of the verification
principle, in the mistaken belief that if this were refuted
there would be no further reason for even considering
an emotive theory. Thus Ross in *The Foundations of
Ethics* seems to regard the emotive theory as an attempt
to 'discredit ethics', which would never have been
undertaken if it had not been for the demands of logical
positivism as a whole. Both parts of this criticism are

misguided, though both are understandable, considering the general iconoclastic tone of *Language, Truth and Logic*. In the introduction to the second edition, Ayer notices that Ross and others have treated the ethical theory as though it were a mere corollary of the verification principle, and he denies that this is so. He says that even if the verification principle is rejected there are still good reasons for accepting an emotive theory of ethics. But naturally he cannot there go into the question of what these good reasons are. But at any rate it is clear that we are justified in considering the theory by itself and on its own merits. It is not *mere* iconoclasm, nor is it a theory just put together for the purposes of a particular argument. It is far more plausible and more serious than either of these descriptions would suggest. Of course there is an important connexion between the emotive theory, and Ayer's general epistemological views. It is only the particular presentation of the connexion which might be called into question.

The most obvious feature of the theory is its firm rejection of naturalism. Moore's formula for the rejection of naturalistic and other definitions of 'good' was as follows: of any proposed definition—let us call the defining phrase D—you could always intelligibly ask 'Is D good?' And this showed that you were not really treating D as equivalent to 'good'. Ayer's formula is that for any proposed definition D, you could always deny without contradiction that it was good, and therefore you could not be using D as equivalent to good. Ayer argues, that is, that it makes sense to deny of any

empirical characteristic whatever that it is good; Moore
argues that it makes sense in every case to *raise the
question* of denying it. Thus Ayer, like Moore, bases his
rejection of naturalism on logical grounds. It would be
perfectly open to him to use the phrase 'naturalistic
fallacy'; and indeed the phrase has come to be used far
more often than not in the context of some sort of
emotive theory, in which the alternative to accepting a
naturalistic definition of ethical terms is to say that
ethical terms are emotive, or at any rate non-descriptive. This leaves the question whether they can be
defined at all somewhat unclear. Ayer, whose version of
the theory we are still considering, is careful to distinguish normative, or properly ethical, uses of ethical
terms from descriptive uses. I may say that something
is good and mean *nothing more* than that it is enjoined
by a certain code; at least this is what he claims. In this
case I am using 'good' descriptively, and in this use it
can be defined. But if I use 'good' properly, then in
using it I am merely expressing my feelings. In this use
'good' cannot be defined, because it does not stand for
any concept which could be analysed. Therefore in the
sense in which definition is equivalent to analysis, 'good'
is indefinable, necessarily. But that is not to say that I
could not be taught when it was proper to use the word.
There are conventions governing the use of ejacula-
tions, and these can be explained. Saying 'That's bad'
when I felt pleased by something would be inappro-
priate and misleading in exactly the same way as saying
'hooray' when I stubbed my toe would be. 'Hooray' or
'damn' cannot be defined, because they do not stand

for characteristics of things. When we utter them we are not stating facts about things but expressing our feelings. The *names* of feelings can of course be defined, and in using *them* I am making factual statements. Thus, if I say 'I am very much put out', what I say may be true or false. Another way of saying that it may, is to say that 'very much put out' stands for a concept, and concepts can be analysed. But 'damn' does not *stand for* anything. The position of ethical terms is the same.

It can perhaps be seen now that the difference between Ayer and Moore is far and away greater and more important than is the agreement between them. In spite of the close similarity in the actual form of their rejection of naturalism, even their purposes in rejecting it are wholly different. Moore's main concern is to state what are the things which are good in themselves. His interest in the *language* of ethics is simply preliminary to this. He needs to expose the mistakes of others in their treatment of the concept of 'goodness', in order to expound the truth; and this truth is not primarily a truth about words at all, but a genuinely ethical truth. This fact cannot be too strongly emphasized. Those philosophers who conceive the business of ethics to be the analysis of the language of morals are not following Moore, though they may claim to do so; but they are, on the other hand, in the true logical positivist tradition. Ayer is perfectly explicit about the task of moral philosophy. He divides ethical propositions into four main classes. There are propositions which express definitions of ethical terms, there are propositions which describe

G

moral experience, there are exhortations to virtue, and
finally there are actual ethical judgements, that such
and such a thing is good or is bad. 'In fact,' he says, 'it
is easy to see that only the first of our four classes,
namely that which comprises the propositions relating
to the definitions of ethical terms, can be said to constitute ethical philosophy.' Descriptions of moral experience are matters for psychology or anthropology;
and the two remaining classes turn out really to be one.
For exhortations to virtue would doubtless be agreed
not only to urge other people to action, but also to
express the speaker's feelings about the action; and we
have already seen that ethical judgements proper, when
analysed, emerge as combined expression of feeling and
command or exhortation. Now it was absolutely to be
expected that Ayer should regard the function of moral
philosophers in this light. It is demanded by his theory
of the function of philosophy in general. In the Preface
to the first edition of *Language, Truth and Logic*, having
explained that any proposition which fails to pass the
test of empirical verifiability is literally senseless, Ayer
says 'it will be found that much of what ordinarily
passes for philosophy is metaphysics (i.e. senseless
according to this criterion and, in particular, that i
cannot be significantly asserted that there is a non-
empirical world of values . . .' and he adds that the
philosopher's function is 'to clarify the propositions o
science by exhibiting their logical relationships and by
defining the symbols which occur in them'. The moral
philosopher, then, has first to show that the proposition
of morals are not scientific, that is, that they do no

state empirical facts, and has then to analyse the terms which they do contain. When this has been done, his task is over. What is perhaps surprising, to look a little ahead, is that this task of analysis of the words of ethics should have continued for so long to dominate English and American moral philosophy. Admittedly great subtleties of analysis turned out to be possible, which were not apparent in the first sketch. But the dogma of the limits of the task—the insistence that one could first mark off ethical propositions from all others and then show how they work, and that this was moral philosophy—these assumptions seem to have outlived the general beliefs about the nature of philosophy out of which they originally arose.

As to the actual analysis which Ayer proposed, the emotive theory itself, this has great plausibility and appeal for any empiricist. Ayer was perfectly right to insist on his empiricist ancestry. For instance Berkeley, in the Introduction to the *Principles of Human Knowledge*, distinguished four different 'ends of language' and suggested that there were more. Besides the communicating of ideas, 'There are other ends, as the raising of some passion, the exciting to or deterring from some action, the putting the mind in some particular disposition.' And Berkeley mentions the word 'good' and the word 'danger' as examples of words which may be so used. The word 'good' may raise a passion without there being any particular characteristic which is referred to by its use. More important is the tradition of Hume. Hume insisted that moral judgements were neither necessary and *a priori*, nor were they descriptions of any actual feature of the world. All that there really is in the world is a series of sense impressions, and whereas we have actual sense impressions of the physical characteristics of things, their moral value is not among these characteristics. When, therefore, we use ethical or aesthetic terms we are not directly referring to things in the world, but to our own attitude towards these things. We have seen that Ayer rejected what he called the subjectivist view that to say something is good is the same as to say that it is approved of, and I suppose that this is the doctrine he would ascribe to Hume. In fact I think Hume did not mean precisely this, but for our present purposes the details of his doctrine are irrelevant. What is clear is that Ayer shares Hume's basic conviction that value is not part of the world. This is the fundamental feature of those empirical theories of morals which have had the most powerful influence in the twentieth century and whose most dramatic statement is to be found at the end of Wittgenstein's *Tractatus*:

The sense of the world must lie outside the world. In the world everything is as it is and happens as it does happen. In it there is no value—and if there were it would be of no value. If there is any value which is of value, it must lie outside all happening and being so. For all happening and being so is accidental.

The logical positivists were professionally interested only in scientific, fact-stating discourse. They thought that such discourse could be marked off once and for all from other uses of language, and they further thought that these other uses, in so far as they often masqueraded as fact-stating when they were not, were actually vicious. This explains the hostility, in *Language, Truth and Logic*, implicit in such expressions as 'pseudo-concepts' and so on. This explains why Wittgenstein in the *Tractatus* said that there could be no propositions of ethics. It explains, finally, why having roughly characterized ethical language as emotive, in very much the same way as Berkeley had, Ayer displays very little further interest in it. His purpose was negative; he wanted to clear the field for significant discourse, and what was thrown out, provided it was shown to be truly non-scientific, was not worth examining very closely. Although as we shall see in a moment, the first crudity of the emotive theory was rubbed off very soon, what was not questioned was the distinction between descriptive and evaluative language. The belief that somewhere behind all discourse there lay a pure array of facts, with pure fact-stating statements belonging to it with which evaluative statements could be contrasted —this belief seems to have had a far longer life in the field of ethics than anywhere else.

I want now to turn to the later developments of the emotive theory. Inevitably a lot of interesting and subtle work will be left out altogether here. All that I can hope to do is to show how the theory developed as it came into contact with various other philosophical tendencies, and as philosophers came to be interested in it for its own sake. The most important name in the history of this development is that of the American philosopher C. L. Stevenson. In 1937 he published in *Mind* an article entitled 'The Emotive Meaning of Ethical

Terms', which was of the greatest importance.[1] I shall consider the arguments contained in this article in some detail. Stevenson says that ethical questions take the form 'Is so and so good?' The aim of his article is to make such ethical questions clear. He sets out a list of requirements which, he says, it has been generally and rightly assumed need to be fulfilled by any satisfactory definition of the word 'good'. These are, first, that on any analysis one must be able to disagree about whether something is good or not; secondly, that 'goodness' must have a certain magnetism. That is, to be told that something is good must at least have a tendency to make one act in its favour. Thirdly, the presence or absence of goodness in a thing must not be verifiable by the use of any scientific method. Stevenson claims that there is some one sense of 'good' which satisfies all these requirements, and this is the sense analysed by the help of the word 'emotive'. He describes this theory as a kind of interest theory; that is, it is related to the theories of Hobbes and Hume. But whereas traditional interest theories have assumed that ethical statements are descriptions of existing states of interest (for instance that the speaker approves or that people in general approve of whatever is under discussion), the emotive theory recognizes that 'the major use of ethical judgements is to create an interest'. It is the emphasis upon description, he says, which renders all the traditional theories irrelevant as analyses of the word 'good'. All this is familiar. There is nothing here, except the air of caution and moderation, which is not in *Language*,

[1] *Mind*, Volume XLVI, p. 14.

Truth and Logic. But Stevenson goes on to raise two further questions of considerable importance. The first is the question how an ethical sentence acquires its power, and the second is, what has this influence to do with the meaning of the sentences. It is to this second question that he goes on to address himself.

Stevenson starts by distinguishing the descriptive from the dynamic use of words. It is important that he is so far saying nothing about the meaning of words, but only about the various uses to which they may be put. Thus, if I know that my companion has a horror of moths, I may say 'moth' not to describe what I see, nor even to inform him that there is a moth in the railway carriage, but specifically in order to get him to leave. Stevenson does not deny that in such a case the word 'moth' does also describe or inform; in fact its dynamic purpose would fail if its ordinary meaning were not understood. His point is simply that we may use the very same words either to inform, or to arouse sympathy, or to drop hints, and so on. He defines the meaning of a word as the psychological causes and effects with which its utterence *tends* to be associated. The meaning, he says, is a causal or dispositional property of the word. There is then, on this interpretation of meaning, a kind of meaning particularly associated with dynamic uses. This is to be called emotive meaning. (The term, as we have seen, was originally used by Ogden and Richards in *The Meaning of Meaning*, but it soon passed into current philosophical language.) 'The emotive meaning of a word is the tendency of a word, arising through the history of its usage, to produce (result from) affective responses in people', and again,

> Certain words, because of their emotive meaning, are suited to a certain kind of dynamic use—so well suited, in fact, that the hearer is likely to be misled if we use them in any other way. The more pronounced a word's emotive meaning is, the less likely people are to use it purely descriptively.

The relation between dynamic use and emotive meaning is contingent, not necessary. But it is a very important relation. If in defining a word with emotive meaning, such as the word 'good', the emotive element of the meaning is left out, people are deceived into thinking that the word is most often used descriptively, while in fact it is most often used dynamically. Stevenson goes on to apply this general principle to the particular question of defining 'good'. He concludes that it is impossible to define it exactly; for in any proposed analysis of its meaning the emotive element, though it may not be left out, will be distorted. Thus he suggests that the meaning of 'This is good' is more or less the same as the meaning of 'I like this. Like it as well.' But in the latter phrase the element of command is explicit, whereas in 'this is good' it is implicit. The emotive force of 'this is good' is therefore subtle while in the supposed analysis it is crude. Nevertheless, Stevenson is not worried by the ultimate failure to find an exact equivalent for 'good'.

> It is possible [he says] to say that 'this is good' is *about* the favourable interest of the speaker and the hearer . . . and that it has a pleasing emotive meaning which fits

the words for use in suggestion. This is a rough description of meaning not a definition. But it serves the same clarifying function that a definition ordinarily does; and that, after all, is enough.

All the requirements with which he started are satisfied by this account of the meaning of 'good'. It is possible for people to disagree about whether something is good, since it is clear that people can have divergent interests. Obviously the requirement that 'good' should have magnetic force is satisfied, for this is precisely what the emotive part of its meaning is. The last requirement was that the presence or absence of goodness in a thing should not be able to be settled by purely scientific methods, and this too is plainly satisfied. If I am commanding you to like something by telling you that it is good, the question how I get to know that it is good need not arise. On the other hand empirical investigations are not wholly ruled out by this analysis since I may offer reasons for issuing the command, and what I give as reasons may be checked by empirical means. Thus if I say 'This book is good, because it will make you laugh', while you cannot verify the command aspect of my statement, you can find out whether or not the book does make you laugh. Finally Stevenson, like Ayer, insists that the function of moral philosophy is precisely to do what he has embarked on in this article, to analyse the meaning of ethical terms.

If 'X is good' is essentially a vehicle for suggestion, it is scarcely a statement which philosophers, any more than many other men, are called upon to make. To the extent that ethics predicates the ethical terms of

anything, rather than explains their meaning, it ceases to
be a reflective study.

The alternatives envisaged for moral philosophy are
either to tell people what things are good, which it has
no right to do, or to tell people what 'good' means,
which Stevenson has done.

In the next year, Stevenson published two more
articles in *Mind*,[1] both of which were intended to show
the emotive theory in action, that is in its application to
some of the traditional problems of moral philosophy.
The articles were entitled 'Ethical Judgments and
Avoidability', and 'Persuasive Definitions'. Both were
of the greatest importance, in that they filled in yet
more details of the theory, and laid down very clearly
the path which moral philosophy was supposed to take,
if it was to continue in the empiricist tradition.

In 'Ethical Judgments and Avoidability', Stevenson
examined the normal assumption that it is only of
avoidable actions that it is proper to use ethical predicates such as 'good' or 'bad'. He argues that the true
reason for this is that ethical predicates, being intended
primarily to influence conduct, would be ineffective, if
they were applied in cases where the agent could not
avoid acting in the way he did.

But he is careful to allow that, though the normal use
of words like 'good' and 'bad' is to encourage or deter
people with regard to conduct such as that which is
being judged, there are also other subordinate uses for
value judgements. Someone may, for instance, evaluate
somebody else's conduct in a certain way so that other

[1] *Mind*, Volume XLVII, 1938, pp. 45 and 331.

people will think better of *him* irrespective of what they think of the agent. This is no doubt true. Doubtless ethical words, like any other words, can be put to a great number of different uses. But I suspect that Stevenson has here partially lost sight of the distinction between the meaning of words and their use for a certain purpose; for I do not think he would want to suggest that, for instance, this snobbish use of ethical words was part of their permanent meaning.

This is a small point, I daresay. More serious is Stevenson's failure to make convincing the central thesis of the article, that it is because ethical words function in a certain way that we cannot apply them to certain things, for instance causally determined or unavoidable behaviour. It is natural to object to this view that it puts the cart before the horse; and if anyone suggested that there is some deeper connexion between the moral character of an act and the fact that it is the free choice of the agent, I do not think that Stevenson would have any argument to bring against him. At least none is even hinted at here. If it were true that ethical words were wholly emotive in their meaning, that they had no descriptive function at all, then it would perhaps seem likely that this would effectively prevent their being intelligibly used of actions which could not have been avoided. But even if this were so, part of the emotive meaning would presumably be an expression of the speaker's feelings; and this part might still be called for by anything whatever, avoidable or not. I may, after all, express, for instance, disgust at things, such as cockroaches, which I do not regard as able to be otherwise.

Why should I not do the same for human actions? But in any case, Stevenson is as a rule very careful to point out that only part of the meaning of any ethical term is emotive, and if this is so, he has not shown why they may not be applied to non-avoidable actions and be at least partially intelligible.

This case does, incidentally, bring out a difference of emphasis, which I think becomes more and more marked, between the first, crude formulation of the emotive theory, as stated by Ayer, and its refined form in Stevenson's articles. In Ayer's version of the theory, as we have seen, the *main* function of ethical words was said to be to evince or express feelings, and Ayer noticed only more or less in passing that they might also function to arouse similar feelings in others. In this second article of Stevenson's it is particularly clear that, in his view, the main function of ethical language is to influence other people. And though in the first article he had tentatively suggested as an analysis of 'good' 'I like this, do so as well', the first part of this analysis tends increasingly to be left out of account. This is not really surprising. In the first place the word 'emotive' itself naturally means 'producing' rather than 'expressing' feelings. Secondly, ethical terms, whatever Ayer may have said about them, are so unlike mere expressions of feelings, that this part of the theory, which was more difficult to justify, tended to get left out in its later developments.

Stevenson's third article, entitled 'Persuasive Definitions', which also appeared in *Mind* during 1938, was even more important than its predecessor as an amplification of the emotive theory. Stevenson starts by defining a persuasive definition as one which gives a new conceptual meaning to a familiar word, without substantially changing its emotive meaning, and which is used with the conscious or unconscious purpose of changing the direction of people's interests. The words which mostly come in for definition of this kind are those which have a relatively vague 'conceptual' meaning but a very rich emotive meaning. People then seek, Stevenson says, to bestow on the word the qualities of their own choice. They steal, as it were, the good will (or bad will) which belongs to the word, and use it for their own ends. The conceptual content of the word may be so indefinite that it may manifest itself only in a feeling that at least one thing must not be left out in the new definition. Aristotle's treatment of the Greek word for happiness would be a case which Stevenson could use. There is little left of the 'conceptual' meaning, except that the word is felt to be necessarily associated somehow or another with pleasure, so that no definition would pass which did not accommodate the idea of pleasure. But apart from that, Aristotle makes few concessions and ends with the definition 'an activity of the soul in accordance with virtue', for which he makes use of the richly emotive word 'happiness' which everyone agrees is the thing to be aimed at. Examples could, of course, be multiplied. Stevenson is very careful to point out that the use of persuasive definitions is only one among many possible ways in which people may seek to influence other people and to change their interests. His contention is only that it is one of the most important methods in philosophical contexts, and this partly because it has so often been employed unknowingly. But if one's attention is drawn to the nature of persuasive definitions, it may become clear what ethical disputes are, and to what extent empirical methods are relevant in settling them. It will be worth while to take one further example to illustrate this point. This time the example is one which Stevenson himself uses. He considers the possible definitions of the word 'just'. He first envisages two men discussing the meaning of 'just' who agree that any law is just which leads to consequences A and B. If they do agree upon this, then trying to find out whether a particular law is just or not will be simply a matter of finding out if A and B do occur in consequence of it. Stevenson speaks as though this investigation is certain to be wholly empirical; and for the sake of formal presentation of his case I suppose this is justified. But in fact it is very unlikely that the supposed consequences A and B will be described in purely factual terms; they are far more likely themselves to be evaluated. And furthermore, dispute may well arise about whether, granted that both A and B occur, they are properly to be described as the consequences of the law under discussion. This is hardly a *straight* matter of fact, but itself involves a certain assessment of the situation. However, Stevenson wants a case which is supposed to be capable of being settled by appeal to the facts alone, since he wants to contrast this with a case where the two disputants disagree about the definition of justice in the following way: one of them says that a law is just if consequences

A and B follow from it, the other says it is just only if consequences B and C follow from it. They may agree in the end that if B follows from it they can both call it just; but it is more likely that they will continue to dispute, not about whether C does or does not follow from the law, but whether the law is just. This kind of disagreement, then, turns into a genuine disagreement in interest, in which one party wishes to *recommend* laws whose consequences are A and B, while the other prefers laws whose consequences combine C with B. Even if they find out that it is wrong to say that the particular law does lead to C, while it is true that it leads to A and B, they may still argue about the justice of the law, even though 'conceptually speaking they have located no point of disagreement'. This disagreement is of the kind that no empirical method will be capable of solving. In analysing the meaning of such ethical terms as 'just', Stevenson suggests that it will usually be necessary to expose what factual elements are, in any given use of the word, being incorporated into its meaning. That is to say, at the beginning of any discussion of justice, for instance, or of generosity, or any other relatively specific ethical term, it will be necessary to set out clearly what definitions of these terms are being assumed. If this is done, the sting will be drawn from the persuasive definitions, since they will be revealed for what they are. These analyses he refers to as 'the second pattern of analysis'. He distinguishes them from the analysis which he recommended for the word 'good' in the first of his articles. There he suggested that the word 'good' had practically no factual content, but that its analysis was more or less of the form 'I like this. Like it as well' where nothing except interests were alluded to. At the end of the third article, he suggests that this first pattern of analysis is suitable for all highly generic ethical or aesthetic words, of which of course 'good' is the best example in both fields, while the second pattern will most probably be needed to deal with any more specific word in either field. But he also suggests that the desirability of using one pattern or the other cannot be laid down in advance of any particular argument.

It can now perhaps be seen in what ways Stevenson developed and improved upon the doctrine sketched in *The Meaning of Meaning* and, with more force, in *Language, Truth and Logic*. The main improvement was the distinction between those ethical terms which he thought had practically no factual or conceptual content, and those which he thought had at least some. His first pattern of analysis, thought to be sufficient for 'good', does not essentially differ from Ayer's. It is the same view of the meaning of 'good' which we noticed was to be found in Berkeley. Even here Stevenson did embark on the valuable distinction between the dynamic *use of* the word and its more permanent emotive meaning. And he did, as I pointed out above, insist more upon the truly emotive function of the word, as against its supposed expressive function, than Ayer had. This too, seems to me to be an improvement. In the second pattern of analysis, on the other hand, he introduces far more scope for the complexity of moral discourse than had hitherto been allowed for in the theory. Even the recognition that 'good' is not the only ethical word in the English language, and that words like 'just' merit discussion as well is enlightened, though it is apparently a lesson which needs to be learned over and over again. Finally, in the discussion of persuasive definitions, Stevenson makes clearly explicit not only his reasons, but the reasons which really weighed with Ayer for rejecting any form of naturalism. Ayer used a logical argument similar to Moore's against any naturalistic definition of ethical terms. Stevenson on the other hand suggests that any such definition will be a cheat. For it will claim to give a total account of a word in terms of some empirically verifiable characteristics, while surreptitiously leaving untouched the emotive content of that word. For instance, if I claim to define 'good' as 'more evolved', a supposedly naturalistic or empirical epithet, although I may state that 'good' means *nothing more than* 'more evolved' I shall in so doing be disingenuous. For even if the factual content of the words were the same, still there is more in 'good' than there is in 'more evolved', namely the emotive meaning. My definition is therefore persuasive, for I have taken over the emotive content of 'good', and if anyone were tempted to accept my definition of 'good' and substitute 'more evolved' for 'good' in every case, they would either be treating 'good' in a new way, or importing into 'more evolved' an emotive sense which did not originally attach to it. Moore recognized that from every naturalistic definition of 'good' some crucial element which belonged *only* to 'good' was left out. Stevenson agrees with this and says that the crucial element in

H

question is the emotive content of 'good'. Wherever Moore would have said that there was a case of the naturalistic fallacy, a wrong attempt to define 'good', which was indefinable, there Stevenson would point to a case of 'persuasive definition'. This insistence that ethics cannot be translated into non-ethical language, that every attempt to do so is a cheat, is the most fundamental principle of the emotive theory. As I have suggested already, the subsequent history of moral philosophy in England reveals philosophers as almost obsessively concerned with the details of this anti-naturalistic campaign. Sometimes it may seem that the doctrines of the emotive theory are almost too obvious to be worth such serious and long-drawn-out investigation. But the feeling that they are obvious is largely due to the extreme patience and lucidity with which Stevenson presented them.

In 1945, Stevenson published a book called *Ethics and Language* which for some years became the bible of the emotive theory. In some ways, however, the earlier articles which are incorporated more or less in full into the book, are more interesting. They are certainly very much more readable. The book seems to me to suffer from inflation and from a resulting failure of impact, compared with the articles. It is as if Stevenson had become over-self-conscious about methodology and there is a good deal of reflexive commenting upon his own procedures, which add little or nothing to the actual ethical theory. The book turns upon the distinction which was already contained in the articles between the 'first pattern of analysis' of ethical terms, in which little or nothing is involved except the laying bare of the interests or feelings expressed, and the 'second pattern' in the course of which the 'conceptual content' of the terms have also to be clearly stated. But I do not intend to say any more about this, or indeed to discuss the book at all. Instead I want to look a little more closely at the history of the theory before Stevenson. For not only was he influenced by the early Wittgenstein, and the logical positivists, as Ayer was, but, in addition, he acknowledges a considerable debt to the American philosophers Dewey and Ralph Barton Perry. In order therefore to make the history of moral philosophy anything like complete it is necessary to take into account, however briefly, the work of these philosophers.

Dewey was, broadly speaking, a pragmatist. His influence on American philosophy has been considerable, though I think he has never exported very well. There are several of his writings which are concerned with ethics, and in particular with the problem of how to distinguish ethical from non-ethical terms. The earlier pragmatists, in particular William James, had held that all possible different kinds of value judgements were judgements of means to ends. To say that anything of any kind was good was to say that it was both fitted for some special purpose, and that it was conducive to the general end of action, namely 'the good'. But this account was extended to cover not only value judgements ordinarily so called, but all judgements whatever. For 'true' and 'real' were also to be viewed as parts of 'the good'; they were each a particular kind of satisfaction of desire. Therefore any fact whatever

would be judged by the same standard. If I state that
something is red, or if I state that it is good, what I say
will be allowed to be true if regarding it as red or
regarding it as good are conducive to the satisfaction of
desires of different kinds. Thus the distinction between
judgements of value and judgements of fact has been
obliterated. (The fullest statement of this view is perhaps to be found in William James's *Philosophical Con-
ceptions and Practical Results* published in 1898.) Dewey
was seeking to reintroduce this very distinction.

But even Stevenson is bound to admit that 'Dewey
does not always write in a way that lends itself to one
and only one interpretation', and therefore I cannot
hope to do more than state what I believe his views to
have been without claiming any kind of finality of interpretation. In a book entitled *The Quest for Certainty*,
which was published in 1929, Dewey made a distinction
between those statements which serve to 'give mere
reports' and those which serve to make judgements as
to the importance of bringing a fact into existence; or
if it is already there of sustaining it in existence'.

A judgement [he says] about what is to be desired and
enjoyed is . . . a claim on future action; it possesses a
de jure and not merely *de facto* quality. . . . It is in effect
a judgement that the thing 'will do'. It involves a prediction; it contemplates a future in which the thing will
continue to serve; it *will* do. It asserts a consequence
that the thing will actively institute; it will *do*.

Part of the trouble with this passage is undoubtedly the
style, which seems to owe more to Henry than to
William James. But the main point may be made as

follows: There is a kind of prediction involved in giving
a scientific description of a thing, namely that the thing
will continue to behave in a certain way and that we
shall reach the truth about it if we describe it in a
certain way. The fact that the truth, even about matters
of science, is partially relative to our purposes need not
here be taken into account. The prediction involved in
a judgement upon the value of a thing is of a different
kind. It is the prediction that the thing in question will
become an end (or will become something to be
avoided), and will therefore direct human activity in the
future. An ethical judgement, that is, is a judgement
that the speaker likes an object and that he regards it as
fit to be liked in future, by himself and other people.
'Moral science', Dewey says (and he presumably means
the knowledge of what things are good and what are
bad), 'is not something with a separate province. It is
physical, biological and historic knowledge placed in a
human context where it will illuminate and guide the
activities of men.' Thus the distinction between judgements of value and judgements of fact, while it has
very properly been reintroduced, is not regarded as a
sharp or absolute one. Both types of judgement involve
predictions, but in describing their objects in different
terms they concentrate upon different aspects of the
future to predict; they concern themselves with different
human purposes. While scientific knowledge does in
fact illuminate and guide the activities of men, ethical
knowledge is specifically intended to do this and nothing else. Good, sober ethical judgements, therefore,
will be those made with an eye to the consequences of

actions which it is thought useful and sensible to pursue. The actions which are likely to have most of these desirable consequences will be those for which terms of praise will be reserved.

Stevenson, while acknowledging his debt to Dewey, and agreeing with him in regarding ethical judgements as particularly intended to redirect attitudes, criticizes him for 'absorbing emotive meaning into predictive suggestion'. He thinks it is odd that Dewey, 'whose views so readily suggest a quasi-imperative element in ethics . . . should have been so neglectful of emotive meaning'. He further criticizes him for over-emphasizing, as a consequence of this neglect, the degree to which empirical methods would be conclusive in settling ethical disputes. To take this second criticism first, it does not seem to me true to say that Dewey was committed to the belief that empirical methods *alone* could settle ethical arguments. No doubt he did think that the most important feature in any ethical judgement was the regard which such judgements necessarily paid to the consequences of the action judged. But part of the point of his theory, as I understand it, is that not only are consequences predicted, to which, of course, empirical investigation is relevant, but these consequences are also themselves assessed; and to assess them is to adopt a certain attitude towards them which is not a matter of empirical investigation. One quotation, again from *The Quest for Certainty*, may serve to show that this is his view: 'Men *like* some of the consequences and *dislike* others. Henceforth . . . attaining or averting similar consequences are aims or ends.

These consequences constitute the meaning and value of an activity as it comes under deliberation.' Not only has one to determine what the consequences of an action will be; one has also to assess them. This at least seems clear. I regard this part of Stevenson's criticism, therefore, as misplaced. As for his general complaint that Dewey unduly neglects emotive meaning, my sympathies here again are rather with Dewey. Stevenson suggests one reason why this neglect may have come about, namely that Dewey concerns himself mainly with describing and analysing situations of *choice*. He constantly tries to set out the considerations which weigh with someone who is trying to decide what he should do, and to analyse the meaning of the terms in which such a man would describe his choice. Stevenson, on the other hand, is all the time primarily concerned with arguments between two people about how to judge some situation, perhaps an action of someone else. This difference may seem trivial, but I think it is not without importance. The obsession which the emotive theorists manifest with the meaning of ethical words, tends to direct their attention more and more to the process of describing things. The difference between ethical and non-ethical terms can be most clearly indicated in the difference between describing something factually, 'descriptively', and describing it emotively, in such a way as to influence people's attitudes towards it. The logical positivists' insistence that ethical language was strictly meaningless derived from the fact that a non-ethical *description* could be empirically checked, while an ethical one could not. The world is regarded as totally composed of facts, of happening and being so, which can be properly described in one and only one way. All language which obscures the bare structure of these facts is at best misleading. Ethical words are marked off as failed descriptions; and in order to bring out this character in them, it is necessary always to represent them as being used quasi-descriptively—that is to denominate things good or bad. Only so can the real distinction between 'good' and 'red' be brought out. This, therefore, leads to these philosophers' interest in how *I* would describe *your* action; their world seems peopled with judges or schoolmasters, perpetually assessing and grading the conduct of others. Of course they would say that whatever they claim of these pseudo-descriptions could be applied *mutatis mutandis* to the judgements one makes about one's own future conduct, that is to one's own inner debates about what to do. But they seldom make the necessary changes, and we remain short of examples. In any case, it is far from clear that the process of deciding what to do *is* exactly like the process of judging somebody else's actions.

This is one reason, then, which Stevenson himself calls attention to, which may have influenced Dewey to neglect the emotive or imperative force of ethical words. It is less easy to think of someone perpetually trying to influence his own tastes, judgements, and actions by applying the pressure of emotive language than it is to think of someone's doing this for somebody else. The other reason why Dewey may have failed, in Stevenson's view, to pay enough attention to the emotive meaning of ethical terms is that perhaps he did not actually think it important enough. Stevenson himself suggests that perhaps his 'seeming omission of emotive meaning is rather a failure to abstract it out and emphasize it'. He can hardly have been unaware that some words have emotive overtones as well as meaning in the normal sense. He was certainly aware that sometimes evaluative words may be used as something like expressions of feeling. (There is a chapter called 'Value Expressions as Ejaculatory' in *Theory of Valuation*.) But this feature of ethical terms may not have seemed to be the central feature which distinguished ethical from non-ethical terms. Of course, if his kind of theory were correct, if it were true that in applying an ethical epithet to something you were saying that it was or was not an end which people would adopt, it would doubtless follow that ethical language would acquire emotive overtones, or even what might be described as a relatively permanent emotive meaning; but this part of the meaning would be based on the other, and therefore to call attention to the emotive meaning alone would not be to give a sufficient analysis of an ethical term. Stevenson himself is of course perfectly aware of this, and, especially in his second pattern analysis, he insists that the emotive and the non-emotive elements of the meaning are present together. But he does not regard the emotive element as secondary and derivative, as I conceive that Dewey would. In this respect, I must confess once more to the belief that Dewey is right.

About Perry, I must be even briefer. His main work on ethics is entitled *General Theory of Value*. He uses the word 'interest' (which has already appeared in the above discussion of Stevenson, who takes the word over from him) to cover all attitudes of liking, disliking, hating, admiring, and so on. His theory is very like that ascribed by Ayer to Hume; that is, he says that to judge that something is good is the same as to judge that most people have a favourable interest in it. He is, of course, criticized by Stevenson for in fact producing 'approved of by everyone' as a definition of 'good'; and this is a typical example, on Stevenson's theory, of a persuasive definition. He is, that is to say, a naturalist in ethics. He takes extremely seriously the consequence of his definition of 'good' that 'better' must necessarily mean 'liked by more people' and 'worse' must mean 'disliked by more people'. Stevenson quotes the following statement, 'An object which is loathed by L and M is worse, other things being equal, than an object which is loathed only by L or only by M'. He does, it must be admitted, introduce various other criteria by which to distinguish the better from the worse, but they are all of them connected with interests, though the way of judging is not always simply numerical as the above passage suggests. There are, for instance, degrees of intensity of dislike, and degrees of inclusiveness of dislike. But what he has produced is a very elaborate hedonistic calculus to help us judge between different things. The difference between his calculus and Bentham's is that his is much harder to apply, since we are asked to weigh up not the pleasure or pain which follows in consequence of a certain type of act, but the pleasure or pain caused in the contemplation of it. For

'Theft is bad' is construed as meaning not 'Theft has consequences which are painful to this or that degree', but as 'Most people dislike theft a very great deal'. The very natural next question might seem to be 'Why do they dislike it so much?' and it might further be tempting to supply a utilitarian answer to this question, in terms of the harm done by theft. But it is this further question and answer which Perry will not accept as relevant (and which, in spite of Ayer, Hume certainly would have accepted). It is mainly because of his insistence on stopping his analysis at just this point that Perry can be said to be influential upon, or at any rate typical of, the emotivist moral philosophers.

The influence of Dewey and Perry on Stevenson was undoubtedly, as he himself says, considerable; and therefore through Stevenson they indirectly influenced the emotivist theory in England as well. But far more important for the *development* of the theory was the pervasive influence of the later Wittgenstein. It is difficult to be precise on this matter, and in any case this is not the place to attempt any full account of the general revolution in the philosophical outlook for which he was responsible, and of which the changed approach to moral philosophy formed a part. But perhaps the most significant feature of the revolution for present purposes may roughly be said to be this: it no longer seemed adequate simply to state what a certain important philosophical concept really was, or how it was to be delimited. Instead, the actual and possible occurrences of the concept in thought had to be investigated; actual and possible languages in which the concept was embedded had to be described. The only way to solve philosophical problems which cluster round some concepts particularly, is to describe in the greatest possible detail the uses which we actually make or might make of them. In so doing we may come to see how we were previously bewildered, and where the preconceptions came from out of which, typically, philosophical problems arise. The application of this treatment to ethical concepts is obvious. The very opposite treatment of them to Wittgenstein's is perhaps that of Prichard, who, though he made some distinctions in meaning with precision, would suddenly insist, without evidence or investigation, that the *real* or *central* meaning of a word was such and such. His treatment of the concept of action, which I quoted in the last chapter, would do as a clear instance of this method; it will be remembered that 'we had in the end to allow' that *really* we meant by 'action' 'bringing about some new state of affairs'. His treatment of what he conceived to be the peculiar and distinct meaning of 'good' is another example. 'Good', he said, just *is* applicable to states of affairs, and only to states of affairs. When someone pointed out that as a child he had often been called a good boy by his Nanny, Prichard, after some thought, austerely replied that the Nanny had been confused. Again, the whole of *Principia Ethica* rests on exactly the assumptions which Wittgenstein aimed to combat. Moore not only thought that he could distinguish ethical from non-ethical uses of 'good' in one sentence, and thereafter leave the non-ethical uses entirely out of account, but he also thought that, within the sphere of the ethical, it was possible, just by inspection, to perceive that 'good' was indefinable, and that it applied uniquely to some things, and not at all to others. In Stevenson's article in *Mind*, for the first time, there are traces of a determination really to find out how ethical words such as 'good' are in fact used. (It is largely because the impact of Wittgenstein upon Stevenson is more clearly revealed in these articles that they are so much more interesting than his book.) It is no longer considered enough just to *state* that 'good' is indefinable, or that it is an expression of a favourable feeling. Examples are used to bring out the complexity of the kinds of disagreement which might actually occur between people about whether something was good or not; and this complexity is reflected especially in Stevenson's 'second pattern' analyses of ethical terms, where it is admitted that a great number of factual considerations may be relevant to determining whether an action is, for instance, an act of generosity or not, but that none of these factual considerations will determine us by themselves to apply a favourable epithet like 'generous', unless we wish also to express our approval, and to urge others to share it. Stevenson's insistence that the most he can give is patterns or models of analyses of such terms is itself an example of the refusal to accept any *single* analysis, derived from 'thinking out the matter clearly' as Prichard would have us do. In Stevenson's articles there is not only the recognition that 'goodness' is a very complex concept, and 'good' a word which we may have to see in use before we can understand it, but there is even, for the first time, the suggestion that 'good' is not the only interesting ethical term. Both these insights appear to be at least partially the result of the influence of Wittgenstein.

Chapter Five

AFTER THE EMOTIVISTS

BECAUSE of the war, Stevenson's book was not generally available in England until 1947. It was then eagerly
read and discussed. By this time the influence of
Wittgenstein upon English philosophy, and particularly
philosophy in Oxford, was extremely strong, although
the *Philosophical Investigations* had not yet been
published. Roughly speaking, the greatest part of moral
philosophy in England for the next ten years may be
divided into two; the first part being in a sense the continuation of the work of Ayer and Stevenson, modified
by an increase in subtlety and, sometimes, in sensiti-
vity to the actual use of language; the second part being
perhaps more directly influenced by Wittgenstein. This
second part I shall refer to as moral psychology, or the
psychology of action, and I shall discuss it in the next
chapter. In this chapter I shall try to deal with the first
of my rough divisions, and I must start with two
preliminary apologies. In the first place, it is obvious
that in dividing up the moral philosophy of the last
ten years in this crude way, I am leaving out a great deal.
What I shall discuss is not necessarily the best moral
philosophy that has been written during that time. My
contention is only that it is in the main stream, for good
or ill. Secondly, it may be thought odd to lump such
authors as Hare and Urmson under the general heading
of continuers of the work of Ayer and Stevenson,

particularly as there is no single writer on moral
philosophy of this decade that I can think of who does
not repudiate emotivism. Of course I do not wish to
call them emotivists; and I admit that there are great
differences between their doctrines and the crude
doctrines of the logical positivists. But still they have far
more in common with Ayer than with, for instance,
Moore, and there is some justification, therefore, in
treating the present chapter as a kind of continuation
of the last. It is futile to speculate too much about what
philosophers will be read in a hundred years' time. But
my guess is that posterity will not distinguish these
authors very carefully one from the other. My second
apology, then, is for guessing in this rash way and
acting on my guess.

The emotivists insisted, like Moore, that ethics was
non-natural. From no set of ordinary empirical statements could you derive, by any means, a single ethical
statement. There was a permanent and all-important
gulf between fact-stating statements and the statements
of ethics. This was one of the foundations of their
doctrine. The second and equally important foundation was that ethical statements were non-descriptive.
They were not, in fact, statements in the proper sense of
the word. They were specially designed to do something other than to convey information. These two
foundations are not questioned by the authors I wish
now to consider. The difference between them and
Stevenson lies in the precise function which they suppose ethical statements to have. One of the clearest and
most straightforward statements of this kind of view

is to be found in an article by Urmson, published in *Mind* for 1950, and entitled 'On Grading'.[1] Urmson confines himself to discussing the word 'good', among ethical words, and expressly states that his explanation does not extend to cover the words 'right' or 'ought', though it is fairly easy to see how, with suitable modifications, these words too could be accommodated. But the main part of his article is not concerned particularly with ethics at all, but with the general features of that particular use of language which he marks off as the grading use. Just as, in Stevenson's book, ethical language was treated as a sub-class of emotive language in general, so here ethical grading, the denomination of things morally good or morally bad, is regarded as a sub-class of grading in general.

Grading is regarded as an *activity*, something which may either be done physically, by moving things into piles, or verbally, by classing things in order of merit. Sometimes grading is spoken of as though it were a possible function of sentences, not of people, but this is an understandable shift. Urmson starts by considering the grading of apples according to the standards laid down by the Ministry of Agriculture. The apples are classified as super, extra fancy, fancy, domestic, and so on, down the scale. The first thing which he notices about the activity of grading these apples is that there are criteria for placing the apples in their different classes which can be precisely specified, and which are listed by the Ministry, under the title 'Definitions of Quality'. Secondly, he calls attention to the fact that

[1] *Mind*, Volume LIX, 1950, p. 145.

I

an apprentice in sorting apples could learn to sort them
into their various categories, by observing the distinguishing criteria for each class, without understanding
that the categories in fact placed the apples in order of
merit. Urmson says that it is doubtful whether this
'blind' sorting of apples should properly be called
grading or not, but decides that it probably should not.
He therefore lays it down as one of the conditions
necessary for proper grading, that the grader should
know what he is doing. He next makes two points
which have obvious importance in the application of the
general description of grading to ethical cases. He
warns us against two opposite mistakes. The first is to
suppose that the presence in a thing of those qualities
which serve as grading criteria *entails* the applicability
of the grading label. The second is to suppose that the
applicability of the grading label to an object shows that
the object has some *further* property, over and above
those properties which served as criteria for placing it
in this class or in that. The first warning can clearly be
seen to be a generalized warning against naturalism.
We must never think that saying that an object has any
particular set of characteristics *comes to the same as*
saying that it has some ethical property, such as goodness; the second warning is against intuitionism, the
supposition that ethical properties are properties over
and above natural properties, which may be the ground
or foundation for them, but can never be identified with
them. The point is that grading labels are not the names
of properties or qualities at all. They simply mark the
presence of this unique and irreducible *activity*, grad-

ing, which cannot be identified with describing in any terms at all, natural or non-natural. The theory is that to say of someone that he is first class is not to describe him; it is to do something to him, namely place him in the first class. Urmson goes on rather briefly to apply his general remarks on grading to the case of ethics. Although he remarks in passing that words like 'brave' and 'cowardly' are grading labels, he confines his attention in the main to the ethical use of the word 'good', though he admits that there are difficulties inherent in discussion of 'good' due to what he calls its vagueness, which I would prefer to call its generality. The important point in the analogy between the ethical and the non-ethical cases is that in both cases, if we grade something, there must exist criteria in accordance with which we are grading it. Urmson goes so far as to say that we should be able to state what these criteria are, and that stating the criteria will be stating what moral standards we adopt. He does not say anything much about where we get these criteria from, nor why we accept as criteria for moral excellence one set of characteristics rather than another. This might well seem to be a matter of great importance, but it is not the subject of this particular article. The consequence of its omission, however, is a certain artificiality in the concept of sets of criteria, or moral standards. Urmson speaks as though we all of us had just one moral standard, and that in the course of arguing about the goodness or badness of something, we could, if need be, trot out a complete set of criteria. This artificiality is of course partly due to the original analogy between moral grading and the grading of apples according to some previously laid down set of rules, which could be discovered by looking them up in the Ministry's hand-out.

The weakness of the analogy comes out most clearly in the brief discussion at the end of the article about moral disagreements. Here Urmson's views are very close to Stevenson's, whose second pattern of analysis he does, rather grudgingly, refer to. Urmson is obliged to hold that, just as when grading apples according to different standards, one could not use any of the grading labels from either list in order to judge which *set of standards* was the best, so with ethics, if it turns out that two people have different moral standards, it is impossible to use moral terms derived from the vocabulary of either of them in order to adjudicate between the standards. He thinks that there may be moral disagreements of a less fundamental kind than this, as where, for instance, two people, though they adopt the same moral standards, may differ about the precise application of one of the set of criteria in a difficult case. But he thinks that when the ultimate disagreement has been revealed, namely a difference in *what criteria are being used*, then no *moral* arbitration between the parties is possible, nor, if they are honest will they be entitled to call each other's view bad or immoral. This seems to me to be exceedingly implausible; and I think that here again the absurdity lie in the suggestion that there is a finite list of moral criteria, which together make up our moral code, the whole of which could, if necessary, be stated. If this were possible, and if two such codes were then laid side by side and seen to be different from one another, it might indeed, as Urmson suggests, be possible to characterize one only as more enlightened than the other, and not as more morally admirable. For the question might then reasonably be raised, 'morally admirable according to which code?' But it is only the persuasive force of the Ministry of Agriculture's finite set of Definitions of Quality, together perhaps with a lurking analogy with legal codes, which could make us think even for a moment that moral codes were like this. It would be perfectly extraordinary if anyone could in fact set out a complete list of all the characteristics which he proposed to use for judging things morally good or bad. And even if he succeeded in listing all the things he could think of which went to make up his moral code, and if he found some other moral code which differed from his own, he would not be very likely just to notice the fact that the other code was different and that therefore the uses of such words as 'good' and 'bad' were ambiguous, according to which code was being employed. This kind of liberality may be all very well in the context of grading apples. No one would do more than express surprise if he came across persons who graded apples as extra fancy on the grounds that they had maggots. But it seems to be one of the peculiar marks of moral beliefs that they cannot be so dispassionately compared. Urmson tries, by the help of his analogy, to make us think that there is some *logical* absurdity in picking a word from our moral vocabulary of grading in order to grade a total set of

moral criteria or a moral code. But there is no logical
reason against doing this. If there seems to be, it is
because we have been misled into thinking of moral
codes as finite statable sets of criteria. As a rule we do
not know what our moral standards are till they are
tested by some new real case. We do not come armed
to the cases with the criteria in our hand, still less with
all the criteria.

But it is unfair to expect more from a single article
than we get from Urmson's. It is a clear statement of an
analogy supposed to throw light on the function of our
ethical language, and to show that this ethical language
is irreducible to any other kind. I now want to mention
two other longer statements of the same kind of views.

The first is to be found in Hare's book *The Language
of Morals*, published in 1952.[1] Hare starts by telling us
that his intention is to write an introduction to ethics
for beginners and to 'bring the beginner as directly as
possible to grips with the fundamental problems of the
subject'. But very soon these fundamental problems
turn out to be the very same problems which exercised
Ayer and Stevenson, namely the correct characteriza-
tion of the language which we use in making ethical
statements. Hare goes on to describe his own book as a
logical study of the language of morals. His contention
is, briefly, that ethical language is a sub-species of prescriptive language, that is to say, language which is
particularly designed to suggest courses of action to
people. Prescriptive language in general may be divided

[1] *The Language of Morals*. R. M. Hare. Oxford University
Press, 1952.

into two classes, the class of overt imperatives, and the class of evaluative words or sentences. When this division is applied to ethics, it seems that 'ought' and 'right' and 'you should' come into the first class, being genuine imperatives, according to Hare; while 'good', 'desirable', and so on come into the second. There is here, therefore, a slight advantage, so far, over Urmson's analogy, since all the commonly discussed ethical words can be accommodated as prescriptive. Hare further maintains that the imperative class of prescriptive language is in a sense fundamental, since value judgements, if they are action-guiding at all, that is if they are truly prescriptive, must be held to entail at least one imperative. Thus from the proposition 'This is a good chocolate', if the proposition is truly evaluative, it must be legitimate to infer 'take it'; or, if this sounds too absurd, perhaps a more complicated imperative should be substituted, namely, 'If there is any question of taking a chocolate, other things being equal, take this one'. There does seem to me to be a danger here. Either the inference rule just stated will turn out to be tautological, since no use of 'good' will be counted as fully prescriptive unless the inference is possible; or, if more uses of 'good' are to count as prescriptive, then the inference will simply not be possible. That is to say, as so often happens with philosophical principles, there is the danger that the principle will turn out to be either uninteresting, because tautological, or false. I do not think that Hare means to restrict very severely the uses of 'good' which he would count as evaluative in the proper sense, or prescriptive; and therefore I think that his claim that one must always be able to infer an imperative from any such use is simply mistaken. It is not at all clear that from 'this is good' you can always infer 'therefore choose it', even when all possible provisos about other things being equal have been made. However, this is the contention. Ethical language is a sub-class of prescriptive language, which is, all of it, either directly imperative, or logically related to an imperative.

A good part of Hare's book is taken up with arguments to show that logical relations such as entailment and inconsistency may hold between propositions in the imperative mood, as well as between those in the indicative mood; and that therefore to say that an argument contains an imperative is not to say that it is irrational or governed by no logical laws. We are, moreover, presented with yet another version of the argument against naturalism, in the form of a proof that from indicative premisses nothing but an indicative conclusion can be deduced.

A good deal more of the book is concerned with the relation I have already discussed between the two main types of prescriptive language, the evaluative and the imperative. This is illustrated with examples, involving the use of the words 'good' and 'ought'. But we are never really told by Hare, any more than we were by Urmson, by what test we decide whether a word or sentence is prescriptive or not. This seems to be supposed to be self-evident. Urmson, in the same way, while insisting that grading was an irreducible activity, and that there was a whole number of words which generally or always functioned as grading labels, did not in the least help us to decide in any given particular cases whether what someone was doing was grading or not. Both Urmson and Hare make it easier for themselves to leave out this important part of the theory by choosing to talk about 'good', which no one would seriously deny was at least very often evaluative. But there are many less general words where it seems to me difficult to say off-hand whether they are evaluative or not, whether they are used to grade, or just to say things. Stevenson, of course, was guilty of the same fault, but to a lesser extent. For he admitted that almost any word *could* have an emotive force, and he did attempt to limit his inquiry to those words whose emotive force had become somehow part of their meaning. He even tried to lay down criteria, by which to test whether this was so or not, for any given word. This was not entirely successful, but at least it was something. Both Hare and Urmson seem to take it for granted that the merest beginner in the consideration of language can tell at a glance whether a word is prescriptive or not, whether it grades or does not grade.

It must be emphasized once again that neither Hare's book nor Urmson's article have any very direct connexion with ethics. They are both of them concerned to show the logical characteristics of a general type of function which language may have, and of which the ethical function is a sub-species. Hare's book *seems* to have more relevance to ethics than Urmson's article, because Hare himself incidentally lets fall some views about morals, which Urmson does not. For instance,

Hare believes that all moral action is action according to some statable principle, and that the more morally grown-up we become, the less simple our principles are. He connects this thesis with the general thesis of the book, by referring to moral principles as general imperatives. For example, he says that 'it is part of our moral development' to turn principles such as 'never say what is false' 'from provisional principles into precise principles with the exceptions definitely laid down'. Thus, as we reach the stage of being morally grown-up we are supposed to approach the question of what we ought to do in any situation with this list of definite instructions, which have been made more and more definite (or rather, precise) over the years. Perhaps this is not so very far from Urmson's implied view too. For if we adopt the grading analogy for moral discourse, we are supposed, as we have seen, to approach the judgement of situations with a definite list of criteria according to which we are going to adjudicate them morally good or bad. In both cases there seems to be an almost ludicrous over-simplification of the actual methods we adopt in deciding what to do or how to live.

The last example of this kind of theory which I want to discuss is Nowell-Smith's. This is to be found in his book *Ethics* published in 1954.[1] This is an altogether more ambitious and comprehensive book than Hare's, and my treatment of it will therefore be proportionately more inadequate. As a matter of fact a good deal of Nowell-Smith's book is devoted to the kind of

[1] *Ethics*. P. H. Nowell-Smith. Pelican Books, 1954.

subject which I have already referred to as the 'psychology of action'; this part of the book is therefore not relevant to the present chapter. But it should be noticed that my discussion of the parts of the book which are relevant may suggest that the whole book is a great deal thinner and less comprehensive than it is. Nowell-Smith has a very wide conception of what is properly a part of ethics, and in this way, if in no other, he is to be sharply distinguished from the writers I have so far discussed in this chapter and the last. But although his view of the subject matter of ethics appears to be wider, his statement of his own purpose sounds familiar. He says that he is trying to 'make clear the complicated connexions between such words as "good", "right", "ought", "choose", "duty", "desire", and "pleasure" '. The best thing about this list is that it is comparatively long. Even more familiar is the note sounded by the editorial foreword to Nowell-Smith's book; and this is not surprising since it was written by Ayer. He says:

There is a distinction, which is not always sufficiently marked, between the activity of a moralist, who sets out to elaborate a moral code, or to encourage its observance, and that of a moral philosopher, whose concern is not primarily to make moral judgements but to analyse their nature. Mr. Nowell-Smith writes as a moral philosopher. He shows how ethical statements are related to, and how they differ from statements of other types, and what are the criteria which are appropriate to them.

We have so far been offered a decent variety of answers to the question how ethical statements differ from statements of other types. We have been told that they are expressions of feeling, that they are designed both to express and to evoke the feelings of others, that they have the function of grading, that they are imperatives, or logically closely related to imperatives. Nowell-Smith does not favour any single simple solution to this problem. In the course of his exposition he has occasion to invent various technical terms, one of which is 'the Janus principle', namely the principle that any one statement or word may be expected to perform at least two functions on any one occasion of its use, and perhaps more than two. Thus, appealing to this principle, he rejects the views that ethical expressions are *just* imperative or *just* emotive, or that they have any other single unique function. But there are words, which can be listed, which characteristically have among other functions, that of suggesting a suitable reaction to something. An example of such a word would be 'horrible', which suggests that the object so described is apt to call forth horror. Nowell-Smith calls these words 'A words', short for Aptness words, 'because they are words that indicate that an object has certain properties which are *apt* to arouse a certain emotion or range of emotions'. These A words are contrasted on the one hand with D words ('Purely descriptive, according to the current distinction between descriptive and evaluative'), and on the other hand with G or Gerundive words, which suggest that an object has properties which *ought* to be regarded in a certain way. Praiseworthy' is an example of a G word. The distinction between A and G would not, I think, be supposed by Nowell-Smith to be hard and fast. It is simply that some words suggest a normal reaction, others a desired or required reaction. In his subsequent discussion of the first class of adjectives, those which suggest emotions, Nowell-Smith covers a good deal of the ground covered by Stevenson. He concludes that these words are used to give explanations and make predictions, not to give reasons. But their use is only proper if the user has in mind reasons of a certain sort which are not stated but contextually implied. Thus it will be proper to say of something that it is horrible only if I have reasons for saying it, among which will be that I dislike the thing in question. Nowell-Smith makes a good deal of use of the concept of 'oddity' or 'logical oddity' and I think that logical oddity is supposed to be the penalty we should pay if we used one of these emotive or A words *without* the normally relevant reasons being present, or, still more, if we used the word but denied the reason. Thus, if I insist both that something is horrible and that I like it, I think that Nowell-Smith would say that I had committed a logical oddity. Exception might be taken to the expression 'logically odd'. It is not, for one thing, very clear. It is supposed to characterize something less than contradiction, but akin to it. So far this is all right. One might at first be tempted to say I had contradicted myself if I said that something which I liked was horrible, and then one might reflect a bit and decide that after all it was less than a contradiction. But if so, then I do not quite see why we need any special name for the kind of surprising thing I am supposed to have said. There could be a number of different explanations of my saying it. I might simply mean that, though the thing was

horrible by other people's standards, it was not so by
mine. This would not count as a case of logical oddity,
for Nowell-Smith would say that in this case I was not
using 'horrible' as a truly A word—that is, I was using
it descriptively. Or it might be that I really did feel
ambivalent about the object; I both hated it and liked
it. In this case I do not see why the oddness is particularly a matter of logic. It may be that my reactions are
odd.

It is valuable, I am sure, to point out that between
'This is horrible' and 'I like this' there is a relation
which is not that of contradiction. This is at least to
suggest that the whole meaning of 'it is horrible' is not
given by the translation 'I dislike this'. For 'I like
this' and 'I dislike this' are, at least on the face of it,
contradictory. And therefore 'this is horrible' must
mean something different from 'I dislike this'. It is
right to point this out. But only the very early pioneering emotivists would ever have maintained that 'this is
horrible' did mean *only* 'I dislike this'. It was very soon
common ground that all emotive words had *some*
descriptive content, some more than others. I do not
think that Nowell-Smith has made this point any
clearer by introducing the notion of 'logical oddity' to
be the name of what happens when the normal con-
comitance of descriptive and emotive meaning falls
apart.

Nowell-Smith connects his Gerundive words with
the possession in the user of them of a favourable
attitude towards some relevant action or choice. Thus,
if I say that something is right, I am using a Gerundive

word and I may also be taken to have a favourable or 'pro' attitude to the doing of the thing in question. He maintains, however, that the connexion is not simple. A person's favourable attitudes, that is, his desires and interests and wishes, form a background without which he could not intelligibly use words like 'ought' and 'right' and 'duty' at all. But he might have all these favourable attitudes without having any concept of duty at all. Favourable attitudes, therefore, are in a sense prior to Gerundive words, and serve to explain them, just as the actual characteristics of things are in a sense prior to our feelings about them, and serve to explain our feelings. Thus both Aptness words and Gerundive words have to be explained in terms of something other than themselves.

These points need, as we have come to expect, have nothing to do with ethics specifically. They are perfectly general points about our use of language in all contexts of appraising, describing (in the real, non-philosophical, sense, in which I may describe things as ghastly or wonderful), advising, and choosing. But once again it is easy to see that they can be applied to specifically ethical language. 'Morally good' will function both as an Aptness word and as a Gerundive word. It will normally both suggest certain appropriate feelings, and suggest that the object so described is a fit object of choice. 'Good', Nowell-Smith says, is the Janus word *par excellence*. It will have at least these two functions in its proper moral use, and perhaps more. All moral words will be used, when properly used, in at least these two ways. They are not then descriptive words;

they do not name properties. Nor are we told at all what things have the characteristics such that we should be justified in having pro feelings and pro attitudes towards them, in the context of morality or outside it. But there is one point for which one may be grateful to Nowell-Smith. He agrees with other philosophers of the twentieth century that the naturalistic fallacy is to be avoided; and he thinks of the naturalistic fallacy, as we should expect, as the mistake of supposing that evaluative words can be defined wholly in terms of non-evaluative or descriptive words. Further, he agrees that the reason why this inter-definition is not possible is that evaluative words are not used to describe at all but to do something different. But he does allow that the philosophers who have mostly been accused of committing the fallacy would not really have been very much shaken if it had been pointed out to them. They were not, and here I quote Nowell-Smith,

primarily interested in the question whether deontological words could be analysed in terms of 'merely empirical' or 'natural' concepts. They believed that, human beings being what they are, there are certain types of activity that are in fact satisfactory to them and that it is possible empirically to discover what these are. . . . They do not seem to have been mistaken in their basic assumptions that the language of obligation is intelligible only in connection with the language of purpose and choice, that men choose to do what they do because they are what they are, and that moral theories which attempt to exclude all consideration of human nature as it is do not even begin to be moral theories.

There is surely good sense in this. We may agree that

ethical language is different from non-ethical; even
that evaluative language in general is different from,
and cannot be derived from, non-evaluative language.
But this does not mean that as a matter of fact what we
value highly cannot be non-evaluatively described; nor
even that no natural explanation can ever be forth-
coming of why we value it as we do. Perhaps the fear
of naturalism in ethics has had too firm a grip.

It can now perhaps be seen how the emotivism which
started with the logical positivists developed. In the
first instance, emotivism was a way out of what had
come to seem like two alternative accounts of ethics,
both unsatisfactory; namely, naturalistic ethics on the
one hand, and intuitionism on the other. Naturalistic
ethics in its most plausible form is utilitarianism, and
in order to reject it, the emotivists had to interpret it as
a theory which stated that the whole meaning of the
word 'good' could be given by some set of non-ethical
words such as 'productive of pleasure'. If this had been
true, ethical statements could have been translated into
fact-stating terms, and would therefore have been
admissible as real statements even by the positivists.
But such a theory seemed to them false. One should
perhaps notice, as I have suggested before, that what
they criticize is a very much enfeebled version of
utilitarianism. I do not think that any utilitarian would
have been inclined to deny that 'good' had emotive
force, or that it was an A word and a G word. And he
might have, therefore, been perfectly prepared to agree
that an actual translation of the word 'good' into something about pleasure might not work. But he would

K

have said that his theory never depended for a moment
on the possibility of such a translation. He was concerned to establish what things people thought were
good, what things people adopted as ultimate ends;
and if some ways of describing the ends had more
emotive power than others, this would not disturb the
theory. But in any case, the positivists were not concerned with questions such as what people actually
adopt as their ends. They thought it was clear that
scientifically verifiable statements could not include
any ethical propositions, or evaluations of any kind, and
therefore they rejected any claim to be able to incor-
porate evaluations indirectly, by means of a translation
into the supposedly non-evaluative word 'pleasure', or
any other non-evaluative word. They also, naturally,
rejected the claims of the intuitionists to be able to
apprehend certain non-scientific properties of things.
Their alternative was to say that ethical and evaluative
language was not informative at all, was not concerned
with the properties of objects, whether scientific or
metaphysical. Evaluative language was concerned to do
something else, namely to express. I think the subsequent history of the theory, in all the various forms
which we have looked at, shows an increased awareness
of the complexity of language. At first there seemed to
be a kind of triumph in the discovery that language
could do anything at all except be used to convey information. Philosophers seemed so pleased to have
found this out that they were content to use the word
'emotive' to cover a large number of quite different
things which language could do. The most notorious

example of this lack of precision is Ayer's initial failure seriously to distinguish between the functions of expressing feelings of one's own, and attempting to arouse the feelings of others. But even Stevenson, who went into the matter so much more thoroughly, and who was clearly under the influence of Wittgenstein, which might have made him cautious about lumping different functions of language together, was fairly vague in his directions for picking out emotive meaning, and for saying precisely what was covered by the term. Nowell-Smith, in contrast, is very much more cautious in putting things together, and more hesitant in claiming completeness. The trouble has always been, partly at least, that while some philosophers have been reasonably detailed in their particular accounts of evaluative language, they have never been at all clear about that with which they were contrasting it. They never even fixed on a wholly satisfactory word for that main body of linguistic use from which the evaluative use was being picked out. 'Non-evaluative' is of course the safest and least harmful. 'Descriptive', as I have already suggested, seems to me the worst. 'Scientific' is perhaps the best, in the sense that the old positivistic contrast comes out most clearly in it. I do not think that this failure is trivial. If a whole ethical theory is meant to turn on the fact that ethical language is some-how importantly to be distinguished from the rest of language, it may surely suggest that the distinction has not been exactly made, if there are not satisfactory ways of referring to *both* sides of the distinction. To mark ethical language off simply from 'the rest' is to say too little. There might be too many ways in which it was different, and 'the rest' might be too internally various. But even to speak of *ethical* language being marked off is perhaps to go too far. For one thing which it common to all the philosophers who have been considered in this chapter and the last is that they were primarily discussing not ethics but evaluation in general. Nothing that they said applied more properly to ethics than to horticulture or fat-stock breeding. Any situation in which assessments and judgements have to be made was distinguished from the situations in which plain statement goes on. But the trouble is that we assess and evaluate practically all the time. Perhaps what prevented them from thinking of a useful description of the supposedly non-evaluative uses of language was that there are practically none of them. In any case the extremely frequent occurrence of evaluation in some form or another may well make us feel, when we come to the end of reading these theories, that we still need to be told something a bit more specific about ethics in particular, as opposed to evaluation in general. All the models and analogies to illuminate ethical language have the air of being preliminary clearings of the ground. We may naturally feel disappointed that, when the ground is cleared, nothing seems to happen.

Chapter Six

MORAL PSYCHOLOGY

IN the last chapter I roughly divided contemporary moral philosophy into two parts, one of which was labelled the Psychology of Action. It is now time to turn to this second division of the subject. But at the outset, a further sub-division seems convenient. There has never been a time when moral philosophers have not concerned themselves with the subject of free will, and the present century is no exception. I want first of all to say something about the course which this traditional discussion has taken in the last ten years or so, and then to consider the more strictly psychological questions which have in many cases seemed to be connected with the traditional problem or even to arise out of it.

Some recent discussions of the freedom of the will have started from Moore's treatment of the subject, in his book called *Ethics*.[1] Moore presented the issue between determinists and libertarians, and his possible solution of the difficulty, in the following way:

Those who hold that we *have* Free Will, think themselves bound to maintain that acts of will sometimes have *no* cause, and those who hold that everything is caused think that this proves completely that we have not Free Will. But in fact it is extremely doubtful whether Free Will is at all inconsistent with the principle

[1] *Ethics*. G. E. Moore. Home University Library. Thornton Butterworth, 1912.

that everything is caused. Whether it is or not, all
depends on a very difficult question as to the meaning of
the word 'could'.

He then goes on to explain that the crucial expression
in the discussion of free choice is 'He could have done
otherwise', since if anyone holds that a man could not
have done otherwise than he did, or could not help
acting as he did, then the man is not held to be fully
responsible for his act, he is not blamed for it, nor
praised for it, and it ceases to be an act to which moral
predicates are properly applied. This is the contention
of both determinists and libertarians alike. And so the
question is whether it is ever the case that a man *could*
have acted otherwise than he did. Moore says that in
the phrase 'I could have done otherwise', 'I could'
means 'I would if I had chosen'; and he goes on to say:

> For my part I must confess that I cannot feel certain
> that this may not be *all* that we mean and understand by
> the assertion that we have free will; so that those who deny
> that we have it are really denying . . . that we ever *should*
> have acted differently even if we had willed differently.

And again,

> It is . . . quite certain (1) that we often should have
> acted differently if we had chosen to; (2) that similarly
> we often should have chosen differently if we had chosen
> so to choose; and (3) that it was almost always *possible*
> that we should have chosen differently in the sense that
> no one could know for certain that we should *not* so
> choose. All these three things are facts, and all of them
> are quite consistent with the principles of causality.

Moore, characteristically, did not present his solution

to the problem as certainly correct; but he was clearly very much inclined towards it. According to this view, then, to say that men have free will is to say that they do choose to perform actions which they need not perform. To say this is the same as to say that there are cases in which a man could have acted otherwise than he did. To say this, again, means the same as to say that he *would have acted differently if he had chosen to*. And if it is objected that after all a man *could not have chosen* differently, Moore's answer is that this is just untrue. There is a perfectly good sense of 'possible' in which it was possible, before the choice was made, either that he would choose as he did, or that he would choose some other way. An observer of the man would not have been able to rule either out as impossible; and this is what is meant by saying it was possible that he could have chosen either of the two things. The essential point of this solution to the problem is that it effects a reconciliation between the determinists and the libertarians by showing that when we speak of freely chosen actions, what we actually mean is something quite precise, which can be precisely shown not to entail an absence of causation. There is no need for the libertarian to try to maintain that there are some uncaused events, namely human choices; he can be granted that choices are really free, once it has been shown to him what he and other people actually mean when they speak of a free choice.

Broadly speaking, there have been two closely interconnected ways of proceeding with the attempt to reinforce and supplement Moore's initial presentation of the case, and to remove the hesitations which he still felt about his reconciliation of the determinists with the libertarians. On the one hand, Moore's own analysis of the meaning of 'could have acted otherwise' has been taken up, and its expansion into 'would have acted otherwise if . . .' has been further elaborated. I shall come back to this development in a moment. On the other hand, further consideration has been given to the question what we do actually mean when we speak of an act as free in general. The conclusion of these second investigations has been that by a freely chosen act is intended an act which a man was not compelled, in any recognized way, to perform. That is to say, the natural opposite of 'free' is not 'caused' but 'compelled' or some similar word. Thus the supposed inconsistency between freedom of choice and universal causation is shown to be non-existent since 'freely chosen' and 'caused' do not rule one another out. Hume offered a solution to the problem on these lines and, still earlier, so did Hobbes. There is nothing new, therefore, in the actual attempt at reconciliation. But the methods of effecting the reconciliation have become more subtle and more precise. Furthermore, a great deal that is interesting in itself has come to light in the course of this kind of examination of the concept of free or voluntary action. Not all the discussions, indeed perhaps not any of them, have been as bald and crude as what I have said may suggest. For instance in the *Proceedings of the Aristotelian Society* for 1948, Professor H. L. A. Hart published an article entitled 'The Ascription of Responsibility and Rights', in which he discussed the concept of responsibility from the legal point of view, and here the many possible opposites of 'voluntary', as applied to actions, were brought out and the whole nature of the concept of responsibility clarified in an important way. Further light was thrown, though less directly, on the concept of freedom by the series of articles which Professor Hart and Mr. Honoré published in the *Law Quarterly Review*, under the title 'Causation in the Law'. Such work as this has not been directed specifically to solving the traditional problem of the freedom of the will, but more generally to clarifying the notions of 'act', 'free act', 'responsibility', and 'choice'. But this clarification has obvious relevance to the traditional problem.

Let us return now to the connexion between 'he acted freely' and 'he could have acted otherwise': Nowell-Smith's book, *Ethics*, contains a discussion of free will which has been influential, and which derives directly from Moore's. His contention is that we call those actions free (and we therefore may praise or blame them), which we believe that a man *could* have chosen not to perform. When we say that he could have chosen not to perform an action, we mean that the man *would* have chosen not to perform it *if* certain conditions had been different. Nowell-Smith's account thus goes beyond Moore's, in that it brings into the actual meaning of 'could have acted otherwise' the concept of conditions—not just the condition 'if he had chosen' but other conditions not yet specified. The main part of the discussion is directed to showing that there are some conditions which we allow as excuses; that is to say, there are some cases where 'he would have acted otherwise if . . .' is filled up with a condition which we feel it would have been impossible to fulfil; and in this sort of case we do not believe that the man really could have acted otherwise, and therefore we do not hold that he acted freely, in acting as he did. But there are other cases where the conditions mentioned in the 'if' clause are not allowed to excuse the man for doing what he did. These are the cases where we feel that he was in some way responsible, not only for what he actually did, but for being subject to the conditions he was subject to. Thus we tend to think that a man did not act freely, let us say, in infecting our children with typhoid, if he really could not have known that he was a carrier of the disease. So if he says 'I would have avoided them if I had known', if we are prepared to allow that he could not have known, we are also prepared to allow that he could not have helped infecting the children. On the other hand, if he says, trying to get out of it, 'I could not help giving them typhoid because I am so forgetful. If I had been more careful I would have avoided the children', we do not allow this as an excuse. We hold the man responsible for what he did, because we hold him responsible for being so careless. Nowell-Smith on the whole presents it simply as a matter of fact that some conditions mentioned in the 'I would have if . . .' clause excuse a man, and others do not; and chief among those which do *not* are conditions relating to a man's moral character. Thus I am never going to be allowed to get away with lying by saying 'I would have done otherwise if I had not been a liar', and hoping you will think I can't help being a liar. But he also has one proposed explanation of the difference between the conditions to which we are subject. He thinks that those conditions are held to be within our power (and are therefore not allowed as excuses) which punishment will alter. This curiously back-to-front view has been mentioned already. It was first fully discussed by Stevenson, who thought that those actions were held to be free which emotive language could influence a man either to perform or to refrain from. Free will could therefore, according to him, be actually defined in terms of the emotive use of language—as that which characterized behaviour with respect to which emotive language was liable to be effective. I do not think this view has any great plausibility. At any rate neither Stevenson nor Nowell-Smith seems to have devised a satisfactory formula for expressing the connexion, if it exists, between free will and the possibility of influence by reprobation and punishment.

A more fundamental doubt about the solutions offered by Moore and Nowell-Smith remains to be expressed. In both theories the solution offered was a demonstration that free choice was compatible with universal causation on the grounds that 'He could have acted otherwise' meant the same as 'He would have acted otherwise if something had been the case' and it was then shown that one way or another the something might, often, have been the case. But if one does not accept the identity of meaning between 'he could have acted otherwise' and 'he would have acted otherwise if ... had been the case' then the demonstration breaks down. Neither Moore nor Nowell-Smith offers a conclusive argument to justify the translations they propose. Moore notices the change from 'could have if I had chosen' to 'should have if I had chosen' but says that he makes the change 'in order to avoid a possible complication', which is not much of a justification (and we are not told what the possible complication was). Nowell-Smith produces an example to show that the expressions 'he could have' and 'he would have if' mean the same, but it is not convincing. He says:

It is logically odd to say 'Smith can run a mile, has had several opportunities, is passionately fond of running, has no ... reason for not doing so, but never has done so'. And, if it is true that this is logically odd, it follows that 'can' is equivalent to 'will ... if ...' and 'could have' to 'would have if ...'

We have already had occasion to regret the expression 'logically odd'. Here it certainly does little to advance the argument. It is difficult to know whether to agree or disagree with the application of the expression to the case of Smith's running, and therefore it is impossible to use its applicability even as a ground for suggesting identity of meaning, let alone as a proof. And on the face of it the two expressions do not, I think, seem to mean the same. In a lecture delivered to the British Academy in 1956, Professor J. L. Austin argues that neither Moore's nor Nowell-Smith's translation of 'he could have' was correct. It is not possible to summarize the argument, much of which was directed against specific points of detail in both Moore's and

Nowell-Smith's discussions. But one distinction of the greatest importance was brought out, and that is the distinction between the conditional or subjunctive use of 'he could have' and the indicative use. The indicative use of 'he could have' means 'he was able to', and this is different from 'he would have been able to, if something or other', and also different from 'he would have, if something or other'. It seems to me absolutely self-evident that to say of someone that he *was able* to do something does not say anything at all about what he *would have done* in certain specifiable circumstances. Admittedly we may collect evidence about what people are able to do from what they have done in the past; but this still does not entitle us to say anything about what they would have done in the past or would do in the future under certain conditions. If this is true, then, as Austin suggests, the compatibility between freedom of choice and determinism may after all be still subject to doubt. The reconciliation was effected by treating 'he could have acted otherwise', the phrase which, for the libertarians, must essentially be saved, as hypothetical, meaning 'he would have acted otherwise if things had been different'. But if this awkward phrase turns out not after all to submit to this treatment, then the question remains to be answered whether it is true that on any given occasion the agent really could have acted otherwise, that is, whether, categorically, he had at the time the ability or the power to do otherwise than he did.

Now if the determinists are right in saying that there must be some causal explanation possible for everything that a man does, it looks as if it cannot be true that when he does one thing he really at that time has the power to do something else, things being as they are. A genuine causal explanation cannot, of its very nature, leave this possibility open. If I explain that your bicycle tyre is flat because I stuck a tin-tack into it, although obviously I can allow that if things had been different the tyre would not have been flat, I cannot allow that, with things as they are, viz. the tyre being capable of puncture by a tin-tack and my having stuck the tin-tack into it, the tyre could be other than flat. If I left this open, I should have failed to give a causal explanation of the thing you wanted explained. It must be possible to justify a properly causal explanation by saying 'whenever this happens, that happens', and this is precisely what would *not* be possible if it were really open to a man, in a given set of circumstances, to choose to do either of two things. Therefore, since we do talk of people choosing, and talk as though they could have chosen what they did not in fact choose, it looks very much as if what we say, and what we feel we need to say, about people's conduct is incompatible with what the determinists claim. This is not of course to say which of us is right. Determinism might be true, even though if we accepted it we should have to alter the way we talk about human conduct.

If, as I believe, then, the attempts which have recently been made to reconcile our ordinary beliefs with determinism break down, however attractive they look at first sight, the next task would obviously be to decide whether determinism is actually true, or whether it can be given up, in favour of what we all naturally incline to believe. But before this task can even be discussed, one other attempt at reconciling the opposing views must be noticed. It is sometimes suggested that although determinism, that is belief in the possibility of a complete causal explanation of all aspects of human behaviour, is not compatible with our ordinary language of choices, motives, and decisions this need not worry us, because it is simply another, different, way of describing the same set of facts. That is, it is claimed that there are different explanations possible of human actions, which run parallel with one another and are not meant to overlap, and which therefore cannot contradict each other in any worrying way. This sort of suggestion was put forward, for instance, by S. E. Toulmin and by A. N. Flew, in *Analysis*, 1948 and 1949.[1] The trouble, however, with this solution is that it is so simple that it fails even to look for very long like a solution. In a recent discussion of the problem Austin Farrer puts this proposed solution into the mouth of an imaginary philosopher, and then goes on to suggest that it does not work.[2] The philosopher says,

Do not we keep describing different aspects of things under different linguistic conventions? Isn't that how language works? And what is there to worry us if we find ourselves talking both personal life language and neuro-physical language about the human body? The physical language is to tell us how it works and what it will do;

[1] *Analysis*, December 1948. 'The Logical Status of Psycho-analysis'. October 1949. 'Psycho-analytic Explanation'.
[2] *The Freedom of the Will*. Austin Farrer. Black, 1958. Chapter IV, p. 63 *sqq.*

the personal life language expresses how it feels itself from inside.

To which the objection is made as follows:

What could sound more unexceptionable? That is how language works: it expresses different aspects of things under different conventions of speech; or, to put it more philosophically, we find that by using different conventions of speech we can arrive at descriptions which are useful in different ways. Certainly. But do we make it a linguistic rule, never to attempt the relating to one another of our different descriptions? . . . Did anyone ever doubt that these two lines of talk employed different types of decription? But it remains to ask, how the matters they describe go together in one world. The general analogy of multiple descriptions will cast no light on so particular a question.

Farrer then proceeds to compare different analogous cases of multiple descriptions with the multiple description of human behaviour, to see whether these help to answer the question of the inter-relation of the two ways of talking, and he finds that they do not. His conclusion, therefore, is that we are left with the question unanswered of which is the *proper* way to describe human behaviour, or whether one type of explanation is not fundamental and the other superficial. Although Farrer's argument from analogy does not conclusively prove that no account could be found which would relate the two ways of talking which he mentions, nor does it conclusively prove even that they need to be related, it does appear strongly to suggest that the proposal of his imagined linguistic philosopher is too weak to be of much use in what we are still inclined to feel is a real issue between determinism and common sense.

If, then, it is an issue, if neither of the proposed methods of reconciliation will work, it would be highly desirable to find out once and for all whether determinism was true or false. The chief obstacle in the way of doing this has so far been that no determinist can be found to state clearly exactly what determinism commits him to. To speak vaguely of causal explanation of human behaviour, is not enough; for although any determinist would presumably hold that causal explanation of some kind was possible, there might be great differences between determinists on such matters as whether the explanation of human conduct was to be mechanical or in terms of regularity of response to stimulus, for example; and about whether the explanation had to be practically, or only theoretically, possible. All these points, and many more, would need to be clarified before a satisfactory argument could even begin. It seems that the doctrines called determinism have usually been stated by persons who either do not wish to accept them, or who wish to show that they are in no way incompatible with our ordinary beliefs about human behaviour. Such persons would not form the best advocates for the view, and it is quite likely that they have constructed a kind of bogus doctrine containing elements from many different sources, which would not stand up to critical examination for long. The difficulty is that so far no one has tried very hard to state the case coherently. But the usual form in which the issue is presented is as turning upon the possibility

Determinism & Freedom. Ed. by Hook, Published by Collier (paperback) in full of determinist!

of the predictability of human choices. If it is true that there could be a genuine causal account of any human choice, then it follows that any human choice should be predictable, by reference to these same causal laws. Now it is clear at once, and has frequently been pointed out, that not all kinds of predictability are incompatible with freedom of choice. If, for instance, I predict that someone whose character I respect and whom I know to be consistent will refuse a bribe, and if I turn out to be right, this does not, even for a moment, suggest that he did not freely choose to refuse the bribe. But the possibility of prediction of this kind is wholly irrelevant to the issue, since although it is doubtless based on inductive evidence, it is not in any sense a causal prediction; it is not the kind of prediction which would be backed up by an explanation of any kind at all, or at least it need not be. It is very different from a prediction that if I give a child soneryl he will go to sleep. This is a prediction which is genuinely based on a causal law, and if I am asked why he will go to sleep I need not just say 'because he is that sort of child'; I can say something about the general effects on people of the ingredients of soneryl. It is prediction of this second, fully causal, kind which would be fatal to human choice. If it is possible for me to say 'Always in this kind of circumstance a person of this kind must choose such and such', and if I really mean that he must, and that his choice is the effect of the circumstances, then the feeling which the agent may have that there is something open, that it is up to him to decide what to do, must be an illusion. But it is not yet certain that prediction of this kind is ever possible, still less that it could ever be widely practised. The onus is upon the determinist, if only one could be found, to show that it does, or even that it might occur. This may seem like an evasion of the issue, but it is very hard to face an issue squarely when one does not know exactly what is supposed to be conflicting with what.

There is one further point which is perhaps worth mentioning before I leave the topic of Free Will: it is not clear that there could ever be a time when the idea of free choice was useless, whatever further discoveries in psychology or neurology were made. For although it might be possible to regard other people as wholly causally determined it would be very difficult if not impossible to regard oneself in the same light. This is a very obvious point which has often been made before, but it is not perhaps wholly irrelevant. It is very often difficult to avoid making a decision, and in some cases passivity is as much a decision as any other. Now even if someone else could tell you in advance the causes which would make you decide one way rather than another, it is unlikely that you would at the time of decision know all the relevant factors in the situation. For some of the things which the other person would have to know in order to predict your choice would be what features in the situation would appeal to you as reasons. You could not discover this for yourself without weighing them up *as* reasons. As soon as you started to do this, instead of trying to predict your own choice you would actually be choosing. For an important part of choice is deciding what is a reason worth taking into account and what is not. Thus it seems unlikely that the concepts of decision and choice could conceivably be eliminated, whatever the theoretical possibilities of prediction might be. But it *is* conceivable that the language which we use of our own choices and that which we use of other people's might come to be rather different, and I am not sure that there is not already a considerable difference between them.

The problem of Free Will, then, has been a good deal discussed in the last few years, but not solved. Some of the discussion, especially that which stemmed from Moore's chapter in *Ethics*, has turned out, in my opinion, to have been misconceived and not to have advanced the subject very far. But this does not mean that it was not worth trying. And in the course of the discussion of Free Will a number of other interesting subjects have been brought to light, among them the nature of such concepts as 'act', 'choice', 'will', 'intention', and others of this general kind. I want now to say a little about the exploratory and analytical work which has been done on these topics.

Like some of the other topics discussed in this book, the group of subjects with which we are now concerned has little specifically to do with ethics. The borderline between moral philosophy and the rest of philosophy becomes at this point impossible to draw. But there is a group of related problems, roughly speaking the philosophy of mind, some of which have particular bearing upon human actions and choices. These may reasonably be considered as a part of moral philosophy, even though they tell us nothing about ethics, or about the difference between right and wrong. It has increasingly come to be felt, indeed, that without an adequate conceptual map of these psychological areas, ethics in the narrow sense is impossible, or at least futile. This feeling has arisen largely as a result of the influence of Ludwig Wittgenstein. As far as concerns moral philosophy, by far the most important change that he brought about was a new interest in description of phenomena, rather than the framing of abstract theories of human behaviour. Wherever a philosophical problem has arisen, as for instance around the concept of 'the Will', in Wittgenstein's view what is needed is a thorough investigation of the language in which the problem has arisen, and still more of the language in the context of which the problematic word is used in real life. Only in this way can the concept be clarified, and the false pictures by which philosophers have been deceived be done away with. It is necessary to find out what the various words we use are used *for*. He says:

We must do away with all *explanation*, and description alone must take its place. And this description gets its power of illumination, i.e. its purpose, from the philosophical problems. These are, of course, not empirical problems, they are solved, rather, by looking into the workings of our language, and that in such a way as to make us recognize those workings: in despite of an urge to misunderstand them. The problems are solved not by giving new information, but by arranging what we have always known. Philosophy is a battle against the bewitchment of our intelligence by means of language.[1]

[1] *Philosophical Investigations.* Ludwig Wittgenstein, translated by G. E. M. Anscombe. Basil Blackwell, 1953, p. 47, paragraph 109.

Let us look at some of the descriptions which Wittgenstein himself embarked upon. In the passage I shall quote, by way of example, he is discussing the concept of the Will. He is examining the view that willing is an experience, something which just happens and cannot be brought about.[1]

[613] In the sense in which I can ever bring anything about (such as stomach-ache through over-eating), I can also bring about an act of willing. In this sense I bring about the act of willing to swim by jumping into the water. Doubtless I was trying to say: I can't will willing; that is it makes no sense to speak of willing willing. 'Willing' is not the name of an action; and so not the name of a voluntary action either. And my use of a wrong expression came from our wanting to think of willing as an immediate non-causal bringing about. A misleading analogy lies at the root of this idea; the causal nexus seems to be established by a mechanism connecting two parts of a machine. The connexion may be broken if the mechanism is disturbed. [614] When I raise my arm 'voluntarily' I do not use any instrument to bring the movement about. My wish is not such an instrument either. [615] Willing, if it is not to be a sort of wishing, must be the action itself. It cannot be allowed to stop anywhere short of the action. If it is the action, then it is so in the ordinary sense of the word; so it is speaking, writing, walking, lifting a thing, imagining something. But it is also trying, attempting, making an effort . . . to speak, to write, to lift a thing, to imagine something etc. One imagines the willing subject here as something without any mass (without any inertia); as a motor which has no inertia in itself to overcome. And so is only a mover not a moved. That is, one can say 'I will, but my body does not obey me' but not 'My will does

[1] op. cit. p. 159, paragraph 613 sqq.

not obey me' (Augustine). But in the sense in which I cannot fail to will, I cannot try to will either.

The discussion moves on, then, to touch upon doing, trying, voluntary action, intention, and meaning. No conclusions are asserted on any of these topics; it is not even always clear when Wittgenstein speaks in his own person and when in the person of someone who has succumbed to the temptations offered by language. But in every case the aim is to make clear, first what we think about the subject, and then how we talk about it, and so finally what is actually true about it. The description is thus always primarily a description of the way to talk about the subject; for only by showing how language is really used can the conceptual confusions which it has generated be cleared up. But describing how to talk about a complicated subject is not very different from describing the complexities of the subject itself. The two cannot properly be distinguished. Our eyes are necessarily directed towards the facts.

The longest and most systematic treatment of this same group of problems is to be found in Ryle's book, *The Concept of Mind*,[1] the central chapters of which have exercised a great influence upon all subsequent discussions. Here, although the intention and purpose of the book are virtually identical with Wittgenstein's, the tone is utterly different, and there is no shortage of conclusions. By way of example I shall quote one short paragraph, once again on the subject of the Will.[2]

[1] *The Concept of Mind*. Gilbert Ryle. Hutchinson's University Library, 1949.
[2] *op. cit.* chapter 3, p. 81 *sqq.*

Men are not machines, not even ghost-ridden machines. They are men . . . a tautology which is sometimes worth remembering. People often pose such questions as 'How does my mind get my hand to make the required movements?' and even 'What makes my hand do what my mind tells it to do?' Questions of these patterns are properly asked of certain chain processes. The question 'What makes the bullet fly out of the barrel?' is properly answered by 'The expansion of gases in the cartridge'; the question 'What makes the cartridge explode?' is answered by reference to the percussion of the detonator; and the question 'How does my squeezing the trigger make the pin strike the detonator?' is answered by describing the mechanism of springs, levers and catches between the trigger and the pin. So when it is asked 'How does my mind get my finger to squeeze the trigger?' the form of the question presupposes that a further chain-process is involved, embodying still further tensions, releases and discharges, though this time mental ones. But whatever is the act or operation adduced as the first step of this postulated chain-process, the performance of it has to be described in just the same way as in ordinary life we describe the squeezing of the trigger by the marksman. Namely we say simply 'he did it' and not 'he did or underwent something else which caused it'.

Perhaps even this single quotation may serve to show both the differences between *The Concept of Mind* and the *Philosophical Investigations*, and their similarity of aim. Professor Ryle shows language at work, in a truly everyday context. The chapters which follow that from which this passage was taken, on Emotions, Dispositions, and Self-knowledge all demonstrate the same refusal to admit nonsensical questions or mysterious answers. Until a word has been shown to be *able* to work in a straightforward and intelligible way, it is not allowed as a proper part of language. So, to return to the particular case of the will, the concept of action in general is clarified by the rejecting of certain bogus concepts which have accumulated round it, such as that of the will as a kind of cause. This is exactly what Wittgenstein too rejected, but less harshly. From the *Investigations* we get the feeling that there was a real reason why people may have come to think of the will as a cause. From *The Concept of Mind* we would infer that only an idiot could ever have thought so. It is the same with the other related subjects discussed in the succeeding chapters: we are induced to think what we really mean by such things as 'feeling', 'motive', 'pleasure', by seeing how these words come into our ordinary discourse. And any philosophical beliefs we may find ourselves half inclined to hold about them are ruled out if they fail to pass the practical test. A concept must have work to do before it is admissible. It may sometimes be felt that Ryle is a little ruthless. A great deal is thrown out, perhaps because he allows us to make use of only rather simple ideas, and therefore only simple language, in our everyday conversations. But all the same, there is a great deal of penetrating observation and accurate description, not so much of actions and feelings themselves as of how we talk about actions and feelings. And there is no other book yet where the same amount of attention has been given to these problems, though they have come to be generally regarded as forming a necessary part of the subject matter of ethics.

Chapter Seven

EXISTENTIALISM: J-P. SARTRE

So far I have been concerned almost exclusively with moral philosophy which, whether written in England or in America, has been essentially written in the tradition of English empiricism. Since 1900, both here and in the United States, metaphysics has been virtually dead. The influence of Wittgenstein, as I hope I have suggested, opened the way for a much wider view of moral philosophy than was generally held at the beginning of the century; and this width of vision may lead to greater descriptive or even classificatory enterprises on the part of philosophers. But it can hardly lead back to metaphysics. Philosophers are more interested in saying what is true than in constructing large-scale super-scientific explanations of things. Moral philosophy shows no signs of being once again swallowed up into a huge philosophical system, built to explain the universe. But on the Continent a very different sort of moral philosophy has been flourishing in the first half of this century, and I must now try to say something about this.

System building has not been discredited on the Continent and metaphysics has been practised in the Hegelian manner. Moral philosophy has taken a place as part of the general theory of man, of human nature and its place in the universe. The metaphysical style, too, has been perpetuated in continental philosophy, and we meet here once again the high tone, the obscurity, the wealth of technical terms, which have been so noticeably absent from English philosophy of the same period. Sometimes, it must be admitted, a kind of despair afflicts one when reading these philosophers, Surely, one feels like saying, we have outgrown all this. We have been through it all and, with the help of Moore and Ayer, we have struggled out the other side. But it would be a mistake to refuse, on either aesthetic or doctrinaire grounds, to make an effort to understand these philosophers. There is a great deal to be found, not only of that peculiar aesthetic satisfaction which, whether we believe in them or not, metaphysical theories of ethics are capable of providing, but also of illumination. For there is, especially in the works of Sartre, much acute criticism of other philosophers, and, most important, there are elaborate serious and imaginative descriptions of moral phenomena. It is at this point that the two different kinds of philosophy meet. With a different purpose, and under the influence of Wittgenstein, English moral philosophers are just beginning to explore this same territory. What we have referred to as the psychology of action and choice, which is coming to be the most interesting part of English moral philosophy, is of the greatest importance in existentialist philosophy. The phenomena thought to be relevant are not always the same, but the descriptive element is common.

It is obvious that in one chapter it would be impossible to give even a sketch of the whole field, and in any case I am not competent to do such a thing. To lump all continental moral philosophers together as existentialists is in itself an absurdity. But existentialism is broadly speaking what I want to discuss, and I shall therefore boldly select for discussion the one philosopher who has actually described himself as an Existentialist, namely Sartre. It is hardly necessary to add that any reasonably complete study would include discussion of at least Kierkegaard, Jaspers, Heidegger, and Marcel as well. But these I shall not mention. Sartre has not only attached to himself this familiar label, but he is also the best known of these philosophers, and there is therefore some justification for discussing him alone. But it must not be forgotten that, in spite of family resemblances between his work and that of other continental philosophers, he does not speak for a group or school, but only for himself.

The term Existentialist is not self-explanatory. Sartre accounts for it in a popular lecture called 'Existentialism is a Humanism', which he delivered in 1946.[1] This lecture is clear, but necessarily over-simplified. By itself it would do little to suggest the depth or complexity of Sartre's thought. It does, however, bring out unambiguously, and indeed with exaggeration, the basic concepts upon which the whole system rests. An existentialist, Sartre says, is one who holds that existence precedes essence. This mysterious belief is meant to have application only to the case of human beings; it is the distinctive feature of human beings, in fact, that

[1] *L'existentialisme est un humanisme.* Published in England as *Existentialism and Humanism*, in U.S.A. as *Existentialism*, in Germany as *Ist der Existenzialismus ein Humanismus?*

their existence does precede their essence. Sartre contrasts a human being with an artifact, a paper-knife, which is first conceived by its maker, and then made. The idea of the paper-knife is that it should be of a certain kind and fulfil a certain function. It is of the essence of a paper-knife to be like this. Once it is conceived, its actual characteristics, when it comes into existence in the workshop, are already determined. This is what is meant by saying that its essence precedes its existence. Human beings, on the other hand, are not first conceived, and then made to a specification, or to fulfil a certain purpose. They exist, and what they are or what they become depends upon what they *do*. For this they are themselves wholly responsible. A man is not, for instance, a born cook, who then fulfils his function by cooking. On the contrary, he *chooses* to be a cook; he elects to fill up the blank space of his life in one way rather than another. His being a cook is not determined by anything, nor is it even justifiable by an appeal to his nature. He is, and has always been, perfectly free to do whatever he likes.

It is, above all, this attitude to human freedom and to human choice that the term 'existentialism' serves to mark off. There is of course very much more to it than this. But already it seems to me that two important points stand out. First, it is no doubt valuable to resist the Greek view that men have a certain function for which they were designed, and that the best anyone can do is to find out what this function is and to fulfil it. But by using the words 'essence' and 'existence' to bring out the difference between the Greek view and his own, Sartre seems to be suggesting not only that people do not have functions, as paper-knives do, but that there is nothing *common to* human beings, or *essential to human nature*, which may limit their freedom of choice. He has to allow that there are common physical characteristics of man, and that physically men are limited by what is 'humanly possible'. But it seems absurd to suggest that there are no common psychological factors which may limit our choice just as much. The example of the paper-knife is in fact unfair. We may well want to agree that it is improper to describe human beings in the sort of terms appropriate for artifacts. But the contrast between essence and existence would be rather different, and rather more difficult to draw, if one took an animal instead of a paper-knife as an example. A horse may not have been designed to do some one job, but still we should want to say that, being a horse, it was determined to behave in certain broadly predictable ways. There is a whole number of things one could say were essential to horses, which limit the ways they can behave; the question of design or purpose need not come into it at all. It seems to me that there are common characteristics of men, too, and of types of men, in terms of which their behaviour is at least partially predictable, which the simple contrast with the paper-knife would not suggest. That Sartre himself was not really able to keep up the belief in pure existence is shown I think by his novels (or at least he could not keep up his interest in it). If the existentialist contention were true, people should be represented as perfectly individualistic, their characters entirely made up of actions which they have chosen themselves. But in fact one may well feel that a defect of Sartre as a novelist is that his characters have no individuality at all. They make decisions, certainly, but they make them as people of a certain type. We tend to forget their names and remember them as 'a traitor', 'a Fascist', 'a homosexual'. It is as if in the last resort Sartre were interested in essences after all, at least in the sense of characteristics in virtue of which people may be regarded as typical of a class. Individual personality which, according to the theory, should be created every moment by free choices, seems to have been squeezed out, and an abstract freedom of choice has taken its place, which demands that the agent be regarded as an abstract entity as well.

The second difficulty in this concept of free choice is perhaps more serious. It seems to me simply false that we choose everything that we do and that we are, from our childhood on. To say that we choose every aspect of our characters, that we are nothing at all except what we *choose* to be, has a certain rhetorical and salutary effect; but, at the very least, it distorts the meaning of the word 'choose'. It is true that we are probably responsible for more of our attitudes and emotions as well as for more of our actions than we are sometimes inclined to think; and it is good for us to be reminded that expressions like 'I could not help feeling . . .' may well be false, or a prelude to mere excuses. Perhaps we are *responsible* for all the attitudes which we find that we have accepted over the years. But to say that we *choose* to adopt them is not true. Choice and responsibility should be distinguished. We need to keep the word 'choice' for some more definite and datable occurrence. We should know when we are choosing, at the very least. But perhaps this objection is not so very serious after all. To say that each one of us has absolute freedom, and to say that he is only what he chooses to be and nothing else—both of these are exaggerations, but they succeed in defining an outlook which is intelligible and from which (more or less), as I hope I shall show, moral philosophy can be fruitfully pursued. In order to show this, it is necessary to go rather more deeply into the metaphysical theory of which Sartre's moral philosophy forms a part.

Sartre's most important philosophical work is *L'Être et le Néant*, of which an English translation was published in 1956.[1] A great deal of the book consists not of arguments but of examples and of long descriptions of psychological phenomena. Moreover, it is written in an extraordinarily thick, obscure style, full of technical terms of a grotesque kind, derived from Hegel. As one reads through the book one comes to accept these terms as perfectly natural and indeed the only terms in which the thought could have been expressed. The danger is that in discussing it one may either reproduce nothing at all except the darkness and obscurity of the original, or, if one tries to expound the thought in plain language, one may be left with something unduly thin and platitudinous, from which all the interest has been

[1] *L'Être et le Néant*. Paris: Gallimard, 1943. Translated into English by Hazel E. Barnes. Philosophical Library of New York, 1956.

removed with the obscurity. In the light of these difficulties I shall attempt not a summary nor a full exposition of Sartre's doctrines but something like an impression of them. It should not be forgotten that to someone else they might appear in a different light.

Sartre, like all French philosophers, starts from Descartes. His aim, like Descartes', is to see how much can be derived from a consideration of consciousness, or thinking in the very widest sense. Like Descartes, he wants to pick on an instantaneous moment of consciousness and derive his conclusions from this. But while Descartes could only prove (at least directly) the existence of himself as a thinking being, Sartre claims to go further. This departure from the master is of the greatest consequence; it marks, in fact, a total rejection of the Cartesian philosophy. He holds that the very essence of consciousness is that it should be directed towards some object. The powerful influence of the phenomenologists, particularly of Husserl, is thus apparent right at the beginning: it is taken as something which hardly needs explanation that consciousness is 'intensional'; that even apparently 'pure' states of mind or feeling have some external object. If a man says to himself, therefore, in a Cartesian spirit, 'I think' he can deduce from this the existence not only of himself but of objects of thought, things in the world and other people, so that merely to be conscious is already to enter into some sort of relation to the world. This is a point of fundamental importance. In trying to state what this relation is, we come upon the first serious difficulty in Sartre's terminology. What distinguishes a

M

conscious being from an unconscious being is that in
consciousness there is a gap between the consciousness
and that which is its object. This gap is referred to as
'nothingness'; but there is an obvious defect in this,
apart from its manifest unintelligibility. To use the
noun 'nothingness' is almost bound in the end to lead
to the suggestion that nothingness is a *thing*, though of
a peculiar kind. If, furthermore, the presence of this
characteristic nothingness is actually the distinguishing
mark of the conscious being, then the temptation to
think of it as a thing of some positive kind is almost
overwhelming. It is better therefore, as far as I can see,
to avoid the word altogether, even though it occurs in
the very title of the book, and to speak instead of 'a gap'
or 'an emptiness' within the conscious being, which he
is always trying to fill by thinking and by acting. But
besides this meaning—that of the emptiness or blank
within the conscious being—there is another meaning
of 'nothingness' which in turn serves to mark off the
conscious being from the unconscious. Conscious beings
are able to form negative judgements, and thus to distinguish both themselves from other things, and other
things one from another. A man who thinks, that is, is
able to realize that a house is not a tree, and that he
himself is not a tree; and he may go further. Through
this possibility of forming negative judgements, he may
realize that today he is not what he will be tomorrow,
and so to understand that what he will be tomorrow is
not anything at all, yet. So the possibility of framing
such judgements is essential to a man's realization of
his own freedom to be this or to be that in the future.

The conscious being is referred to by Sartre, borrowing from Hegel, as the *being-for-itself*. Unconscious beings are *beings-in-themselves*. They are thought of as thoroughly existing in a solid concrete way. The whole of their possibilities are, as it were, absorbed in being a chair or a tree. Whatever thoughts or attitudes we may have concerning them, beings-in-themselves go on existing undisturbed, and completely determined by their own nature to be as they are. They are more than just our perception of them. Consciousness is regarded as the very opposite of this. Beings-for-themselves bring nothingness into the world, both in the sense of emptiness—a failure to be *anything*, and in the sense of negation—a being-for-itself knows that it does *not* have this pure concrete solid existence which trees and chairs have, and it strives above all things to have such existence, unsuccessfully. Consciousness, therefore, consisting as it does of this emptiness waiting to be filled up, and of this knowledge that it is *not* any of the solid and permanent beings-in-themselves, must, if it exists at all, exist in relation to external objects, whose existence in the world does not need further proof. From this starting-point Sartre sets out to explore more completely the relations which do in fact hold between conscious beings and the rest of the world.

It is noticeable that even into what purports to be a bare statement of Sartre's most general views, words like 'strive' and 'unsuccessful' inevitably creep in. This is not chance. In exploring further the relations which he supposes to hold between conscious beings and the outside world, we shall need to employ a whole battery of such words. Conscious beings, beings-for-them-selves, *desire* being-in-itself; they feel *nausea* at the contemplation of the multiplicity and disorderliness of things in the world; they feel *anguish* at the realization of their own freedom. Now it may well be objected that the words 'nausea' and 'anguish' are emotive to a very high degree, that Sartre could have made the very same philosophical points in different terms. When he wished to express the thought, fundamental to his system, that human life is not determined, and that it cannot be justified by any appeal to something outside itself, he says that human life is 'absurd'. Once again it may be objected that he could make a perfectly good point against any theorists who want to explain or justify human life, by simply denying what they say, and without using the powerfully emotive word 'absurd'. It is necessary to notice this objection straight away since the offending words play so important a part in the whole structure of existentialist thought. There is, I think, a perfectly good reason why words of this type come into the exposition of Sartre's views. His meta-physical system is concerned with human nature not as the uniquely cognitive element in the world, but as the uniquely active, non-determined element. The contrast he is constantly insisting upon is not that between the knower and what he knows, between mind-substance and body-substance (which is the typically Cartesian dualism); he is concerned with the contrast between the natural world, governed by rigidly deterministic laws, and dynamic human nature, which has its own power of action within it, and which is free to make itself what it chooses. Sartre is of course not the first to concern himself with this dualism instead of the other. It has indeed quite properly been characterized as Kantian. But it follows that any description of the human situation in relation to the external world will inevitably be in terms of doing things, of choices, projects, and attitudes. Emotions are regarded as partial and frustrated actions; therefore what a man *feels* on contemplating the world is as relevant to his situation as what he actually does. Any account of human nature must above all, on this view, concern itself with human motives. Thus the concepts of desiring, striving, trying —all these must necessarily be employed. But what about nausea and anguish? and what about absurdity? Here once again what there is, I think, is exaggeration. It is not that such concepts are irrelevant altogether to philosophy; it is that the actual words used go too far. They may mislead, if people pick just on them without seeing how they fit into the whole metaphysical picture of man. But just as it is not accidental that Sartre should exaggerate in his insistence upon human responsibility and freedom of choice, so his use of words like 'absurd' to describe the human situation is not accidental. He means to produce a certain impression, as well as to expound a system. Nor is he the first metaphysician to have such an intention.

To return now to the exposition: when confronted by the awareness of the variety, contingency, and senselessness of the world, a conscious being feels nausea. He longs to be able to class things neatly into kinds, and to see some sort of necessity of their being in this kind or in that. When he thinks of his own life, he wants to be able to regard that in the same way, as something which is orderly and which has a certain pattern. But he finds that he cannot. Even language turns out to be misleading, simply because it does suggest that things can be pinned down by having their appropriate name attached to them. But in fact the existence of things escapes from this artificial restraint imposed by words. Of peculiar importance in explaining this nausea which we are supposed to feel, is the concept of the viscous. In Part Four, Chapter Two, of *Being and Nothingness*, in a section called 'Quality as a revelation of being', Sartre says that what we need is a psycho-analysis of things. He then considers the case of viscous sticky things, half liquid half solid, and he finds that this viscosity is a fundamental category of material things, which has a peculiar fascination for us, as well as filling us with disgust. That our attitude to it should be of this kind is wholly natural; we do not have to be taught to regard it in this way; as soon as we are aware of objects at all we are aware of this aspect of them. The secret of our attitude is that the viscous is naturally ambiguous. It is neither solid nor liquid. We may think we can touch it, or pick it up like solid stuff, but it eludes us. It is not, on the other hand, like water which we know we cannot pick up and possess. If something is viscous and sticky we may think we can pick it up 'only, at the very moment when I believe that I possess it, by a curious reversal, it possesses me'. It is impossible to get rid of. It clings to our hands. Now it is clear how we may use the viscous as a symbol of things in the external world, and Sartre says that we do so use it. His point is also that we are not *taught* to regard it as symbolic. It comes to us already symbolizing other objects and ourselves, which we constantly feel we should be able to grasp and possess, only to find that we cannot. Just when we may think that we have it, we are sucked back into the sticky, senseless mass of objects and of our own random and pointless acts in the past. To escape from the viscosity of things would be to be able to see one's own life as an ordered inevitable pattern, and to see oneself as a solid being-in-itself, moving inevitably among other hard, solid, predictable objects. The viscous, then, is a ready-made symbol of the situation in which we find ourselves. That is why we feel a sickly horror when we contemplate it.

Connected with the nausea which we feel when we realize our situation with regard to the objects around us is the anguish which we experience when we turn our attention to ourselves. Nausea is brought on by our inability to organize and separate objects, and our tendency to be overwhelmed by them and sucked into the general mess. Anguish is brought on by the reflection that there is nothing at all to determine our choices. Our past is separated from us by the perpetual gap which arises in our consciousness. We may suppose that by acting in this way or in that, we have determined ourselves to a certain course in the future. But, if we are still conscious at all, as soon as our acts become past acts, the emptiness within us reasserts itself. We are forced to *think* about our past, not just to have it drive us forward. And just as there thus arises a gap between the past and the present, which prevents our ever saying we were *caused* to do this or that by what had happened before, so there is equally a gap between us and the future, which may be filled in anyhow we choose. But whatever we choose, we can never hope finally to justify it, nor can we be sure that any value attaches to it at all. Thus we feel anguish before the recognition that we have to choose, but that the choice is for nothing.

But of course Sartre is perfectly prepared to allow that we do not feel either nausea or anguish all, or even much, of the time. How then do we avoid them? Sartre's answer to this is absolutely fundamental to what may be called his moral philosophy and his psychology. The answer is that we avoid them by means of *Mauvaise Foi*—Bad Faith. The whole of the first part of *L'Être et le Néant* is indeed centred round the question, 'How must we describe the human consciousness if it is to be capable of bad faith?' Let us examine, as far as we can, what Sartre understands by bad faith. Essentially it is a denial of our freedom of choice. If we see ourselves as bound to act in a certain way, if we feel inclined to say 'I have no choice in the matter', then we are deceiving ourselves. Bad faith is a kind of self-deception. It involves playing a role, and regarding our behaviour as determined by the role we play. It is the failure to realize that even what role to play has originally been a matter of choice and that it remains a matter of choice whether to continue in the role or not. Bad faith operates at various levels. It covers the superficial self-deception with the help of which, for instance, we might justify some extravagance by saying 'I really need it', or 'This is a good time to buy; next year they will be even more expensive'. It also covers more basic self-deceptions by means of which one might, for instance, excuse one's political inertia by claiming that it was just not part of one's character to interest oneself in such things, or that one had been brought up not to do so. The moment one is introduced to the concept of bad faith, it can be seen to have infinite explanatory possibilities. There are many people, for instance, about whom one would hesitate to say that they were insincere, or that they knowingly or fully deliberately pretended to be what they were not. But nevertheless one feels about these people that they are always seeing themselves as a such and such—a member of some social group, an intellectual, a mother; and that all their tastes and views are, for the time being, dictated by the part they see themselves in. For this kind of person the concept of bad faith is useful. It is worth considering some of the examples which Sartre himself gives in *Being and Nothingness*.

Take the example [he says][1] of a woman who has consented to go out with a particular man for the first time. She knows very well the intentions which the man who is speaking to her cherishes regarding her, she knows also that it will be necessary sooner or later for her to make a decision. But she does not want to realize the urgency. She does not apprehend this conduct as an attempt to achieve what we call 'the first approach': that is she does not want to see possibilities of temporal development which his conduct presents. She restricts this behaviour to what is present; she does not wish to read into the

[1] *op. cit.* chapter 2, part 2.

phrases which he addresses to her anything except their explicit meaning. If he says to her 'I find you so attractive', she disarms this phrase of its sexual background; she attaches to the conversation and to the behaviour of the speaker, the immediate meanings, which she imagines as objective qualities. The man who is speaking to her appears to her sincere and respectful, just as the table is round or square, as the wall colouring is grey or blue. The qualities thus attached to the person she is listening to are in this way fixed in a permanence like that of things. . . . But then suppose he takes her hand. This act of her companion risks changing the situation by calling for an immediate decision. To leave the hand there is to consent in herself to flirt, to engage herself. To withdraw it is to break the troubled and unstable harmony which gives the hour its charm. The aim is to postpone the moment of decision as long as possible. We know what happens next; the young woman leaves her hand there, but she *does not notice* that she is leaving it. She does not notice it because it happens by chance that she is at this moment all intellect. She draws her companion up to the most lofty regions of sentimental speculation; she speaks of life, of her life, she shows herself in her essential aspect—a personality, a consciousness. And during this time the divorce of the body from the soul is accomplished; the hand rests inert between the warm hands of her companion—neither consenting nor resisting . . . a thing.

I shall quote extensively from one further example, from the same part of the book, which seems to me particularly illuminating.

Let us consider [Sartre says] the waiter in the café. His movement is quick and forward, a little too precise, a little too rapid. He comes towards the patrons with a step a little too quick. He bends forward a little too eagerly; his voice, his eyes express an interest a little too solicitous for the order of the customer. Finally he returns, trying to imitate in his walk the inflexible stiffness of some kind of automaton while carrying his tray with the recklessness of a tight rope walker by putting it in a perpetually unstable, perpetually broken equilibrium which he perpetually re-establishes by a light movement of the arm and hand. All his behaviour seems to us a game, but what is he playing? We need not watch long before we can explain it: he is playing *at being* a waiter in a café. There is nothing there to surprise us. The game is a kind of marking out and investigating. The child plays with his own body in order to explore it, to take inventory of it; the waiter in the café plays with his condition in order to *realize it*. This obligation is not different from that which is imposed on all tradesmen. Their condition is wholly one of ceremony. The public demands of them that they realize it as a ceremony; there is the dance of the grocer, of the tailor, of the auctioneer, by which they endeavour to persuade their clientele that they are nothing but a grocer, an auctioneer, a tailor. A grocer who dreams is offensive to the buyer, because such a grocer is not wholly a grocer. Society demands that he limit himself to his function as a grocer, just as a soldier on duty makes himself into a soldier-thing with a direct regard which does not see at all, which is no longer meant to see, since it is the rule and not the interest of the moment which determines the point he must fix his eyes on. . . . There are indeed many precautions to imprison a man in what he is, as if we lived in perpetual fear that he might escape from it, that he might break away and suddenly elude his condition. . . . From within, the waiter in the café cannot immediately be a café waiter in the sense that this inkwell is an inkwell or the glass is a glass. It is by no means that he cannot form reflective judgements or concepts concerning his condition. He knows well what it 'means': the obligation of getting up at five o'clock, of sweeping the floor of the shop before the restaurant opens, of starting the coffee pot going, etc. He knows the rights which it allows: the right to the tips, the right to belong to a union, etc. But all these concepts, all these judgements refer to the transcendent. It is a matter of abstract possibilities, of rights and duties conferred on a 'person possessing rights'. And it is precisely this person *who I have to be* (if I am the waiter in question) and who I am not. . . . If I represent myself as him, I am not he: I am separated from him as the object from the subject, separated by *nothing*, but this nothing isolates me from him. I cannot be he, I can only play at *being* him, that is imagine to myself that I am he. What I attempt to realize is a being-in-itself of the café waiter, as if it were not in my power to confer their value and their urgency upon my duties and the rights of my position, as if it were not my free choice to get up at five o'clock each morning or to remain in bed, even though it meant getting fired. As if from the very fact that I sustain this role in existence I did not transcend it on every side, as if I did not constitute myself as one beyond my condition. Yet there is no doubt that I *am* in a sense a café waiter . . . otherwise could I not just as well call myself a diplomat or a reporter? But if I am one, this cannot be in the mode of being-in-itself. I am a waiter in the mode of *Being-what-I-am-not*.

These examples, each in its different way, show that the person who exhibits bad faith does so in order to try to become an object, a being-in-itself, without consciousness and without, therefore, the necessity of choosing what to do. He wishes to be something with fixed describable properties in virtue of the possession of which he is *determined to* behave in this way or in that. In the first example, the woman not only wishes to regard herself in this light but she wishes to regard the man in the same way. She has attached to him the label 'sincerity' and therefore she simply does not choose to notice anything except what bears out this description of him. She treats herself equally as an object. There is her hand, lying there. She is not responsible for it. It is simply a thing occupying a certain spatial position, and meanwhile *she* is concerned with higher things. But of course she has *chosen* to dissociate herself in this way from her hand. She is trading on the undeniable fact that her hand is an object in the world. But it is not only this and cannot, with good faith, be treated as if it were. In the second example, the waiter is likewise attempting to be a waiter in the way in which an inkwell is an inkwell. That is to say, he is pretending that waiters are simply *compelled* to behave in the way he behaves, in virtue of the fact that they are waiters. But he is not, as the woman was, trying to pretend that he is an object in the world. He is trading rather on the fact that everybody is an object of attention to other people. He knows that in the eyes of others he is just a waiter, that indeed they want him to be just a waiter; and therefore he aims to live up to this view and be nothing except what they think him. By doing this he manages, more or less, to obscure from himself the truth, namely that at any moment he could stop behaving as he does; and that if he gets up at five each morning it is because he chooses to do so. This concept of being-for-others is of great importance, and I want to come back to it in a moment. First, however, there are one or two points which arise out of the concept of bad faith in general.

Bad faith is the protection which we assume against the torments of nausea and anguish. Any evasion of responsibility is an instance of bad faith; any denial that we can be other than we are. One of the kinds of bad faith which Sartre attacks is a reliance upon Freudian psycho-analysis as an explanation of human conduct. The subconscious mind he regards as magic— a pseudo-explanation invoked by persons who cannot or will not understand their true motives. Nearly all his descriptions of psychological phenomena and of human behaviour have the precise point of offering an alternative explanation, to supersede the Freudian. But there is in Sartre's explanations a defect which is at times shared by Freud's, namely that it is absolutely impossible to refute it, or even deny its applicability, since every refusal to accept it is taken as yet one more piece of evidence in its favour. For instance, suppose that one denied, as I think one very well might, that nausea was what one experienced when contemplating the external world. Suppose that, to be more specific still, one denied that the viscosity of things had any particular effect on one at all; suppose one said the suggestion that viscosity is an important category of the material was nothing but neurotic . . . would not all these denials be taken simply as instances of bad faith? They probably would. If bad faith can be crudely defined as the refusal to face disagreeable facts, then one's denials can always be construed as such a refusal. And the more vigorous one's protests that this is not self-deception, that it is only to falsehoods or exaggerations that one is objecting, the more serious the accusation of bad faith would become. Such obstinacy could be interpreted as a fault of character, not a desire for truth. At the very least, Sartre has neurotically over-emphasized what may be a tiny fact about some people's attitude to the world. And it cannot be denied that there is something insanely arbitrary and partial in picking out just *this* quality of things for so much attention. The difficulty with any philosophy whose method is largely descriptive is brought out by this case. It is impossible to describe *all* the objects or situations or qualities in the universe. So whatever is selected is likely to have the appearance of having been selected at random. There can be no justification, as far as I can see, for picking on one aspect of the world rather than another. The test cannot be completeness; it must be rather whether the description succeeds in conveying *some* kind of feeling, some attitude to the world. By this test, Sartre's descriptions certainly succeed. But it is going too far, in the light of this partial success, to hope to explain the whole of the universe and human conduct in the terms introduced into the description.

As I have suggested already there is one important aspect of existentialism which must still be discussed. This is the question of a man's relation not to objects in the external world, but to other men. We have seen that in two different ways a man of bad faith may try to become a *thing* and thus deny his responsibility for what he does. The first way is to try to become just a physical object: it is worth remarking here that Sartre, like Berkeley and other metaphysicians, has a powerful feeling for the texture of the universe. It does not seem

to him extraordinary to search for some one word
which would characterize all physical things—indeed
the word he picks on is 'massif' . . . solid. 'The in-itself
has nothing secret.' 'It has no within which is opposed
to a without.' In a sense we can designate it as a
synthesis; but it is the most indissoluble of all: the
synthesis of itself with itself. Human beings, then, are
not 'massif' in this way, and part of their perpetual
quest is to become so—to have no opposition of the
within to the without. Since no one wants to become
unconscious, although he longs for solid being-in-itself,
and since consciousness is what produces the lack of
solidity in men, the quest is contradictory. But sometimes it may take the form of seeking to be God—for
God could be described as the possessor of just these
contradictory qualities—namely consciousness and
being-in-itself. (It is therefore senseless, Sartre says, to
ask whether God exists. 'God' is the name of something
to be arrived at, which it is impossible to achieve.)

The second thing that a man of bad faith may attempt
to do is to become nothing but an object for others. The
fact that we are each of us an object for others is an
essential component in our existence as human beings.
It helps to define our situation as specifically human.
For instance, suppose I had been on a desert island
alone for so long that I had lost the concept of other
people. Then I might come to think that the way I
chose to do things was literally the only possible way.
The fact that things could be looked at from another
viewpoint would escape me, and therefore I might fail
to realize that I myself occupied some particular view-

point which I could change at will, and by thus being
unaware of my freedom I would be less than human.
In the third part of *Being and Nothingness*, Sartre sets
out to explore the concept of the existence of others. In
spite of its extreme length and repetitiveness, this seems
to me one of the most interesting parts of the whole
book. He starts with a criticism of solipsism, and an
account of the views of Husserl, Heidegger, and Hegel.
In the section entitled 'The look' [1] he finally states his
own view of what the relation is between myself and
other people. He argues that in our awareness of other
people we do not first apprehend them as physical
objects of a particular kind, and then argue, by analogy,
that they have consciousness, that they can feel and
think. It is rather that our first apprehension of them
strikes us immediately as incomplete. We have the feeling that, unlike other material objects which we perceive, here is one which can escape us, and which
necessarily partially eludes us. This is neither an inference from perception, nor a kind of mysterious or
mystical awareness of someone else's mind. It is, Sartre
says, like ordinary perception with a hole in it. He takes
the example of seeing a man reading a book as he walks
in the park.

There is a full object for me to grasp. In the midst of
the universe I can say 'man reading' as I could say 'cold
stone', 'fine rain'. I apprehend a closed 'gestalt' in which
the reading forms an essential quality; for the rest, it
remains blind and mute, lets itself be known as a pure
and simple temporal-spatial thing. . . . The quality 'man

[1] *loc. cit.* part 3, chapter 1, section IV.

N

reading' as the relation of the man to the book is simply a little particular crack in my universe. At the heart of this solid visible form, he makes himself a particular emptying. The form is solid only in appearance; its peculiar meaning is to be—in the midst of my universe, at ten paces from me, at the heart of that solidity—a closely consolidated localized flight.

But this is not the whole truth about the relation between myself and the Other. So far the Other still appears as a mere object, though of a peculiar kind. The key to the unique relation between me and the Other is that I am an object for him; he can look at me. I am not able to consider this exactly as I consider his looking at anything else—say grass. The difference is that being looked at by another person actually affects me. Sartre considers the case of soldiers who are trying to escape the notice of the enemy. In this case they do not think of the look of the enemy as necessarily connected with a particular man whose eyes they can see looking at them. They regard bushes and houses—all sorts of cover—as places from which the look may come.

What I apprehend immediately when I hear the branches crackling behind me is not that there is some-one there; it is that I am vulnerable, that I have a body which can be hurt, that I occupy a place, and that I can not in any case escape from the space in which I am without defence—in short that I am seen.

He then goes on to raise the question 'What does being seen mean for me?' In the next example he considers the case of a man who out of curiosity, or jealousy, looks and listens at a keyhole. While he is engaged in this, his whole concentration is fixed upon what he is doing, and upon what he hears and sees. In a sense he is unaware of himself; in a sense his 'self' does not yet exist, because he is nothing except the act of looking and listening. But then, while he is in this attitude, he becomes aware that he has heard footsteps, and that someone has come up behind him. The realization that there is someone watching him alters his whole mode of existence. He becomes aware of himself in a way that he was not before. He suddenly feels ashamed. Shame, Sartre says, is a confession that it was HE doing the act of which he is ashamed; later he will try to get round the memory of the incident by bad faith. But even bad faith is a confession. So self-awareness, guilt, shame, and pride all come into existence at the glance of the other, and it is in this sense that it is possible to say that the existence of the person, the for-itself, is actually dependent on the existence of another person. Without it, no one would be able to conceive any definition of himself. The discussion of shame and pride is curiously perfunctory, and it is impossible not to be reminded of Hume's discussions of the same subject, and to feel that his conclusions were not so very different and his manner of reaching them less exhausting. But all the same Sartre has, in the discussion of the Other in general, called attention to a number of extremely import- ant points. First, he has noticed the inadequacy of any theory which suggests that other people are, for us, just material objects which we invest, imaginatively, with inner life on an analogy with our own. Of course analogy plays an enormous part in our understanding of individual human beings; but it is very hard to believe that our primary awareness of the existence of others can be explained in these terms. The fact that we are objects of perception, of attention for them, the fact that they are obstacles for us, and make plans in which we have no share, but which affect our plans—these things seem to me, as Sartre suggests, far more basic to our realization both of other people and of our own consequent situation in the world. Secondly, Sartre draws our attention to the difficulties inherent in the difference between our own view of ourselves and other people's view of us. These are partly difficulties of language; from our own point of view it is usually very difficult to accept any description of ourselves. Even though I might admit that, for instance, I worked in a bank, I should repudiate the suggestion that I was a bank clerk. Though I might admit that I sometimes took things which did not belong to me, I should resist the designation 'thief'. But for other people, who see me from the outside, there is no other appropriate description except 'bank clerk' or 'thief'. And reflecting on these words, I may come to feel that since I would not use them, while someone else would, of the very same object, therefore their meaning is somehow destroyed. Again, there is a familiar difficulty about the predictability of a man's behaviour. He is filled with horror when he first realizes that people regard him as in certain ways predictable. He suddenly sees himself as a *thing* in the world, subject to laws; or at least as an obsessive character with virtually no free choice. Sartre imagines a terrible little conversation which illustrates this difference of viewpoint:

'I swear to you that I will do it.'

'Maybe so. You tell me so. I want to believe you. It is indeed possible that you will do it.'

From this conversation, a doubt may arise for the first speaker as to whether he is really in a position to make promises at all. One cannot commit oneself to a future action unless one is conceived as a free agent, with a continuous ability to frame resolutions and stick to them. The ability to do this indeed is one of the most important aspects of human personality. But the second speaker clearly regards the promise as futile, since the behaviour of the promiser is determined quite independently of any promise or undertaking. If I observe a man's behaviour inductively for a long time, as I might observe the behaviour of an ant or a bee, then I feel justified in making inductively based predictions about his conduct. To see oneself as the subject of this kind of inductive prediction is to see oneself suddenly as an object in the natural world, distinguished from other animals only by the ridiculous characteristic of being able to mouth such expressions as 'I promise'. The look of the other is partly important because of the reduction in status which it is thus capable of effecting. And then the question arises of which view is right. Am I right to take my own promises and resolutions seriously; or is he right to regard them as totally irrelevant to the way I will in fact behave? This is analogous to the difficulty of description which I sketched just now. Am I right to regard myself as a complex person with complex motives for doing what I do, or is the other right in regarding me as simply a thief? Which of these points of view is to be taken seriously, if the question arises of how to *treat* me? Sartre is constantly aware of the possibility of a total shift in the point of view, which may radically affect our attitude towards one and the same person. Becoming aware of how I seem to others may, of course, be the origin of bad faith, as we have seen already. To take seriously someone's view of you as incapable of altering your conduct by means of any number of promises or resolutions might lead you to feel that you were determined by your character to go on behaving as you always had; and this would be bad faith. There is, therefore, a perpetual contradiction between a man's actual freedom and his appearance as an object for the other. This is only another version of the familiar debate about responsibility; but it is a version with a peculiar force, since its questions are raised not merely by difficult cases, cases of 'diminished responsibility', or of hypnotism, but by the continuous possibility of a shifting point of view about every aspect of our life.

Other people do not, however, exist merely to look at us and thereby affect our self-awareness. We are constantly entering into various different relations with them, which Sartre sets out to explore. All this part of *Being and Nothingness* has a kind of bewildering power which derives from the intensity of Sartre's imaginative vision of each of us forming his own interpretations of the world, and locked in a constant battle with other people, whom we are obliged to recognize as possessing as much freedom as we do ourselves. For in spite of his repudiation of solipsism, Sartre rejects as bad faith any suggestion that we take over our understanding of the world from other people, that we are taught under what headings to classify it and that we regard it from a common, characteristically human standpoint. We are responsible for our own categories. Each man is therefore left isolated, attempting to sort out his impression of the world for himself. But there is a constant danger of self-deception, as we have seen, even in this attempted sorting out. For the acceptance of any category as necessary or given, the failure to analyse anything, or the mere acceptance of a given way of talking, may all of them be bad faith. This virtual isolation in our own consciousness leads to perpetual failure in our relations with other people. We aim all the time to achieve stability for ourselves, to fill up the emptiness within us, and to take on the status of beings-in-themselves though without losing our consciousness. We try to use other people as means to this self-contradictory end. For instance, if a man is loved by another person, the loving gaze of the other gives him this solid, stable existence which he aims at. But the freedom of the other is an impediment; there is the constant possibility that the gaze may be withdrawn; and furthermore the lover is himself seeking his own stability, and therefore demands the same loving look. There is a struggle therefore between the lovers, each seeking to capture and deny the freedom of the other. But this struggle is in any case self-defeating, since only love or admiration freely given can have the effect of stabilizing the existence of the one loved. To fall in love is therefore to embark on a series of battles which are doomed from the start to futility.

If this is the human situation with regard to the world of external objects and other people, it remains to ask how Sartre thinks we ought actually to behave. Is there anything which it is worth while our trying to be or to do? First, it is essential that we realize that, if there is anything which has value for us, it is a contingent matter. We have created the value for ourselves. The main lesson which we are to learn from the description of our situation is that we must 'repudiate the spirit of seriousness'. Sartre defines the spirit of seriousness as follows: 'It considers values as transcendent given independent of human subjectivity, and it transfers the quality of "desirable" from the ontological structure of things to their simple material constitution.' Thus the belief that some things are good in themselves, and the belief that some things are always good because their consequences are desirable, are both equally expressions of this spirit. Above all, non-naturalism in ethics must be abandoned; though ordinary naturalism too is 'serious'. A morality based on such beliefs is a morality of bad faith.

It has obscured all its goals in order to free itself from anguish. Man pursues being blindly by hiding from himself the free project which is this pursuit. He makes himself such that he is *waited for* by all the tasks along his way. Objects are mute demands, and he is nothing in himself but the passive obedience to these demands.

But the fact remains that even though values have no independent existence, we do assign values to things, and regard some things as goals worth pursuing. It is indeed in the word 'goal' that the clue to the concept of value is to be found. You cannot describe something as good in the same way as you can describe it as red. This truth which has so much exercised English moral philosophers is familiar to Sartre as well. If you describe it as good you are uttering a normative expression, and you are suggesting that here is something to be aimed at. Goodness is a quality which does not have existence in the ordinary sense; but to say that something is good or generous or noble is to see it as an instance of a quality which is always to be pursued and will never be reached. This unattainability of the morally perfect is, for Sartre, the reason why properties like goodness have always seemed to moral philosophers both to exist unconditionally and in some sense not to exist at all. It is impossible for any conscious human being not to assign values to things. The essential human characteristic is to form projects and intentions and to pursue aims. To these necessarily and as part of their existence, value attaches. Therefore there is no question of *knowing* that something is good or that it is noble. A project is formed and value 'haunts' this project.

Value is everywhere and nowhere; at the heart of the nihilating relation 'reflection-reflecting' it is present and out of reach, and it is simply lived as the concrete meaning of that lack which makes my present being. . . . Thus reflective consciousness can properly be called moral consciousness since it cannot arise without at the same moment disclosing values.

Now all this may seem disquietingly vague. What

Sartre seems to be expressing is a romantic view of morality, according to which there is nothing but the conscience of each of us as a guide, and for each one of us, whatever solitary goal he pursues, he is sure only of never attaining it. And this is, I think, a not unfair estimate of the doctrine in *Being and Nothingness*. But sometimes, particularly in the lecture 'Existentialism is a Humanism', to which I have already referred, Sartre puts forward a theory of morality which has more content and which he expressly compares with the theories of Kant. He there says that if I really aim at my own freedom, which, as a human being, I must necessarily do, I cannot help aiming at the freedom of others. It would be self-contradictory to desire freedom as an end, without universalizing this end, and including in it the freedom of others. It is fairly clear, furthermore, that in this argument he is thinking of freedom not only as the freedom to choose which is the opposite of determinism, but more specifically as political freedom. This view, therefore, could lead to concrete aims, and to a programme of moral and political action not unlike that of Mill and the utilitarians. But it must be admitted that this Kantian-utilitarian view, comforting though it is to come across anything so familiar in the metaphysical jungle, is not really connected in any way with the main part of Sartre's theory. It is given nothing in the way of metaphysical backing; and he does nothing to show that to assign a value to something necessarily entails a universal judgement. We know from the novels, and indeed from everything that Sartre has written, that freedom is in his view the supreme value. But we must admit that it is not wholly clear to what a man is committed if he chooses freedom, or what his alternatives are.

Sartre explains, as an integral part of his whole metaphysical system, how value arises in the world, and how it is that men are so situated that they must always be attempting something which they cannot achieve. But he tells us little about how, for instance, it is possible to argue about matters of value, or how someone would set about showing that one course of action was better than another. There is no formula which can readily be derived from *Being and Nothingness* for deciding what I ought to do; it is difficult even to conceive what form such a decision would take. But it must be remembered that Sartre does not yet suppose himself to have written any kind of moral philosophy. At the very end of *Being and Nothingness* he says that once the moral agent has realized that he is himself the source of all values, 'His freedom will become conscious of itself and reveal itself in anguish as the unique source of value and the emptiness by which the *world* exists'. But the possibility of acting will always be realized only in the context of other people who can also choose and whose choices may affect my own. The question becomes one of trying to find out how far a free agent can escape from his particular situation in his choices; and of how much responsibility he can be brought to accept for being as he is. To these questions Sartre promises to devote another, specifically ethical, work.

But there are two things which may perhaps be said

about the form which moral questions will take, according to existentialist theory. The first is that it is impossible on such a theory sharply to distinguish moral from political questions. It is not *just* an accident of time and place that for Sartre the pressing moral question seems to be 'Shall I join the Communist party?' Marxist philosophy, like existentialism, insists that morality is a matter not of knowing this or that but of acting; but the action is in accordance with a shared creed. The question for Sartre therefore is always whether the adopting of any shared creed whatever is not going to plunge the believer into bad faith. Though you may freely choose to join the party, this may well be your last free act. This leads to the second point. Apart from his rather uneasy flirtation with utilitarianism, Sartre seems inclined to think that to give any concrete general rules, or to frame any political programme, is to come perilously near to bad faith. It is impossible not to be involved in the political and social situation in which one finds oneself, but the way through it must be found for each one by himself. It is to this highly romantic, individualist view of morality that Sartre is most deeply committed. If there is any typically moral question it is of the form 'What, here and now, would be the least *phoney* thing for me to choose?'

Chapter Eight
CONCLUSION

IT is now time to attempt some general remarks on the course of the history of Ethics in the last sixty years. Is there anything which can profitably be said about all of the different philosophers we have considered in this book? At first sight it may appear that there is one interest which all of them without exception have shared, and that is an interest in refuting Ethical Naturalism. If hostility could nullify the influence of a philosophical view, then utilitarianism ought by now to be stone dead. This hostility is surprising, particularly in English empirical philosophers, many of whom would in their non-philosophical moments turn out to be utilitarians of an enlightened liberal kind. But this anti-naturalism, although it has been universally a part of recent ethical theories, has taken radically different forms, and the differences are far greater than the similarities.

It has commonly been held that Moore exercised a great influence upon the course of moral philosophy during this century, and this for two reasons. First, he was the inventor of the phrase 'The Naturalistic Fallacy'; and secondly, he directed the attention of philosophers towards the problem of analysing the concept of goodness. As far as the first point goes, Bradley and the other metaphysical philosophers were just as deeply opposed to naturalism as Moore was.

Anti-naturalism is not, therefore, in itself a sufficient reason for insisting on the influence of Moore. The name Naturalistic Fallacy, it is true, we have all learned from Moore; but I should be inclined to say that we had learned little else. As to the second point, Moore's interests, as I hope to have suggested already, were not in the *language* of morals. He did not care at all how the word 'good' was used. He was interested in what things were good in themselves. He was concerned to show, as all anti-naturalists are, that values are distinct from facts, and that no amount of reflection upon facts, in the ordinary sense, will entitle anyone to make a single value judgement upon them. But he thought that this was because goodness was a special and unique kind of property, the possession of which was different from the possession of other properties. Now if any philosopher is an ethical intuitionist, as Moore was, it is necessary for him to be prepared actually to give examples of those things which have the intuitable property of goodness, or rightness, or whatever it is. Moore was perfectly prepared to do this; in fact, as we have seen, he thought it the easiest thing in the world to do. He told us, in a perfectly straightforward way, what things were as a matter of fact the best things in the world, and therefore what, in general, we should aim at. Sometimes people have objected to recent moral philosophy that it has been, at least in England and America, uncommitted; that it has taken no sides, and given no guidance about how to behave. People who have made this complaint cannot have read the philosophy of Moore. The other intuitionists also told us what things were obligatory, but unfortunately they, for the most part, failed to hold our attention. They cheated by telling us to do only the things we would have done anyway, like returning books we have borrowed. They did not tell us how to live, or how to treat other people in serious matters. But from *Principia Ethica* we could, if we tried, derive this information. This difference between Moore and the other intuitionists brings out, I think, the real reason why we continue to read *Principia Ethica*, and why in the history of this period of moral philosophy Moore looms so large. The reason is that the book is so good and so eccentric. Moore dominates us through its pages just as he dominated his contemporaries in Cambridge. There is no comparable book on ethics in this century. But to be great is not the same as to be influential.

There is one respect, however, in which subsequent philosophers did follow Moore. Whereas Bradley, following Hegelian, and ultimately Kantian models of ethical theory, regarded human choice as the only proper subject matter of morals, and further, thought of choice as something which must essentially be viewed from inside, from behind the eyes of the agent, Moore and moral philosophers after him were concerned only secondarily with choices. Their main interest was in judging things to be good or bad, right or wrong. The central question became 'What is a moral judgement?' It was inevitable that Moore himself should adopt this standpoint, since his concern was with the property of goodness, which was a property of things in the external world, there to be discovered. It was states of consciousness which were good, and it did not matter whose state of consciousness it was; all could equally come up for judgement.

It was equally natural that Ayer and the logical positivists should adopt the same standpoint. Their concern was to mark off scientific from non-scientific discourse, statements of fact from pseudo-statements which purported to, but did not, state facts. Their attention was therefore naturally drawn to the differences between statements such as 'the boy is a diabetic' and 'the boy is a good influence in the house'. Once again the proper function of moral philosophy appeared to be to discuss moral judgements, though now in a new way.

From the positivists, and the heyday of the emotive theory, it was, as I hope I have shown, only a short step to the post-war linguistic analyses which issued mainly from Oxford. Here again the point of view is the same. Anti-naturalism still characterizes this philosophy as well; but it has moved very far from the anti-naturalism of Moore. What distinguishes a moral from a non-moral judgement is now not the kind of property which they each call attention to, but the logic of the words used in the statement of each. Ethical judgements are seen as a sub-class of value judgements in general, and the most general form of the question raised by these philosophers is 'What is it to evaluate things?' or 'What is the difference between evaluating things and describing them?'

It may be thought that I am unfair to some philosophers of the last ten years; they have not all, it may be urged, concentrated so exclusively on the judging and assessing, the grading and marking aspect of morality. After all, Hare regarded moral judgements as imperatives, and the point of an imperative is that it should galvanize someone into activity. It is not just a spectator's judgement of the scene. Nowell-Smith, equally, maintained that many moral words, at least much of the time, were specifically intended to indicate that something ought to be done about the situation to which they were applied. (One of his examples was the word 'weed' which was supposed to suggest the necessity of action in any keen gardener.) I do not deny that these philosophers, like Hume and Berkeley before them, recognized that the language which we use about things may affect our attitude towards these things, and therefore even our actions. But this does not seem to me to constitute a real difference between them and the emotive theorists. Their interest was still concentrated upon the actual words used in the framing of what they called ethical propositions. An ethical proposition may, it is true, take various forms, but there was supposed to be a connexion between all the different forms it might take, and this connexion lay in the logical characteristics of the words used. The differences between 'I ought to do this' and 'this is right' or 'this is good' were not really represented as serious or important differences. Therefore in the end, it did not make very much difference whether cases of personal choice were taken as examples, or cases of public advice, or cases of judgement after the event. The same analysis would do, with a few adjustments,

o

for all the cases. The standpoint was still that of the judge or the schoolmaster, even if sometimes the judgement was passed or the report written with an eye to the future.

This, then, seems to me the most important way in which, whether under the influence of Moore or not, later philosophers have followed his practice. There is one other less important feature common to their writings. Moore was convinced that *goodness* was the central concept of ethics and, apart from an extension to cover 'ought', right', and 'duty', most philosophers of the last sixty years have agreed with him. There is a small and general set of concepts which have been singled out for treatment in books about ethics. It is a great pity, however, to concentrate on this small group of words, especially as they are not words which, with the exception of 'duty', have any particular relevance to ethics. If it is the logic of ethical language which is interesting, then it might have been better to start to analyse some words which appear only in ethical contexts, instead of insisting on first of all examining these extremely general and virtually contentless words. Admittedly 'ought' and 'right' come into our moral vocabulary, but they do not exhaust it. As for 'good', I doubt whether it even comes in very much except in the pages of books about moral philosophy.

One of the consequences of treating ethics as the analysis of ethical language is, as I have suggested earlier, that it leads to the increasing triviality of the subject. This is not a general criticism of linguistic analysis, but only of this method applied to ethics. In ethics, alone among the branches of philosophical study, the subject matter is not so much the categories which we use to describe or to learn about the world, as our own impact upon the world, our relation to other people and our attitude to our situation and our life. We do need to categorize and to describe, even in the sphere of morals, but we should still exist as moral agents even if we seldom did so; and therefore the subject matter of ethics would still exist. How we describe the world cannot be the primary concern of moral philosophers; and it is an evasion to say that by distinguishing between evaluating and describing, moral philosophers have avoided assimilating ethics to epistemology. Evaluating is not the distinctive function of moral agents either. Deliberating, wishing, hating, loving, choosing; these are things which characterize us as people, and therefore as moral agents, and these are the things to which the emotive theory and its later developments paid insufficient attention.

One aspect of this trivializing of the subject is the refusal of moral philosophers in England to commit themselves to any moral opinions. They have for the most part fallen in happily with the positivist distinction between moral philosophers, who analyse the logic of moral discourse, and moralists, who practise it. It follows that they are inclined to believe that, in theory at least, absolutely anything could count as a moral opinion, or a moral principle, provided it was framed in the way laid down for such principles, and used, as they are used, to guide conduct. It would be generally agreed that some opinions might be outrageous, and some principles harmful, but where we get our principles and opinions from, how we should decide between them, and what would be an example of a good one—these things they will not tell us, for to do so would be actually to express a moral opinion. This caution derives, as it is easy to see, at least in part from the obsessive fear of naturalism. If it were possible for these philosophers to say that some moral principles are derived from what people actually want, or desire in the long run, then they could say what these principles were without appearing to be dogmatic, or to be merely voicing their private preferences. Hume and Mill would have been happy to give any number of examples of good moral principles, and to derive each of them directly or indirectly from some general desire for security or human happiness. But this would be to destroy the autonomy of ethics, or so they say. Thus the concentration upon the most general kind of evaluative language, combined with the fear of committing the naturalistic fallacy, has led too often to discussions of grading fruit, or choosing fictitious games equipment, and ethics as a serious subject has been left further and further behind.

But I believe that the most boring days are over. I cannot risk much speculation about the future, but there is no doubt that in at least three different but related ways an interest in the subject matter of ethics is reviving. First, under the general influence of Wittgenstein, it is increasingly recognized that in order to discuss any subject properly, it is necessary to see the language which is appropriate to it actually at work. This leads to the consideration of a more interesting set of concepts than the right and the good. Virtues and vices may now be considered, as well as feelings, scruples, desires, intentions, and other psychological phenomena. Secondly, an increasing interest in the question of what specially characterizes a moral as opposed to any other evaluative judgement, is leading philosophers at least to reopen the question of ethical naturalism. Is it after all perhaps not so self-evident that empirical considerations about what does people good and what does them harm are irrelevant to deciding what is a moral principle and what is not? In this connexion I should call attention to two very persuasive articles by Philippa Foot, in *Mind*, 1958, and the *Proceedings of the Aristotelian Society*, 1958, which display both the tendencies I have mentioned, and which have aroused great interest.

Finally, there is at least the possibility that we may in England learn a little from the Continent. I do not for a moment mean to suggest that we should all become Hegelian metaphysicians. That would be both undesirable and anyway impossible. Philosophy progresses, and it has now progressed beyond the stage at which a philosopher can simply invent a system which pleases him and by means of which he can explain everything in the universe. But even if total explanations are no longer possible, that is no reason why we should not still look at human beings in general in their context in the world. If we do this, it is likely that the most important thing about them should appear to us, as it did to Kant, to Hegel, to Bradley, and to Sartre, to be their capacity for acting spontaneously, and choosing between alternatives; for making and keeping resolutions, for regretting their decisions and rationally changing their minds, for feeling guilt and feeling pride in their achievements. If this capacity is what makes morality possible, then it should surely be in this group of phenomena that moral philosophers should, at least partly, interest themselves. I think that in the past, philosophers have been too much concerned with moral *theories* to pay very much attention to how people actually decide, or what moral decisions are really like. For instance, it has too often been suggested, without sufficient support, that all moral decisions must be decisions *on principle*, or decisions to do something *because it is a duty*. Reading Sartre, if it taught us nothing else, might perhaps open our eyes to the suggestion that not all moral decisions are of this kind; and indeed that sometimes to do something on the supposition that it is a duty, waiting to be fulfilled, would be bad faith.

Moral philosophy might in this way properly include both description of the complexities of actual choices and actual decisions, and also discussion of what would count as reasons for making this or that decision. I believe that this is what philosophers are beginning gradually to do. It is impossible to predict what kind of books they will actually write. But the examples which they contain will necessarily have to be long, complicated, and realistic. I think that the days of shouting to revive the fainting man, and the days of grading apples, are over. Moral philosophy will be much more difficult, perhaps much more embarrassing, to write than it has been recently, but it will be far more interesting to read.

SHORT BIBLIOGRAPHY

THE following list includes those books and articles discussed in the text and several others which seem to be essential reading for anyone interested in the ethical writings of this period. There is, however, no claim to completeness.

I. BOOKS

G. E. Moore. *Principia Ethica*. Cambridge University Press, 1903.
      Ethics. Home University Library, 1912.
F. H. Bradley. *Ethical Studies*. 2nd edition, Oxford University Press, 1927.
C. K. Ogden and I. A. Richards. *The Meaning of Meaning*. Kegan Paul, London, 1923.
W. D. Ross. *The Right and the Good*. Oxford University Press, 1930.
      The Foundations of Ethics. Oxford University Press, 1939.
H. A. Prichard. *Moral Obligation: Essays and Lectures*. Oxford University Press, 1949.
E. F. Carritt. *Theory of Morals*. Oxford University Press, 1928.
H. W. B. Joseph. *Some Problems in Ethics*. Oxford University Press, 1931.
C. D. Broad. *Ethics and the History of Philosophy*. Routledge & Kegan Paul, 1952.
A. J. Ayer. *Language, Truth and Logic*. Gollancz, 1936; 2nd ed., 1946.
C. L. Stevenson. *Ethics and Language*. Yale University Press, 1945.
A. C. Ewing. *The Definition of Good*. Routledge & Kegan Paul, 1947.
G. Ryle. *The Concept of Mind*. Hutchinson, 1949.
A. N. Prior. *Logic and the Basis of Ethics*. Oxford University Press, 1949.
S. E. Toulmin. *An Examination of the Place of Reason in Ethics*. Cambridge, 1950.

R. M. Hare. *The Language of Morals*. Oxford University Press, 1952.

L. Wittgenstein. *Philosophical Investigations*. Blackwell, Oxford, 1953.

Iris Murdoch. *Sartre*. Bowes & Bowes, Cambridge, 1953.

P-H. Nowell-Smith. *Ethics*. Penguin Books, 1954; Blackwell, Oxford, 1957.

G. E. M. Anscombe. *Intention*. Blackwell, Oxford, 1957.

J-P. Sartre. *Being and Nothingness*. Translated Hazel E. Barnes. Methuen, 1957.

K. Baier. *The Moral Point of View, a Rational Basis of Ethics*. Ithaca, N.Y., 1958.

A. Farrer. *The Freedom of the Will*. Black, 1958.

A. Montefiore. *A Modern Introduction to Moral Philology*. Routledge & Kegan Paul, 1958.

S. Hampshire. *Thought and Action*. Chatto & Windus, 1959.

II. ARTICLES

C. L. Stevenson. 'The Emotive Meaning of Ethical Terms'. *Mind*, 1937.

'Ethical Judgments andAvoidability'. *Mind*, 1938.

'Persuasive Definitions'. *Mind*, 1938.

J. N. Findlay. 'Morality by Convention'. *Mind*, 1944.

'The Justification of Attitudes'. *Mind*, 1954.

P. F. Strawson. 'Ethical Intuitionism'. *Philosophy*, 1949.

J. O. Urmson. 'On Grading'. *Mind*, 1950.

J. L. Austin. 'Ifs and Cans'. Henrietta Hertz Lecture to the British Academy, 1956.

P. R. Foot. 'Moral Arguments'. *Mind*, 1958.

'Moral Beliefs'. *Proceedings of the Aristotelian Society*, 1958.

'When is a principle a moral principle?' *Proceedings of the Aristotelian Society*, Supplementary Volume 28.

INDEX

JOHN BULL'S OTHER ISLAND

Bernard Shaw was born in Dublin in 1856. Although essentially shy, he created the persona of G.B.S., the showman, satirist, controversialist, critic, pundit, wit, intellectual buffoon and dramatist. Commentators brought a new adjective into English: Shavian, a term used to embody all his brilliant qualities.

After his arrival in London in 1876 he became an active Socialist and a brilliant platform speaker. He wrote on many social aspects of the day: on *Commonsense about the War* (1914), *How to Settle the Irish Question* (1917) and *The Intelligent Woman's Guide to Socialism and Capitalism* (1928). He undertook his own education at the British Museum and consequently became keenly interested in cultural subjects. Thus his prolific output included music, art and theatre reviews, which were collected into several volumes, such as *Music in London 1890–1894* (3 vols., 1931); *Pen Portraits and Reviews* (1931); and *Our Theatres in the Nineties* (3 vols., 1931). He also wrote five novels and some shorter fiction including *The Black Girl in Search of God and some Lesser Tales* and *Cashel Byron's Profession*, both published in Penguin.

He conducted a strong attack on the London theatre and was closely associated with the intellectual revival of British theatre. His many plays fall into several categories: 'Plays Unpleasant'; comedies, chronicle-plays; 'metabiological Pentateuch' (*Back to Methuselah*, a series of plays) and 'political extravaganzas'. Bernard Shaw died in 1950.

BERNARD SHAW

JOHN BULL'S OTHER ISLAND

DEFINITIVE TEXT
under the editorial supervision of
Dan H. Laurence

PENGUIN BOOKS

PENGUIN BOOKS

Published by the Penguin Group
Penguin Books Ltd, 80 Strand, London, WC2R 0RL, England
Penguin Books USA Inc., 375 Hudson Street, New York, New York 10014, USA
Penguin Books Australia Ltd, Ringwood, Victoria, Australia
Penguin Books Canada Ltd, 10 Alcorn Avenue, Toronto, Ontario, Canada M4V 3B2
Penguin Books (NZ) Ltd, 182–190 Wairau Road, Auckland 10, New Zealand

Penguin Books Ltd, Registered Offices: 80 Strand, London, WC2R 0RL, England

First published 1907
This revised text first published 1930
Published in Penguin Books 1984

012

Printed in Great Britain by
Clays Ltd, St Ives plc

In Great Britain, all business connected with Bernard Shaw's plays is in the
hands of THE SOCIETY OF AUTHORS, 84 Drayton Gardens, London SW10 9SB
(Telephone: 071-373 6642), to which all inquiries and applications for licences
should be addressed and fees paid. Dates and places of contemplated
performances must be precisely stated in all applications.

In the United States of America and Canada, applications for permission
to give stock and amateur performances of Bernard Shaw's plays should be
made to Samuel French, Inc., 45 West 25th Street, New York, New York 10010.
In all other cases, whether for stage, radio, or television, application should
be made to the Society of Authors, 84 Drayton Gardens,
London SW10 9SB, England.

ISBN 978-0-14-045044-6

www.greenpenguin.co.uk

MIX
Paper from
responsible sources
FSC
www.fsc.org   FSC® C018179

Penguin Books is committed to a sustainable
future for our business, our readers and our planet.
This book is made from Forest Stewardship
Council™ certified paper.

ALWAYS LEARNING   PEARSON

Contents

Preface for Politicians

(written in 1906)

John Bull's Other Island was written in 1904 at the request of Mr William Butler Yeats, as a patriotic contribution to the repertory of the Irish Literary Theatre. Like most people who have asked me to write plays, Mr Yeats got rather more than he bargained for. The play was at that time beyond the resources of the new Abbey Theatre, which the Irish enterprise owed to the public spirit of Miss A. E. F. Horniman (an Englishwoman, of course), who, twelve years ago, played an important part in the history of the modern English stage as well as in my own personal destiny by providing the necessary capital for that memorable season at the Avenue Theatre which forced my Arms and The Man and Mr Yeats's Land of Heart's Desire on the recalcitrant London playgoer, and gave a third Irish playwright, Dr John Todhunter, an opportunity which the commercial theatres could not have afforded him.

There was another reason for changing the destination of John Bull's Other Island. It was uncongenial to the whole spirit of the neo–Gaelic movement, which is bent on creating a new Ireland after its own ideal, whereas my play is a very uncompromising presentment of the real old Ireland. The next thing that happened was the production of the play in London at the Court Theatre by Messrs Vedrenne and Barker, and its immediate and enormous popularity with delighted and flattered English audiences. This constituted it a successful commercial play, and made it unnecessary to resort to the special machinery or tax the special resources of the Irish Literary Theatre for its production.

HOW TOM BROADBENT TOOK IT

Now I have a good deal more to say about the relations between the Irish and the English than will be found in my play. Writing the play for an Irish audience, I thought it would be good for them to be shewn very clearly that the loudest laugh they could raise at the expense of the absurdest Englishman was not really a laugh on their side; that he would succeed where they would fail; that he could inspire strong affection and loyalty in an Irishman who knew the world and was moved only to dislike, mistrust, impatience and even exasperation by his own countrymen; that his power of taking himself seriously, and his insensibility to anything funny in danger and destruction, was the first condition of economy and concentration of force, sustained purpose, and rational conduct. But the need for this lesson in Ireland is the measure of its demoralizing superfluousness in England. English audiences very naturally swallowed it eagerly and smacked their lips over it, laughing all the more heartily because they felt that they were taking a caricature of themselves with the most tolerant and large-minded goodhumor. They were perfectly willing to allow me to represent Tom Broadbent as infatuated in politics, hypnotized by his newspaper leader-writers and parliamentary orators into an utter paralysis of his common sense, without moral delicacy or social tact, provided I made him cheerful, robust, goodnatured, free from envy, and above all, a successful muddler-through in business and love. Not only did no English critic allow that the success in business of Messrs English Broadbent and Irish Doyle might possibly have been due to some extent to Doyle, but one writer actually dwelt with much feeling on the pathos of Doyle's failure as an engineer (a circumstance not mentioned nor suggested in my play) in contrast with Broadbent's solid success. No doubt, when the play is performed in Ireland, the Dublin critics will regard it as self-evident that without Doyle Broadbent would have become bankrupt in six months. I should say, myself, that the combination was probably much more effective than either of the partners would have been alone. I am persuaded further – without pretending to know more about it than anyone else – that Broadbent's special contri- bution was simply the strength, self-satisfaction, social confidence and cheerful bumptiousness that money, comfort, and good feeding bring to all healthy people; and that Doyle's special contribution was the freedom from illusion, the power of facing facts, the nervous industry, the sharp- ened wits, the sensitive pride of the imaginative man who has fought his way up through social persecution and poverty. I do not say that the con- fidence of the Englishman in Broadbent is not for the moment justified. The virtues of the English soil are not less real because they consist of coal and iron, not of metaphysical sources of character. The virtues of Broad- bent are not less real because they are the virtues of the money that coal and iron have produced. But as the mineral virtues are being discovered and developed in other soils, their derivative virtues are appearing so rapidly in other nations that Broadbent's relative advantage is vanishing. In truth I am afraid (the misgiving is natural to a by-this-time slightly elderly playwright) that Broadbent is out of date. The successful Englishman of today, when he is not a transplanted Scotchman or Irishman, often turns out on investigation to be, if not an American, an Italian, or a Jew, at least to be depending on the brains, the nervous energy, and the freedom from romantic illusions (often called cynicism) of such foreigners for the management of his sources of income. At all events I am persuaded that a modern nation that is satisfied with Broadbent is in a dream. Much as I like him, I object to be governed by him, or entangled in his political destiny. I therefore propose to give him a piece of my mind here, as an Irishman, full of an instinctive pity for those of my fellow-creatures who are only English.

WHAT IS AN IRISHMAN?

When I say that I am an Irishman I mean that I was born in Ireland, and that my native language is the English of Swift and not the unspeakable jargon of the mid-XIX century London newspapers. My extraction is the extraction of most Englishmen: that is, I have no trace in me of the commercially imported North Spanish strain which passes for aboriginal Irish: I am a genuine typical Irishman of the Danish, Norman, Cromwellian, and (of course) Scotch invasions. I am violently and arrogantly Protestant by family tradition; but let no English Government therefore count on my allegiance: I am English enough to be an inveterate Republican and Home Ruler. It is true that one of my grandfathers was an Orangeman; but then his sister was an abbess; and his uncle, I am proud to say, was hanged as a rebel. When I look round me on the hybrid cosmopolitans, slum poisoned or square pampered, who call themselves Englishmen today, and see them bullied by the Irish Protestant garrison as no Bengalee now lets himself be bullied by an Englishman; when I see the Irishman everywhere standing clearheaded, sane, hardily callous to the boyish sentimentalities, susceptibilities, and credulities that make the Englishman the dupe of every charlatan and the idolater of every numskull, I perceive that Ireland is the only spot on earth which still produces the ideal Englishman of history. Blackguard, bully, drunkard, liar, foulmouth, flatterer, beggar, backbiter, venal functionary, corrupt judge, envious friend, vindictive opponent, unparalleled political traitor: all these your Irishman may easily be, just as he may be a gentleman (a species extinct in England, and nobody a penny the worse); but he is never quite the hysterical, nonsense-crammed, fact-proof, truth-terrified, unballasted sport of all the bogey panics and all the silly enthusiasms that now calls itself 'God's Englishman'. England cannot do without its Irish and its Scots today, because it cannot do without at least a little sanity.

THE PROTESTANT GARRISON

The more Protestant an Irishman is – the more English he is, if it flatters you to have it put that way, the more intolerable he finds it to be ruled by English instead of Irish folly. A 'loyal' Irishman is an abhorrent phenomenon, because it is an unnatural one. No doubt English rule is vigorously exploited in the interests of the property, power, and promotion of the Irish classes as against the Irish masses. Our delicacy is part of a keen sense of reality which makes us a very practical, and even, on occasion, a very coarse people. The Irish soldier takes the King's shilling and drinks the King's health; and the Irish squire takes the title deeds of the English settlement and rises uncovered to the strains of the English national anthem. But do not mistake this cupboard loyalty for anything deeper. It gains a broad base from the normal attachment of every reasonable man to the established government as long as it is bearable; for we all, after a certain age, prefer peace to revolution and order to chaos, other things being equal. Such considerations produce loyal Irishmen as they produce loyal Poles and Fins, loyal Hindoos, loyal Filipinos, and faithful slaves. But there is nothing more in it than that. If there is an entire lack of gall in the feeling of the Irish gentry towards the English, it is because the Englishman is always gaping admiringly at the Irishman as at some clever child prodigy. He overrates him with a generosity born of a traditional conviction of his own superiority in the deeper aspects of human character. As the Irish gentleman, tracing his pedigree to the conquest or one of the invasions, is equally convinced that if this superiority really exists, he is the genuine true blue heir to it, and as he is easily able to hold his own in all the superficial social accomplishments, he finds English society agreeable, and English houses very comfortable, Irish establishments being generally straitened by an attempt to keep a park and a stable on an income which would not justify an Englishman in venturing upon a wholly detached villa.

OUR TEMPERAMENTS CONTRASTED

But however pleasant the relations between the Protestant garrison and the English gentry may be, they are always essentially of the nature of an *entente cordiale* between foreigners. Personally I like Englishmen much better than Irishmen (no doubt because they make more of me) just as many Englishmen like Frenchmen better than Englishmen, and never go on board a Peninsular and Oriental steamer when one of the ships of the Messageries Maritimes is available. But I never think of an Englishman as my countryman. I should as soon think of applying that term to a German. And the Englishman has the same feeling. When a Frenchman fails to make the distinction, we both feel a certain disparagement involved in the misapprehension. Macaulay, seeing that the Irish had in Swift an author worth stealing, tried to annex him by contending that he must be classed as an Englishman because he was not an aboriginal Celt. He might as well have refused the name of Briton to Addison because he did not stain himself blue and attach scythes to the poles of his sedan chair. In spite of all such trifling with facts, the actual distinction between the idolatrous Englishman and the fact-facing Irishman, of the same extraction though they be, remains to explode those two hollowest of fictions, the Irish and English 'races'. There is no Irish race any more than there is an English race or a Yankee race. There *is* an Irish climate, which will stamp an immigrant more deeply and durably in two years, apparently, than the English climate will in two hundred. It is reinforced by an artificial economic climate which does some of the work attributed to the natural geographic one; but the geographic climate is eternal and irresistible, making a mankind and a womankind that Kent, Middlesex, and East Anglia cannot produce and do not want to imitate.

How can I sketch the broad lines of the contrast as they strike me? Roughly I should say that the Englishman is wholly at the mercy of his imagination, having no sense of reality to check it. The Irishman, with a far subtler and more fastidious imagination, has one eye always on things as they are. If you compare Moore's visionary Minstrel Boy with Mr Rudyard Kipling's quasi-realistic Soldiers Three, you may yawn over Moore or gush over him, but you will not suspect him of having had any illusions about the contemporary British private; whilst as to Mr Kipling, you will see that he has not, and unless he settles in Ireland for a few years will always remain constitutionally and congenitally incapable of having, the faintest inkling of the reality which he idolizes as Tommy Atkins. Perhaps you have never thought of illustrating the contrast between English and Irish by Moore and Mr Kipling, or even by Parnell and Gladstone. Sir Boyle Roche and Shakespear may seem more to your point. Let me find you a more dramatic instance. Think of the famous meeting between the Duke of Wellington, that intensely Irish Irishman, and Nelson, that intensely English Englishman. Wellington's contemptuous disgust at Nelson's theatricality as a professed hero, patriot, and rhapsode, a theatricality which in an Irishman would have been an insufferably vulgar affectation, was quite natural and inevitable. Wellington's formula for that kind of thing was a well-known Irish one: 'Sir: dont be a damned fool.' It is the formula of all Irishmen for all Englishmen to this day. It is the formula of Larry Doyle for Tom Broadbent in my play, in spite of Doyle's affection for Tom. Nelson's genius, instead of producing intellectual keenness and scrupulousness, produced mere delirium. He was drunk with glory, exalted by his fervent faith in the sound British patriotism of the Almighty, nerved by the vulgarest anti-foreign prejudice, and apparently unchastened by any reflections on the fact that he had never had to fight a technically capable and properly equipped enemy except on land, where he had never been successful. Compare Wellington, who had to fight Napoleon's armies, Napoleon's marshals, and finally Napoleon himself, without one moment of illusion as to the human material he had to command, without one gush of the 'Kiss me, Hardy' emotion which enabled Nelson to idolize his crews and his staff, without forgetting even in his dreams that the normal British officer of that time was an incapable amateur (as he still is) and the normal British soldier a never-do-well (he is now a depressed and respectable young man). No wonder Wellington became an accomplished comedian in the art of anticlimax, scandalizing the unfortunate Croker, responding to the demand for glorious sentiments by the most disenchanting touches of realism, and, generally, pricking the English windbag at its most explosive crises of distention. Nelson, intensely nervous and theatrical, made an enormous fuss about victories so cheap that he would have deserved shooting if he had lost them, and, not content with lavishing splendid fighting on helpless adversaries like the heroic De Brueys or Villeneuve (who had not even the illusion of heroism when he went like a lamb to the slaughter), got himself killed by his passion for exposing himself to death in that sublime defiance of it which was perhaps the supreme tribute of the exquisite coward to the King of Terrors (for, believe me, you cannot be a hero without being a coward: supersense cuts both ways), the result being a tremendous effect on the gallery. Wellington, most capable of captains, was neither a hero nor a patriot: perhaps not even a coward; and had it not been for the Nelsonic anecdotes invented for him – 'Up guards, and at em' and so forth – and the fact that the antagonist with whom he finally closed was such a master of theatrical effect that Wellington could not fight him without getting into his limelight, nor overthrow him (most unfortunately for us all) without drawing the eyes of the whole world to the catastrophe, the Iron Duke would have been almost forgotten by this time. Now that contrast is English against Irish all over, and is the more delicious because the real Irishman in it is the Englishman of tradition, whilst the real Englishman is the traditional theatrical foreigner.

The value of the illustration lies in the fact that Nelson and Wellington were both in the highest degree efficient, and both in the highest degree incompatible with one another on any other footing than one of independence. The government of Nelson by Wellington or of Wellington by Nelson is felt at once to be a dishonorable outrage to the governed and a finally impossible task for the governor.

I daresay some Englishman will now try to steal Wellington as Macaulay tried to steal Swift. And he may plead with some truth that though it seems impossible that any other country than England could produce a hero so utterly devoid of common sense, intellectual delicacy, and international chivalry as Nelson, it may be contended that Wellington was rather an eighteenth century aristocratic type, than a specifically Irish type. George IV and Byron, contrasted with Gladstone, seem Irish in respect of a certain humorous blackguardism, and a power of appreciating art and sentiment without being duped by them into mistaking romantic figments for realities. But faithlessness and the need for carrying off the worthlessness and impotence that accompany it, produce in all nations a gay, sceptical, amusing, blaspheming, witty fashion which suits the flexibility of the Irish mind very well; and the contrast between this fashion and the energetic infatuations that have enabled intellectually ridiculous men, without wit or humor, to go on crusades and make successful revolutions, must not be confused with the contrast between the English and Irish idiosyncrasies. The Irishman makes a distinction which the Englishman is too lazy intellectually (the intellectual laziness and slovenliness of the English is almost beyond belief) to make. The Englishman, impressed with the dissoluteness of the faithless wits of the Restoration and the Regency, and with the victories of the wilful zealots of the patriotic, religious, and revolutionary wars, jumps to the conclusion that wilfulness is the main thing. In this he is right. But he overdoes his jump so far as to conclude also that stupidity and wrong-headedness are better guarantees of efficiency and trustworthiness than intellectual vivacity, which he mistrusts as a common symptom of worthlessness, vice, and instability. Now in this he is most dangerously wrong. Whether the Irishman grasps the truth as firmly as the Englishman may be open to question; but he is certainly comparatively free from the error. That affectionate and admiring love of sentimental stupidity for its own sake, both in men and women, which shines so steadily through the novels of Thackeray would hardly be possible in the works of an Irish novelist. Even Dickens, though too vital a genius and too severely educated in the school of shabby-genteel poverty to have any doubt of the national danger of fatheadedness in high places, evidently assumes rather too hastily the superiority of Mr Meagles to Sir John Chester and Harold Skimpole. On the other hand, it takes an Irishman years of residence in England to learn to respect and like a blockhead. An Englishman will not respect nor like anyone else. Every English statesman has to maintain his popularity by pretending to be ruder, more ignorant, more sentimental, more super-stitious, more stupid than any man who has lived behind the scenes of public life for ten minutes can possibly be. Nobody dares to publish really intimate memoirs of him or really private letters of his until his whole generation has passed away, and his party can no longer be compromised by the discovery that the platitudinizing twaddler and hypocritical opportunist was really a man of some perception as well as of strong constitution, pegaway industry, personal ambition, and party keenness.

ENGLISH STUPIDITY EXCUSED

I do not claim it as a natural superiority in the Irish nation that it dislikes and mistrusts fools, and expects its political leaders to be clever and humbug-proof. It may be that if our resources included the armed force and virtually unlimited money which push the political and military figureheads of England through bungled enterprises to a muddled success, and create an illusion of some miraculous and divine innate English quality that enables a general to become a conqueror with abilities that would not suffice to save a cabman from having his license marked, and a member of parliament to become Prime Minister with the outlook on life of a sporting country solicitor educated by a private governess, we should lapse into gross intellectual sottishness, and prefer leaders who encouraged our vulgarities by sharing them, and flattered us by associating them with purchased successes, to our betters. But as it is, we cannot afford that sort of encouragement and flattery in Ireland. The odds against which our leaders have to fight would be too heavy for the fourth-rate Englishmen whose leadership consists for the most part in marking time ostentatiously until they are violently shoved, and then stumbling blindly forward (or backward) wherever the shove sends them. We cannot crush England as a Pickford's van might crush a perambulator. We are the perambulator and England the Pickford. We must study her and our real weaknesses and real strength; we must practise upon her slow conscience and her quick terrors; we must deal in ideas and political principles since we cannot deal in bayonets; we must outwit, outwork, outstay her; we must embarrass, bully, even conspire and assassinate when nothing else will move her, if we are not all to be driven deeper and deeper into the shame and misery of our servitude. Our leaders must be not only determined enough, but clever enough to do this. We have no illusions as to the existence of any mysterious Irish pluck, Irish honesty, Irish bias on the part of Providence, or sterling Irish solidity of character, that will enable an Irish blockhead to hold his own against England. Blockheads are of no use to us: we were compelled to follow a supercilious, unpopular, tongue-tied, aristocratic Protestant Parnell, although there was no lack among us of fluent imbeciles, with majestic presences and oceans of dignity and sentiment, to promote into his place could they have done his work for us. It is obviously convenient that Mr Redmond should be a better speaker and rhetorician than Parnell; but if he began to use his powers to make himself agreeable instead of making himself reckoned with by the enemy; if he set to work to manufacture and support English shams and hypocrisies instead of exposing and denouncing them; if he constituted himself the permanent apologist of doing nothing, and, when the people insisted on his doing something, only roused himself to discover how to pretend to do it without really changing anything, he would lose his leadership as certainly as an English politician would, by the same course, attain a permanent place on the front bench. In short, our circumstances place a premium on political ability whilst the circumstances of England discount it; and the quality of the supply naturally follows the demand. If you miss in my writings that hero-worship of dotards and duffers which is planting England with statues of disastrous statesmen and absurd generals, the explanation is simply that I am an Irishman and you an Englishman.

IRISH PROTESTANTISM REALLY PROTESTANT

When I repeat that I am an Irish Protestant, I come to a part of the relation between England and Ireland that you will never understand unless I insist on explaining it to you with that Irish insistence on intellectual clarity to which my English critics are so intensely recalcitrant.

First, let me tell you that in Ireland Protestantism is really Protestant. It is true that there is an Irish Protestant Church (disestablished some 35 years ago) in spite of the fact that a Protestant Church is, fundamentally, a contradiction in terms. But this means only that the Protestants use the word Church to denote their secular organization, without troubling themselves about the metaphysical sense of Christ's famous pun, 'Upon this rock I will build my church.' The Church of England, which is a reformed Anglican Catholic Anti-Protestant Church, is quite another affair. An Anglican is acutely conscious that he is not a Wesleyan; and many Anglican clergymen do not hesitate to teach that all Methodists incur damnation. In Ireland all that the member of the Irish Protestant Church knows is that he is not a Roman Catholic. The decorations of even the 'lowest' English Church seem to him to be extravagantly Ritualistic and Popish. I myself entered the Irish Church by baptism, a ceremony performed by my uncle in 'his own church'. But I was sent, with many boys of my own denomination, to a Wesleyan school where the Wesleyan catechism was taught without the least protest on the part of the parents, although there was so little presumption in favor of any boy there being a Wesleyan that if all the Church boys had been withdrawn at any moment, the school would have become bankrupt. And this was by no means analogous to the case of those working class members of the Church of England in London, who send their daughters to Roman Catholic schools rather than to the public elementary schools. They do so for the definite reason that the nuns teach girls good manners and sweetness of speech, which have no place in the County Council curriculum. But in Ireland the Church parent sends his son to a Wesleyan school (if it is convenient and socially eligible) because he is indifferent to the form of Protestantism provided it is Protestantism. There is also in Ireland a characteristically Protestant refusal to take ceremonies and even sacraments very seriously except by way of strenuous objection to them when they are conducted with candles or incense. For example, I was never confirmed, although the ceremony was specially needed in my case as the failure of my appointed godfather to appear at my baptism had led to his responsibilities being assumed on the spot, at my uncle's order, by the sexton. And my case was a very common one, even among people quite untouched by modern scepticisms. Apart from the weekly churchgoing, which holds its own as a respectable habit, the initiations are perfunctory, the omissions regarded as negligible. The distinction between churchman and dissenter, which in England is a class distinction, a political distinction, and even occasionally a religious distinction, does not exist. Nobody is surprised in Ireland to find that the squire who is the local pillar of the formerly established Church is also a Plymouth Brother, and, except on certain special or fashionable occasions, attends the Methodist meeting-house. The parson has no priestly character and no priestly influence: the High Church curate of course exists and has his vogue among religious epicures of the other sex; but the general attitude of his congregation towards him is that of Dr Clifford. The clause in the Apostles' creed professing belief in a Catholic Church is a standing puzzle to Protestant children; and when they grow up they dismiss it from their minds more often than they solve it, because they really are not Catholics but Protestants to the extremest practicable degree of individualism. It is true that they talk of church and chapel with all the Anglican contempt for chapel; but in Ireland the chapel means the Roman Catholic church, for which the Irish Protestant reserves all the class rancor, the political hostility, the religious bigotry, and the bad blood generally that in England separates the Establishment from the non-conforming Protestant organizations. When a vulgar Irish Protestant speaks of a 'Papist' he feels exactly as a vulgar Anglican vicar does when he speaks of a Dissenter. And when the vicar is Anglican enough to call himself a Catholic priest, wear a cassock, and bless his flock with two fingers, he becomes horrifically incomprehensible to the Irish Protestant Churchman, who, on his part, puzzles the Anglican by regarding a Methodist as tolerantly as an Irishman who likes grog regards an Irishman who prefers punch.

A FUNDAMENTAL ANOMALY

Now nothing can be more anomalous, and at bottom impossible, than a Conservative Protestant party standing for the established order against a revolutionary Catholic party. The Protestant is theoretically an anarchist as far as anarchism is practicable in human society: that is, he is an individualist, a freethinker, a self-helper, a Whig, a Liberal, a mistruster and vilifier of the State, a rebel. The Catholic is theoretically a Collectivist, a self-abnegator, a Tory, a Conservative, a supporter of Church and State one and undivisible, an obeyer. This would be a statement of fact as well as of theory if men were Protestants and Catholics by temperament and adult choice instead of by family tradition. The peasant who supposed that Wordsworth's son would carry on the business now the old gentleman was gone was not a whit more foolish than we who laugh at his ignorance of the nature of poetry whilst we take it as a matter of course that a son should 'carry on' his father's religion. Hence, owing to our family system, the Catholic Churches are recruited daily at the font by temperamental Protestants, and the Protestant organizations by temperamental Catholics, with consequences most disconcerting to those who expect history to be deducible from the religious professions of the men who make it.

Still, though the Roman Catholic Church may occasionally catch such Tartars as Luther and Voltaire, or the Protestant organizations as Newman and Manning, the general run of mankind takes its impress from the atmosphere in which it is brought up. In Ireland the Roman Catholic peasant cannot escape the religious atmosphere of his Church. Except when he breaks out like a naughty child he is docile; he is reverent; he is content to regard knowledge as something not his business; he is a child before his Church, and accepts it as the highest authority in science and philosophy. He speaks of himself as a son of the Church, calling his priest father instead of brother or Mister. To rebel politically, he must break away from tutelage and follow a Protestant leader on national questions. His Church naturally fosters his submissiveness. The British Government and the Vatican may differ very vehemently as to whose subject the Irishman is to be; but they are quite agreed as to the propriety of his being a subject. Of the two, the British Government allows him more liberty, giving him as complete a democratic control of local government as his means will enable him to use, and a voice in the election of a formidable minority in the House of Commons, besides allowing him to read and learn what he likes – except when it makes a tufthunting onslaught on a seditious newspaper. But if he dared to claim a voice in the selection of his parish priest, or a representative at the Vatican, he would be denounced from the altar as an almost inconceivable blasphemer; and his educational opportunities are so restricted by his Church that he is heavily handicapped in every walk of life that requires any literacy. It is the aim of his priest to make him and keep him a submissive Conservative; and nothing but gross economic oppression and religious persecution could have produced the strange phenomenon of a revolutionary movement not only tolerated by the Clericals, but, up to a certain point, even encouraged by them. If there is such a thing as political science, with natural laws like any other science, it is certain that only the most violent external force could effect and maintain this unnatural combination of political revolution with Papal reaction, and of hardy individualism and independence with despotism and subjugation.

That violent external force is the clumsy thumb of English rule. If you would be good enough, ladies and gentlemen of England, to take your thumb away and leave us free to do something else than bite it, the unnaturally combined elements in Irish politics would fly asunder and recombine according to their proper nature with results entirely satisfactory to real Protestantism.

THE NATURE OF POLITICAL HATRED

Just reconsider the Home Rule question in the light of that very English characteristic of the Irish people, their political hatred of priests. Do not be distracted by the shriek of indignant denial from the Catholic papers and from those who have witnessed the charming relations between the Irish peasantry and their spiritual fathers. I am perfectly aware that the Irish love their priests as devotedly as the French loved them before the Revolution or as the Italians loved them before they imprisoned the Pope in the Vatican. They love their landlords too: many an Irish gentleman has found in his nurse a foster-mother more interested in him than his actual mother. They love the English, as every Englishman who travels in Ireland can testify. Please do not suppose that I speak satirically: the world is full of authentic examples of the concurrence of human kindliness with political rancor. Slaves and schoolboys often love their masters; Napoleon and his soldiers made desperate efforts to save from drowning the Russian soldiers under whom they had broken the ice with their cannon; even the relations between nonconformist peasants and country parsons in England are not invariably unkindly; in the southern States of America planters are often traditionally fond of negroes and kind to them, with substantial returns in humble affection; soldiers and sailors often admire and cheer their officers sincerely and heartily; nowhere is actual personal intercourse found compatible for long with the intolerable friction of hatred and malice. But people who persist in pleading these amiabilities as political factors must be summarily bundled out of the room when questions of State are to be discussed. Just as an Irishman may have English friends whom he may prefer to any Irishman of his acquaintance, and be kind, hospitable, and serviceable in his intercourse with Englishmen, whilst being perfectly prepared to make the Shannon run red with English blood if Irish freedom could be obtained at that price; so an Irish Catholic may like his priest as a man and revere him as a confessor and spiritual pastor whilst being implacably determined to seize the first opportunity of throwing off his yoke. This is political hatred: the only hatred that civilization allows to be mortal hatred.

THE REVOLT AGAINST THE PRIEST

Realize, then, that the popular party in Ireland is seething with rebellion against the tyranny of the Church. Imagine the feelings of an English farmer if the parson refused to marry him for less than £20, and if he had virtually no other way of getting married! Imagine the Church Rates revived in the form of an unofficial Income Tax scientifically adjusted to your taxable capacity by an intimate knowledge of your affairs verified in the confessional! Imagine being one of a peasantry reputed the poorest in the world, under the thumb of a priesthood reputed the richest in the world! Imagine a Catholic middle class continually defeated in the struggle of professional, official, and fashionable life by the superior education of its Protestant competitors, and yet forbidden by its priests to resort to the only efficient universities in the country! Imagine trying to get a modern education in a seminary of priests, where every modern book worth reading is on the index, and the earth is still regarded, not perhaps as absolutely flat, yet as being far from so spherical as Protestants allege! Imagine being forbidden to read this preface because it proclaims your own grievance! And imagine being bound to submit to all this because the popular side must hold together at all costs in the face of the Protestant enemy! That is, roughly, the predicament of Roman Catholic Ireland.

PROTESTANT LOYALTY: A FORECAST

Now let us have a look at Protestant Ireland. I have already said that a 'loyal' Irishman is an abhorrent phenomenon, because he is an unnatural one. In Ireland it is not 'loyalty' to drink the English king's health and stand uncovered to the English national anthem: it is simply exploitation of English rule in the interests of the property, power, and promotion of the Irish classes as against the Irish masses. From any other point of view it is cowardice and dishonor. I have known a Protestant go to Dublin Castle to be sworn in as a special constable, quite resolved to take the baton and break the heads of a patriotic faction just then upsetting the peace of the town, yet back out at the last moment because he could not bring himself to swallow the oath of allegiance tendered with the baton. There is no such thing as genuine loyalty in Ireland. There is a separation of the Irish people into two hostile camps: one Protestant, gentlemanly, and oligarchical: the other Roman Catholic, popular, and democratic. The oligarchy governs Ireland as a bureaucracy deriving authority from the king of England. It cannot cast him off without casting off its own ascendancy. Therefore it naturally exploits him sedulously, drinking his health, waving his flag, playing his anthem, and using the foolish word 'traitor' freely in its cups. But let the English Government make a step towards the democratic party, and the Protestant garrison revolts at once, not with tears and prayers and anguish of soul and years of trembling reluctance, as the parliamentarians of the XVII century revolted against Charles I, but with acrid promptitude and strident threatenings. When England finally abandons the garrison by yielding to the demand for Home Rule, the Protestants will not go under, nor will they waste much time in sulking over their betrayal, and comparing their fate with that of Gordon left by Gladstone to perish on the spears of heathen fanatics. They cannot afford to retire into an Irish Faubourg St Germain. They will take an energetic part in the national government, which will be sorely in need of parliamentary and official forces independent of Rome. They will get not only the Protestant votes, but the votes of Catholics in that spirit of toleration which is everywhere extended to heresies that happen to be politically serviceable to the orthodox. They will not relax their determination to hold every inch of the government of Ireland that they can grasp; but as that government will then be a national Irish government instead of as now an English government, their determination will make them the vanguard of Irish Nationalism and Democracy as against Romanism and Sacerdotalism, leaving English Unionists grieved and shocked at their discovery of the true value of an Irish Protestant's loyalty.

But there will be no open break in the tradition of the party. The Protestants will still be the party of Union, which will then mean, not the repeal of Home Rule, but the maintenance of the Federal Union of English-speaking commonwealths, now theatrically called the Empire. They will pull down the Union Jack without the smallest scruple; but they know the value of the Channel Fleet, and will cling closer than brothers to that and any other Imperial asset that can be exploited for the protection of Ireland against foreign aggression or the sharing of expenses with the British taxpayer. They know that the Irish coast is for the English invasion-scaremonger the heel of Achilles, and that they can use this to make him pay for the boot.

PROTESTANT PUGNACITY

If any Englishman feels incredulous as to this view of Protestantism as an essentially Nationalist force in Ireland, let him ask himself which leader he, if he were an Irishman, would rather have back from the grave to fight England: the Catholic Daniel O'Connell or the Protestant Parnell. O'Connell organized the Nationalist movement only to draw its teeth, to break its determination, and to declare that Repeal of the Union was not worth the shedding of a drop of blood. He died in the bosom of his Church, not in the bosom of his country. The Protestant leaders, from Lord Edward Fitzgerald to Parnell, have never divided their devotion. If any Englishman thinks that they would have been more sparing of blood than the English themselves are, if only so cheap a fluid could have purchased the honor of Ireland, he greatly mistakes the Irish Protestant temper. The notion that Ireland is the only country in the world not worth shedding a drop of blood for is not a Protestant one, and certainly not countenanced by English practice. It was hardly reasonable to ask Parnell to shed blood *quant. suff.* in Egypt to put an end to the misgovernment of the Khedive and replace him by Lord Cromer for the sake of the English bondholders, and then to expect him to become a Tolstoyan or an O'Connellite in regard to his own country. With a wholly Protestant Ireland at his back he might have bullied England into conceding Home Rule; for the insensibility of the English governing classes to philosophical, moral, social considerations – in short, to any considerations which require a little intellectual exertion and sympathetic alertness – is tempered, as we Irish well know, by an absurd susceptibility to intimidation.

For let me halt a moment here to impress on you, O English reader, that no fact has been more deeply stamped into us than that we can do nothing with an English Government unless we frighten it, any more than you can yourself. When power and riches are thrown haphazard into children's cradles as they are in England, you get a governing class without industry, character, courage, or real experience; and under such circumstances reforms are produced only by catastrophes followed by panics in which 'something must be done'. Thus it costs a cholera epidemic to achieve a Public Health Act, a Crimean War to reform the Civil Service, and a gunpowder plot to disestablish the Irish Church. It was by the light, not of reason, but of the moon, that the need for paying serious attention to the Irish land question was seen in England. It cost the American War of Independence and the Irish Volunteer movement to obtain the Irish parliament of 1782, the constitution of which far overshot the nationalist mark of today in the matter of independence.

It is vain to plead that this is human nature and not class weakness. The Japanese have proved that it is possible to conduct social and political changes intelligently and providentially instead of drifting along helplessly until public disasters compel a terrified and inconsiderate rearrangement. Innumerable experiments in local government have shewn that when men are neither too poor to be honest nor too rich to understand and share the needs of the people – as in New Zealand, for example – they can govern much more providently than our little circle of aristocrats and plutocrats.

THE JUST ENGLISHMAN

English Unionists, when asked what they have to say in defence of their rule of subject peoples, often reply that the Englishman is just, leaving us divided between our derision of so monstrously inhuman a pretension, and our impatience with so gross a confusion of the mutually exclusive functions of judge and legislator. For there is only one condition on which a man can do justice between two litigants, and that is that he shall have no interest in common with either of them, whereas it is only by having every interest in common with both of them that he can govern them tolerably. The indispensable preliminary to Democracy is the representation of every interest: the indispensable preliminary to justice is the elimination of every interest. When we want an arbitrator or an umpire, we turn to a stranger: when we want a government, a stranger is the one person we will not endure. The Englishman in India, for example, stands, a very statue of justice, between two natives. He says, in effect, 'I am impartial in your religious disputes because I believe in neither of your religions. I am impartial in your conflicts of custom and sentiment because your customs and sentiments are different from, and abysmally inferior to, my own. Finally, I am impartial as to your interests because they are both equally opposed to mine, which is to keep you both equally powerless against me in order that I may extract money from you to pay salaries and pensions to my self and my fellow Englishmen as judges and rulers over you. In return for which you get the inestimable benefit of a government that does absolute justice as between Indian and Indian, being wholly preoccupied with the maintenance of absolute injustice as between India and England.'

It will be observed that no Englishman, without making himself ridiculous, could pretend to be perfectly just or disinterested in English affairs, or would tolerate a proposal to establish the Indian or Irish system in Great Britain. Yet if the justice of the Englishman is sufficient to ensure the welfare of India or Ireland, it ought to suffice equally for England. But the English are wise enough to refuse to trust to English justice themselves, preferring democracy. They can hardly blame the Irish for taking the same view.

In short, dear English reader, the Irish Protestant stands outside that English Mutual Admiration Society which you call the Union or the Empire. You may buy a common and not ineffective variety of Irish Protestant by delegating your powers to him, and in effect making him the oppressor and you his sorely bullied and bothered catspaw and military maintainer; but if you offer him nothing for his loyalty except the natural superiority of the English character, you will – well, try the experiment, and see what will happen! You would have a ten-times better chance with the Roman Catholic; for he has been saturated from his youth up with the Imperial idea of foreign rule by a spiritually superior international power, and is trained to submission and abnegation of his private judgment. A Roman Catholic garrison would take its orders from England and let her rule Ireland if England were Roman Catholic. The Protestant garrison simply seizes on the English power; uses it for its own purposes; and occasionally orders the English Government to remove an Irish secretary who has dared to apply English ideas to the affairs of the garrison. Whereupon the English Government abjectly removes him, and implores him, as a gentleman and a loyal Englishman, not to reproach it in the face of the Nationalist enemy.

Such incidents naturally do not shake the sturdy conviction of the Irish Protestant that he is more than a match for any English Government in determination and intelligence. Here, no doubt, he flatters himself; for his advantage is not really an advantage of character, but of comparative directness of interest, concentration of force on one narrow issue, simplicity of aim, with freedom from the scruples and responsibilities of world-politics. The business is Irish business, not English; and he is Irish. And his object, which is simply to secure the dominance of his own caste and creed behind the power of England, is simpler and clearer than the confused aims of English Cabinets struggling ineptly with the burdens of empire, and biassed by the pressure of capital anywhere rather than in Ireland. He has no responsibility, no interest, no status outside his own country and his own movement, which means that he has no conscience in dealing with England; whereas England, having a very uneasy conscience, and many hindering and hampering responsibilities and interests in dealing with him, gets bullied and driven by him, and finally learns sympathy with Nationalist aims by her experience of the tyranny of the Orange party.

IRISH CATHOLICISM FORECAST

Let us suppose that the establishment of a national government were to annihilate the oligarchic party by absorbing the Protestant garrison and making it a Protestant National Guard. The Roman Catholic laity, now a cipher, would organize itself; and a revolt against Rome and against the priesthood would ensue. The Roman Catholic Church would become the official Irish Church. The Irish parliament would insist on a voice in the promotion of churchmen; fees and contributions would be regulated; blackmail would be resisted; sweating in conventual factories and workshops would be stopped; and the ban would be taken off the universities. In a word, the Roman Catholic Church, against which Dublin Castle is powerless, would meet the one force on earth that can cope with it victoriously. That force is Democracy, a thing far more Catholic than itself. Until that force is let loose against it, the Protestant garrison can do nothing to the priesthood except consolidate it and drive the people to rally round it in defence of their altars against the foreigner and the heretic. When it *is* let loose, the Catholic laity will make as short work of sacerdotal tyranny in Ireland as it has done in France and Italy. And in doing so it will be forced to face the old problem of the relations of Church and State. A Roman Catholic party must submit to Rome: an anti-clerical Catholic party must of necessity become an Irish Catholic party. The Holy Roman Empire, like the other Empires, has no future except as a Federation of national Catholic Churches; for Christianity can no more escape Democracy than Democracy can escape Socialism. It is noteworthy in this connection that the Anglican Catholics have played and are playing a notable part in the Socialist movement in England in opposition to the individualist Secularists of the urban proletariat; but they are quit of the preliminary dead lift that awaits the Irish Catholic. Their Church has thrown off the yoke of Rome, and is safely and permanently Anglicized. But the Catholic Church in Ireland is still Roman. Home Rule will herald the day when the Vatican will go the way of Dublin Castle, and the island of the saints assume the headship of her own Church. It may seem incredible that long after the last Orangeman shall lay down his chalk for ever, the familiar scrawl on every blank wall in the north of Ireland 'To hell with the Pope!' may reappear in the south, traced by the hands of Catholics who shall have forgotten the traditional counter legend, 'To hell with King William!' (of glorious, pious, and immortal memory); but it may happen so. 'The island of the saints' is no idle phrase. Religious genius is one of our national products; and Ireland is no bad rock to build a Church on. Holy and beautiful is the soul of Catholic Ireland: her prayers are lovelier than the teeth and claws of Protestantism, but not so effective in dealing with the English.

ENGLISH VOLTAIREANISM

Let me familiarize the situation by shewing how closely it reproduces the English situation in its essentials. In England, as in France, the struggle between the priesthood and the laity has produced a vast body of Voltaireans. But the essential identity of the French and English movements has been obscured by the ignorance of the ordinary Englishman, who, instead of knowing the distinctive tenets of his church or sect, vaguely believes them to be the eternal truth as opposed to the damnable error of all the other denominations. He thinks of Voltaire as a French 'infidel', instead of as the champion of the laity against the official theocracy of the State Church. The Nonconformist leaders of our Free Churches are all Voltaireans. The warcry of the Passive Resisters is Voltaire's warcry, 'Écrasez l'infâme.' No account need be taken of the technical difference between Voltaire's 'infâme' and Dr Clifford's. One was the unreformed Roman Church of France; the other is the reformed Anglican Church; but in both cases the attack has been on a priestly tyranny and a professional monopoly. Voltaire convinced the Genevan ministers that he was the philosophic champion of their Protestant, Individualistic, Democratic Deism against the State Church of Roman Catholic France; and his heroic energy and beneficence as a philanthropist, which now only makes the list of achievements on his monument at Ferney the most impressive epitaph in Europe, then made the most earnest of the Lutheran ministers glad to claim a common inspiration with him. Unfortunately Voltaire had an irrepressible sense of humor. He joked about Habakkuk; and jokes about Habakkuk smelt too strongly of brimstone to be tolerated by Protestants to whom the Bible was not a literature but a fetish and a talisman. And so Voltaire, in spite of the church he 'erected to God', became in England the bogey-atheist of three generations of English ignoramuses, instead of the legitimate successor of Martin Luther and John Knox.

Nowadays, however, Voltaire's jokes are either forgotten or else fall flat on a world which no longer venerates Habakkuk; and his true position is becoming apparent. The fact that Voltaire was a Roman Catholic layman, educated at a Jesuit college, is the conclusive reply to the shallow people who imagine that Ireland delivered up to the Irish democracy – that is, to the Catholic laity – would be delivered up to the tyranny of the priesthood.

SUPPOSE!

Suppose, now, that the conquest of France by Henry V of England had endured, and that France in the XVIII century had been governed by an English viceroy through a Huguenot bureaucracy and a judicial bench appointed on the understanding that loyalty for them meant loyalty to England, and patriotism a willingness to die in defence of the English conquest and of the English Church, would not Voltaire in that case have been the meanest of traitors and self-seekers if he had played the game of England by joining in its campaign against his own and his country's Church? The energy he threw into the defence of Calas and Sirven would have been thrown into the defence of the Frenchmen whom the English would have called 'rebels'; and he would have been forced to identify the cause of freedom and democracy with the cause of 'l'infâme'. The French revolution would have been a revolution against England and English rule instead of against aristocracy and ecclesiasticism; and all the intellectual and spiritual forces in France, from Turgot to De Tocqueville, would have been burnt up in mere anti-Anglicism and nationalist dithyrambs instead of contributing to political science and broadening the thought of the world.

What would have happened in France is what has happened in Ireland; and that is why it is only the small-minded Irish, incapable of conceiving what religious freedom means to a country, who do not loathe English rule. For in Ireland England is nothing but the Pope's policeman. She imagines she is holding the Vatican cardinals at bay when she is really strangling the Voltaires, the Foxes and Penns, the Cliffords, Hortons, Campbells, Walters, and Silvester Hornes, who are to be found among the Roman Catholic laity as plentifully as among the Anglican Catholic laity in England. She gets nothing out of Ireland but infinite trouble, infinite confusion and hindrance in her own legislation, a hatred that circulates through the whole world and poisons it against her, a reproach that makes her professions of sympathy with Finland and Macedonia ridiculous and hypocritical, whilst the priest takes all the spoils, in money, in power, in pride, and in popularity.

IRELAND'S REAL GRIEVANCE

But it is not the spoils that matter. It is the waste, the sterilization, the perversion of fruitful brain power into flatulent protest against unnecessary evil, the use of our very entrails to tie our own hands and seal our own lips in the name of our honor and patriotism. As far as money or comfort is concerned, the average Irishman has a more tolerable life – especially now that the population is so scanty – than the average Englishman. It is true that in Ireland the poor man is robbed and starved and oppressed under judicial forms which confer the imposing title of justice on a crude system of bludgeoning and perjury. But so is the Englishman. The Englishman, more docile, less dangerous, too lazy intellectually to use such political and legal power as lies within his reach, suffers more and makes less fuss about it than the Irishman. But at least he has nobody to blame but himself and his fellow countrymen. He does not doubt that if an effective majority of the English people made up their minds to alter the Constitution, as the majority of the Irish people have made up their minds to obtain Home Rule, they could alter it without having to fight an overwhelmingly powerful and rich neighboring nation, and fight, too, with ropes round their necks. He can attack any institution in his country without betraying it to foreign vengeance and foreign oppression. True, his landlord may turn him out of his cottage if he goes to a Methodist chapel instead of to the parish church. His customers may stop their orders if he votes Liberal instead of Conservative. English ladies and gentlemen who would perish sooner than shoot a fox do these things without the smallest sense of indecency and dishonor. But they cannot muzzle his intellectual leaders. The English philosopher, the English author, the English orator can attack every abuse and expose every supersitition without strengthening the hands of any common enemy. In Ireland every such attack, every such exposure, is a service to England and a stab to Ireland. If you expose the tyranny and rapacity of the Church, it is an argument in favor of Protestant ascendency. If you denounce the nepotism and jobbery of the new local authorities, you are demonstrating the unfitness of the Irish to govern themselves, and the superiority of the old oligarchical grand juries.

And there is the same pressure on the other side. The Protestant must stand by the garrison at all costs: the Unionist must wink at every bureaucratic abuse, connive at every tyranny, magnify every official blockhead, because their exposure would be a victory for the Nationalist enemy. Every Irishman is in Lancelot's position: his honor rooted in dishonor stands; and faith unfaithful keeps him falsely true.

THE CURSE OF NATIONALISM

It is hardly possible for an Englishman to understand all that this implies. A conquered nation is like a man with cancer: he can think of nothing else, and is forced to placé himself, to the exclusion of all better company, in the hands of quacks who profess to treat or cure cancer. The windbags of the two rival platforms are the most insufferable of all windbags. It requires neither knowledge, character, conscience, diligence in public affairs, nor any virtue, private or communal, to thump the Nationalist or Orange tub: nay, it puts a premium on the rancor or callousness that has given rise to the proverb that if you put an Irishman on a spit you can always get another Irishman to baste him. Jingo oratory in England is sickening enough to serious people: indeed one evening's mafficking in London produced a determined call for the police. Well, in Ireland all political oratory is Jingo oratory; and all political demonstrations are maffickings. English rule is such an intolerable abomination that no other subject can reach the people. Nationalism stands between Ireland and the light of the world. Nobody in Ireland of any intelligence likes Nationalism any more than a man with a broken arm likes having it set. A healthy nation is as unconscious of its nationality as a healthy man of his bones. But if you break a nation's nationality it will think of nothing else but getting it set again. It will listen to no reformer, to no philosopher, to no preacher, until the demand of the Nationalist is granted. It will attend to no business, however vital, except the business of unification and liberation.

That is why everything is in abeyance in Ireland pending the achievement of Home Rule. The great movements of the human spirit which sweep in waves over Europe are stopped on the Irish coast by the English guns of the Pigeon House Fort. Only a quaint little offshoot of English pre-Raphaelitism called the Gaelic movement has got a footing by using Nationalism as a stalking-horse, and popularizing itself as an attack on the native language of the Irish people, which is most fortunately also the native language of half the world, including England. Every election is fought on nationalist grounds; every appointment is made on nationalist grounds; every judge is a partisan in the nationalist conflict; every speech is a dreary recapitulation of nationalist twaddle; every lecture is a corruption of history to flatter nationalism or defame it; every school is a recruiting station; every church is a barrack; and every Irishman is unspeakably tired of the whole miserable business, which nevertheless is and perforce must remain his first business until Home Rule makes an end of it, and sweeps the nationalist and the garrison hack together into the dustbin.

There is indeed no greater curse to a nation than a nationalist movement, which is only the agonizing symptom of a suppressed natural function. Conquered nations lose their place in the world's march because they can do nothing but strive to get rid of their nationalist movements by recovering their national liberty. All demonstrations of the virtues of a foreign government, though often conclusive, are as useless as demonstrations of the superiority of artificial teeth, glass eyes, silver windpipes, and patent wooden legs to the natural products. Like Democracy, national self-government is not for the good of the people: it is for the satisfaction of the people. One Antonine emperor, one St Louis, one Richelieu, may be worth ten democracies in point of what is called good government; but there is no satisfaction for the people in them. To deprive a dyspeptic of his dinner and hand it over to a man who can digest it better is a highly logical proceeding; but it is not a sensible one. To take the government of Ireland away from the Irish and hand it over to the English on the ground that they can govern better would be a precisely parallel case if the English had managed their own affairs so well-as to place their superior faculty for governing beyond question. But as the English are avowed muddlers – rather proud of it, in fact – even the logic of that case against Home Rule is not complete. Read Mr Charles Booth's account of London, Mr Rowntree's account of York, and the latest official report on Dundee; and then pretend, if you can, that Englishmen and Scotchmen have not more cause to hand over their affairs to an Irish parliament than to clamor for another nation's cities to devastate and another people's business to mismanage.

A NATURAL RIGHT

The question is not one of logic at all, but of natural right. English universities have for some time past encouraged an extremely foolish academic exercise which consists in disproving the existence of natural rights on the ground that they cannot be deduced from the principles of any known political system. If they could, they would not be natural rights but acquired ones. Acquired rights are deduced from political constitutions; but political constitutions are deduced from natural rights. When a man insists on certain liberties without the slightest regard to demonstrations that they are not for his own good, nor for the public good, nor moral, nor reasonable, nor decent, nor compatible with the existing constitution of society, then he is said to claim a natural right to that liberty. When, for instance, he insists on living, in spite of the irrefutable demonstrations of many able pessimists, from the author of the book of Ecclesiastes to Schopenhauer, that life is an evil, he is asserting a natural right to live. When he insists on a vote in order that his country may be governed according to his ignorance instead of the wisdom of the Privy Council, he is asserting a natural right to self-government. When he insists on guiding himself at 21 by his own inexperience and folly and immaturity instead of by the experience and sagacity of his father, or the well-stored mind of his grandmother, he is asserting a natural right to independence. Even if Home Rule was as unhealthy as an Englishman's eating, as intemperate as his drinking, as filthy as his smoking, as licentious as his domesticity, as corrupt as his elections, as murderously greedy as his commerce, as cruel as his prisons, and as merciless as his streets, Ireland's claim to self-government would still be as good as England's. King James the First proved so cleverly and conclusively that the satisfaction of natural rights was incompatible with good government that his courtiers called him Solomon. We, more enlightened, call him Fool, solely because we have learnt that nations insist on being governed by their own consent – or, as they put it, by themselves and for themselves – and that they will finally upset a good government which denies them this even if the alternative be a bad government which at least creates and maintains an illusion of democracy. America, as far as one can ascertain, is much worse governed, and has a much more disgraceful political history than England under Charles I; but the American Republic is the stabler government because it starts from a formal concession of natural rights, and keeps up an illusion of safeguarding them by an elaborate machinery of democratic election. And the final reason why Ireland must have Home Rule is that she has a natural right to it.

A WARNING

Finally, some words of warning to both nations. Ireland has been deliberately ruined again and again by England. Unable to compete with us industrially, she has destroyed our industries by the brute force of prohibitive taxation. She was perfectly right. That brute force was a more honorable weapon than the poverty which we used to undersell her. We lived with and as our pigs, and let loose our wares in the Englishman's market at prices which he could compete with only by living like a pig himself. Having the alternative of stopping our industry altogether, he very naturally and properly availed himself of it. We should have done the same in his place. To bear malice against him on that score is to poison our blood and weaken our constitutions with unintelligent rancor. In wrecking all the industries that were based on the poverty of our people England did us an enormous service. In omitting to do the same on her own soil, she did herself a wrong that has rotted her almost to the marrow. I hope that when Home Rule is at last achieved, one of our first legislative acts will be to fortify the subsistence of our people behind the bulwark of a standard wage, and to impose crushing import duties on every English trade that flourishes in the slum and fattens on the starvation of our unfortunate English neighbors.

DOWN WITH THE SOLDIER!

Now for England's share of warning. Let her look to her Empire; for unless she makes it such a Federation for civil strength and defence that all free peoples will cling to it voluntarily, it will inevitably become a military tyranny to prevent them from abandoning it; and such a tyranny will drain the English taxpayer of his money more effectually than its worst cruelties can ever drain its victims of their liberty. A political scheme that cannot be carried out except by soldiers will not be a permanent one. The soldier is an an anachronism of which we must get rid. Among people who are proof against the suggestions of romantic fiction there can no longer be any question of the fact that military service produces moral imbecility, ferocity, and cowardice, and that the defence of nations must be undertaken by the civil enterprise of men enjoying all the rights and liberties of citizenship, and trained by the exacting discipline of democratic freedom and responsibility. For permanent work the soldier is worse than useless: such efficiency as he has is the result of dehumanization and disablement. His whole training tends to make him a weakling. He has the easiest of lives: he has no freedom and no responsibility. He is politically and socially a child, with rations instead of rights, treated like a child, punished like a child, dressed prettily and washed and combed like a child, excused for outbreaks of naughtiness like a child, forbidden to marry like a child, and called Tommy like a child. He has no real work to keep him from going mad except housemaid's work: all the rest is forced exercise, in the form of endless rehearsals for a destructive and terrifying performance which may never come off, and which, when it does come off, is not like the rehearsals. His officer has not even housekeeper's work to keep him sane. The work of organizing and commanding bodies of men, which builds up the character and resource of the large class of civilians who live by it, only demoralizes the military officer, because his orders, however disastrous or offensive, must be obeyed without regard to consequences: for instance, if he calls his men dogs, and perverts a musketry drill order to make them kneel to him as an act of personal humiliation, and thereby provokes a mutiny among men not yet thoroughly broken in to the abjectness of the military condition, he is not, as might be expected, shot, but, at worst, reprimanded, whilst the leader of the mutiny, instead of getting the Victoria Cross and a public testimonial, is condemned to five years' penal servitude by Lynch Law (technically called martial law) administered by a trade union of officers. Compare with this the position of, for instance, our railway managers or our heads of explosive factories. They have to handle large bodies of men whose carelessness or insubordination may cause wholesale destruction of life and property; yet any of these men may insult them, defy them, or assault them without special penalties of any sort. The military commander dares not face these conditions: he lives in perpetual terror of his men, and will undertake their command only when they are stripped of all their civil rights, gagged, and bound hand and foot by a barbarous slave code. Thus the officer learns to punish, but never to rule; and when an emergency like the Indian Mutiny comes, he breaks down; and the situation has to be saved by a few untypical officers with character enough to have retained their civilian qualities in spite of the messroom. This, unfortunately, is learnt by the public, not on the spot, but from Lord Roberts fifty years later.

Besides the Mutiny we have had the Crimean and South African wars, the Dreyfus affair in France, the incidents of the anti-militarist campaign by the Social-Democrats in Germany, and now the Denshawai affair in the Nile delta, all heaping on us sensational demonstrations of the fact that soldiers pay the penalty of their slavery and outlawry by becoming, relatively to free civilians, destructive, cruel, dishonest, tyrannical, hysterical, mendacious, alarmists at home and terrorists abroad, politically reactionary, and professionally incapable. If it were humanly possible to militarize all the humanity out of a man, there would be absolutely no defence to this indictment. But the military system is so idiotically academic and impossible, and renders its victims so incapable of carrying

it out with any thoroughness except when, in an occasional hysterical
outburst of terror and violence, that hackneyed comedy of civil life, the
weak man putting his foot down, becomes the military tragedy of the
armed man burning, flogging, and murdering in a panic, that a body of
soldiers and officers is in the main, and under normal circumstances,
much like any other body of laborers and gentlemen. Many of us count
among our personal friends and relatives officers whose amiable and
honorable character seems to contradict everything I have just said about
the military character. You have only to describe Lynch courts and acts
of terrorism to them as the work of Ribbonmen, Dacoits, Moonlighters,
Boxers, or – to use the general term most familiar to them – 'natives', and
their honest and generous indignation knows no bounds: they feel about
them like men, not like soldiers. But the moment you bring the professional side of them uppermost by describing precisely the same proceedings to them as the work of regular armies, they defend them, applaud
them, and are ready to take part in them as if their humanity had been
blown out like a candle. You find that there is a blind spot on their moral
retina, and that this blind spot is the military spot.

The excuse, when any excuse is made, is that discipline is supremely
important in war. Now most soldiers have no experience of war; and to
assume that those who have are therefore qualified to legislate for it, is as
absurd as to assume that a man who has been run over by an omnibus is
thereby qualified to draw up wise regulations for the traffic of London.
Neither our military novices nor our veterans are clever enough to see that
in the field, discipline either keeps itself or goes to pieces; for humanity
under fire is a quite different thing from humanity in barracks: when there
is danger the difficulty is never to find men who will obey, but men who
can command. It is in time of peace, when an army is either a police force
(in which case its work can be better done by a civilian constabulary) or
an absurdity, that discipline is difficult, because the wasted life of the
soldier is unnatural, except to a lazy man, and his servitude galling and
senseless, except to a docile one. Still, the soldier is a man, and the officer
sometimes a gentleman in the literal sense of the word; and so, what with
humanity, laziness, and docility combined, they manage to rub along
with only occasional outbursts of mutiny on the one side and class rancor
and class cowardice on the other.

They are not even discontented; for the military and naval codes

PREFACE FOR POLITICIANS 37

simplify life for them just as it is simplified for children. No soldier is asked to think for himself, to judge for himself, to consult his own honor and manhood, to dread any consequence except the consequence of punishment to his own person. The rules are plain and simple; the ceremonies of respect and submission are as easy and mechanical as a prayer wheel; the orders are always to be obeyed thoughtlessly, however inept or dishonorable they may be. As the late Laureate said in the two stinging lines in which he branded the British soldier with the dishonor of Esau, 'theirs not to reason why, theirs but to do and die.' To the moral imbecile and political sluggard these conditions are as congenial and attractive as they are abhorrent and intolerable to the William Tell temperament. Just as the most incorrigible criminal is always, we are told, the best behaved convict, so the man with least conscience and initiative makes the best behaved soldier, and that not wholly through mere fear of punishment, but through a genuine fitness for and consequent happiness in the child-like military life. Such men dread freedom and responsibility as a weak man dreads a risk or a heavy burden; and the objection to the military system is that it tends to produce such men by a weakening disuse of the moral muscles. No doubt this weakness is just what the military system aims at, its ideal soldier being, not a complete man, but a docile unit of cannon-fodder which can be trusted to respond promptly and certainly to the external stimulus of a shouted order, and is intimidated to the pitch of being afraid to run away from a battle. It may be doubted whether even in the Prussian heyday of the system, when floggings of hundreds and even thousands of lashes were matters of ordinary routine, this detestable ideal was ever realized; but your courts-martial are not practical enough to take that into account: it is characteristic of the military mind continually to ignore human nature and cry for the moon instead of facing modern social facts and accepting modern democratic conditions. And when I say the military mind, I repeat that I am not forgetting the patent fact that the military mind and the humane mind can exist in the same person; so that an officer who will take all the civilian risks, from city traffic to foxhunting, without uneasiness, and who will manage all the civil employees on his estate and in his house and stables without the aid of a Mutiny Act, will also, in his military capacity, frantically declare that he dare not walk about in a foreign country unless every crime of violence against an Englishman in uniform is punished by the bombardment and destruction of a whole village, or the wholesale flogging and execution of every native in the neighborhood, and also that unless he and his fellow-officers have power, without the intervention of a jury, to punish the slightest self-assertion or hesitation to obey orders, however grossly insulting or disastrous those orders may be, with sentences which are reserved in civil life for the worst crimes, he cannot secure the obedience and respect of his men, and the country will accordingly lose all its colonies and dependencies, and be helplessly conquered in the German invasion which he confidently expects to occur in the course of a fortnight or so. That is to say, in so far as he is an ordinary gentleman he behaves sensibly and courageously; and in so far as he is a military man he gives way without shame to the grossest folly, cruelty and poltroonery. If any other profession in the world had been stained by these vices, and by false witness, forgery, swindling, torture, compulsion of men's families to attend their executions, digging up and mutilation of dead enemies, all wantonly added to the devastation proper to its own business, as the military profession has been within recent memory in England, France, and the United States of America (to mention no other countries), it would be very difficult to induce men of capacity and character to enter it. And in England it is, in fact, largely dependent for its recruits on the refuse of industrial life, and for its officers on the aristocratic and plutocratic refuse of political and diplomatic life, who join the army and pay for their positions in the more or less fashionable clubs which the regimental messes provide them with – clubs which, by the way, occasionally figure in ragging scandals as circles of extremely coarse moral character.

Now in countries which are denied Home Rule: that is, in which the government does not rest on the consent of the people, it must rest on military coercion; and the bureaucracy, however civil and legal it may be in form and even in the character of its best officials, must connive at all the atrocities of military rule, and become infected in the end with the chronic panic characteristic of militarism. In recent witness whereof, let me shift the scene from Ireland to Egypt, and tell the story of the Denshawai affair of June 1906 by way of object-lesson.

THE DENSHAWAI HORROR

Denshawai is a little Egyptian village in the Nile delta. Besides the dilapidated huts among the reeds by the roadside, and the palm trees, there are towers of unbaked brick, as unaccountable to an English villager as a Kentish oast-house to an Egyptian. These towers are pigeon-houses; for the villagers keep pigeons just as an English farmer keeps poultry.

Try to imagine the feelings of an English village if a party of Chinese officers suddenly appeared and began shooting the ducks, the geese, the hens, and the turkeys, and carried them off, asserting that they were wild birds, as everybody in China knew, and that the pretended indignation of the farmers was a cloak for hatred of the Chinese, and perhaps for a plot to overthrow the religion of Confucius and establish the Church of England in its place! Well, that is the British equivalent of what happened at Denshawai when a party of English officers went pigeon-shooting there the year before last. The inhabitants complained and memorialized; but they obtained no redress: the law failed them in their hour of need. So one leading family of pigeon farmers, Mahfouz by name, despaired of the law; and its head, Hassan Mahfouz, aged 60, made up his mind not to submit tamely to a repetition of the outrage. Also, British officers were ordered not to shoot pigeons in the villages without the consent of the Omdeh, or headman, though nothing was settled as to what might happen to the Omdeh if he ventured to refuse.

Fancy the feelings of Denshawai when on the 13th of June last there drove to the village four khaki-clad British officers with guns, one of them being a shooter of the year before, accompanied by one other officer on horseback, and also by a dragoman and an Ombashi, or police official! The oriental blood of Hassan Mahfouz boiled; and he warned them that they would not be allowed to shoot pigeons; but as they did not understand his language, the warning had no effect. They sent their dragoman to ask the Omdeh's permission to shoot; but the Omdeh was away; and all the interpreter could get from the Omdeh's deputy, who knew better than to dare an absolute refusal, was the pretty obvious reply that they might shoot if they went far enough away from the village. On the strength of this welcome, they went from 100 to 300 yards away from the houses (these distances were afterwards officially averaged at 500 yards), and began shooting the villagers' pigeons. The villagers remonstrated and finally seized the gun of the youngest officer. It went off in the struggle, and wounded three men and the wife of one Abd-el-Nebi, a young man of 25. Now the lady, though, as it turned out, only temporarily disabled by a charge of pigeon shot in the softest part of her person, gave herself up for dead; and the feeling in the village was much as if our imaginary Chinese officers, on being interfered with in their slaughter of turkeys, had killed an English farmer's wife. Abd-el-Nebi, her husband, took the matter to heart, not altogether without reason, we may admit. His threshing-floor also caught fire somehow (the official English theory is that he set it on fire as a signal for revolt to the entire Moslem world); and all the lads and loafers in the place were presently on the spot. The other officers, seeing their friend in trouble, joined him. Abd-el-Nebi hit the supposed murderer of his wife with a stick; Hassan Mahfouz used a stick also; and the lads and loafers began to throw stones and bricks. Five London policemen would have seen that there was nothing to be done but fight their way out, as there is no use arguing with an irritated mob, especially if you do not know its language. Had the shooting party been in the charge of a capable non-commissioned officer, he would perhaps have got it safely off. As it was, the officers tried propitiation, making their overtures in pantomime. They gave up their guns; they offered watches and money to the crowd, crying Baksheesh; and the senior officer actually collared the junior and pretended to arrest him for the murder of the woman. Naturally they were mobbed worse than before; and what they did not give to the crowd was taken from them, whether as payment for the pigeons, blood money, or simple plunder was not gone into. The officers, two Irishmen and three Englishmen, having made a hopeless mess of it, and being now in serious danger, made for their carriages, but were dragged out of them again, one of the coachmen being knocked senseless. They then 'agreed to run', the arrangement being that the Englishmen, being the juniors, should run away to camp and bring help to the Irishmen. They bolted accordingly; but the third, the youngest, seeing the two Irishmen hard put to it, went back and stood by them. Of the two fugitives, one, after a long race in the Egyptian afternoon sun, got to the next village and there dropped, smitten by sunstroke, of which he died. The other ran on and met a patrol, which started to the rescue.

Meanwhile, the other three officers had been taken out of the hands of the lads and the loafers, of Abd-el-Nebi and Hassan Mahfouz, by the elders and watchmen, and saved from further injury, but not before they had been severely knocked about, one of them having one of the bones of his left arm broken near the wrist – simple fracture of the thin end of the ulna. They were also brought to the threshing-floor; shewn the wounded woman; informed by gestures that they deserved to have their throats cut for murdering her; and kicked (with naked feet, fortunately); but at this point the elders and constables stopped the mobbing. Finally the three were sent off to camp in their carriages; and the incident ended for that day.

No English mob, under similar provocation, would have behaved any better; and few would have done as little mischief. It is not many months since an old man – not a foreigner and not an unbeliever – was kicked to death in the streets of London because the action of a park constable in turning him out of a public park exposed him to suspicion of misconduct. At Denshawai, the officers were not on duty. In their private capacity as sportsmen, they committed a serious depredation on a very poor village by slaughtering its stock. In an English village they would have been tolerated because the farmers would have expected compensation for damage, and the villagers coals and blankets and employment in country house, garden and stable, or as beaters, huntsmen and the like, from them. But Denshawai had no such inducements to submit to their thoughtless and selfish aggression. One of them had apparently killed a woman and wounded three men with his gun: in fact his own comrade virtually convicted him of it before the crowd by collaring him as a prisoner. In short, the officers had given outrageous provocation; and they had shewn an amiable but disastrous want of determination and judgment in dealing with the riot they provoked. They should have been severely reprimanded and informed that they had themselves to thank for what happened to them; and the villagers who assaulted them should have been treated with leniency, and assured that pigeon-shooting would not be allowed in future.

That is what should have ensued. Now for what actually did ensue.

Abd-el-Nebi, in consideration of the injury to his wife, was only sentenced to penal servitude for life. And our clemency did not stop there. His wife was not punished at all – not even charged with stealing the shot which was found in her person. And lest Abd-el-Nebi should feel lonely at 25 in beginning penal servitude for the rest of his days, another young man, of 20, was sent to penal servitude for life with him.

No such sentimentality was shewn to Hassan Mahfouz. An Egyptian pigeon farmer who objects to Brtish sport; threatens British officers and gentlemen when they shoot his pigeons; and actually hits those officers with a substantial stick, is clearly a ruffian to be made an example of. Penal servitude was not enough for a man of 60 who looked 70, and might not have lived to suffer five years of it. So Hassan was hanged; but as a special mark of consideration for his family, he was hanged in full view of his own house, with his wives and children and grandchildren enjoying the spectacle from the roof. And lest this privilege should excite jealousy in other households, three other Denshavians were hanged with him. They went through the ceremony with dignity, professing their faith ('Mahometan, I regret to say,' Mr Pecksniff would have said). Hassan, however, 'in a loud voice invoked ruin upon the houses of those who had given evidence against him'; and Darweesh was impatient and presumed to tell the hangman to be quick. But then Darweesh was a bit of a brigand: he had been imprisoned for bearing false witness; and his resistance to the British invasion is the only officially recorded incident of his life which is entirely to his credit. He and Abd-el-Nebi (who had been imprisoned for theft) were the only disreputable characters among the punished. Ages of the four hanged men respectively, 60, 50, 22 and 20.

Hanging, however, is the least sensational form of public execution: it lacks those elements of blood and torture for which the military and bureaucratic imagination lusts. So, as they had room for only one man on the gallows, and had to leave him hanging half an hour to make sure work and give his family plenty of time to watch him swinging ('slowly turning round and round on himself', as the local papers described it), thus having two hours to kill as well as four men, they kept the entertainment going by flogging eight men with fifty lashes each: eleven more than the utmost permitted by the law of Moses in times which our Army of Occupation no doubt considers barbarous. But then Moses conceived his law as being what he called the law of God, and not simply an instrument for the gratification of his own cruelty and terror. It is unspeakably reassuring to learn from the British official reports laid before parliament that 'due dignity was observed in carrying out the executions', and 'all possible humanity was shewn in carrying them out', and that 'the arrangements were admirable, and reflect great credit on all concerned'. As this last testimonial apparently does not refer to the victims, they are evidently officially considered not to have been concerned in the proceedings at all. Finally, Lord Cromer certifies that the Englishman in charge of the proceedings is 'a singularly humane man, and is very popular amongst the natives of Egypt by reason of the great sympathy he has always shewn for them'. It will be seen that Pariamentary Papers, Nos. 3 and 4, Egypt, 1906, are not lacking in unconscious humor. The official walrus pledges himself in every case for the kindliness of the official carpenter.

One man was actually let off, to the great danger of the British Empire perhaps. Still, as he was an epileptic, and had already had several fits in the court of Judge Lynch, the doctor said Better not; and he escaped. This was very inconvenient; for the number of floggees had been made up solely to fill the time occupied by the hangings at the rate of two floggings per hanging; and the breakdown of the arrangement through Said Suleiman Kheirallah's inconsiderate indisposition made the execution of Darweesh tedious, as he was hanging for fully quarter of an hour without any flogging to amuse his fellow villagers and the officers and men of the Inniskilling Dragoons, the military mounted police, and the mounted infantry. A few spare sentences of flogging should have been kept in hand to provide against accidents.

In any case there was not time to flog everybody, not to flog three of the floggees enough; so these three had a year's hard labor apiece in addition to their floggings. Six others were not flogged at all, but were sent to penal servitude for seven years each. One man got fifteen years. Total for the morning's work: four hanged, two to penal servitude for life, one to fifteen years penal servitude, six to seven years penal servitude, three to imprisonment for a year with hard labor and fifty lashes, and five to fifty lashes.

Lord Cromer certifies that these proceedings were 'just and necessary'. He also gives his reasons. It appears that the boasted justice introduced into Egypt by the English in 1882 was imaginary, and that the real work of coping with Egyptian disorder was done by Brigandage Commissions, composed of Egyptians. These Commissions, when an offence was reported, descended on the inculpated village; seized everybody concerned; and plied them with tortures, mentionable and unmentionable, until they accused everybody they were expected to accuse. The accused were in turn tortured until they confessed anything and everything they were accused of. They were then killed, flogged, or sent to penal servitude.

This was the reality behind the illusion that soothed us after bombarding Alexandria. The bloodless, white-gloved native courts set up to flatter our sense of imperial justice had, apparently, about as much to do with the actual government of the fellaheen as the annual court which awards the Dunmow flitch of bacon has to do with our divorce court. Eventually a Belgian judge, who was appointed Procureur-Général, exposed the true state of affairs.

Then the situation had to be faced. Order had to be maintained somehow; but the regular native courts which saved the face of the British Occupation were useless for the purpose; and the Brigandage Commissions were so abominable and demoralizing that they made more mischief than they prevented. Besides, there was Mr Wilfrid Scawen Blunt on the warpath against tyranny and torture, threatening to get questions asked in parliament. A new sort of tribunal in the nature of a court-martial had therefore to be invented to replace the Brigandage Commissions; but simple British military courts-martial, though probably the best available form of official Lynch Law, were made impossible by the jealousy of the 'loyal' (to England) Egyptians, who, it seems, rule the Occupation and bully England exactly as the 'loyal' Irish rule the Garrison and bully the Unionists nearer home. That kind of loyalty, not being a natural product, has to be purchased; and the price is an official job of some sort with a position and a salary attached. Hence we got, in 1895, a tribunal constituted in which three English officials sat with two Egyptian officials, exercising practically unlimited powers of punishment without a jury and without appeal. They represent the best of our judicial and military officialism. And what that best is may be judged by the sentences on the Denshawai villagers.

Lord Cromer's justification of the tribunal is practically that, bad as it is, the Brigandage Commissions were worse. Also (lest we should propose to carry our moral superiority any further) that the Egyptians are so accustomed to associate law and order with floggings, executions, torture and Lynch Law, that they will not respect any tribunal which does not continue these practices. This is a far-reaching argument: for instance, it suggests that Church of England missionaries might do well to adopt the rite of human sacrifice when evangelizing tribes in whose imagination that practice is inseparably bound up with religion. It suggests that the sole reason why the Denshawai tribunal did not resort to torture for the purpose of extorting confessions and evidence was that parliament might not stand it – though really a parliament which stood the executions would, one would think, stand anything. The tribunal had certainly no intention of allowing witnesses to testify against British officers; for, as it happened, the Ombashi who accompanied them on the two shooting expeditions, one Ahmed Hassan Zakzouk, aged 26, was rash enough to insist that after the shot that struck the woman, the officers fired on the mob twice. This appears in the parliamentary paper; but the French newspaper *L'Égypte* is quoted by Mr Wilfrid Scawen Blunt as reporting that Zakzouk, on being asked by one of the English judges whether he was not afraid to say such a thing, replied 'Nobody in the world is able to frighten me: the truth is the truth,' and was promptly told to stand down. Mr Blunt adds that Zakzouk was then tried for his conduct in connection with the affair before a Court of Discipline, which awarded him two years imprisonment and fifty lashes. Without rudely calling this a use of torture to intimidate anti-British witnesses, I may count on the assent of most reasonable people when I say that Zakzouk probably regards himself as having received a rather strong hint to make his evidence agreeable to the Occupation in future.

Not only was there of course no jury at the trial, but considerably less than no defence. Barristers of sufficient standing to make it very undesirable for them to offend the Occupation were instructed to 'defend' the prisoners. Far from defending them, they paid high compliments to the Occupation as one of the choicest benefits rained by Heaven on their country, and appealed for mercy for their miserable clients, whose conduct had 'caused the unanimous indignation of all Egyptians'. 'Clemency,' they said, 'was above equity.' The Tribunal in delivering judgment remarked that 'the counsel for the defence had a full hearing: nevertheless the defence broke down completely, and all that their counsel could say on behalf of the prisoners practically amounted to an appeal to the mercy of the Court'.

Now the proper defence, if put forward, would probably have convinced Lord Cromer that nothing but the burning of the village and the crucifixion of all its inhabitants could preserve the British Empire. That defence was obvious enough: the village was invaded by five armed foreigners who attempted for the second time to slaughter the villagers' farming stock and carry it off; in resisting an attempt to disarm them four villagers had been wounded; the villagers had lost their tempers and knocked the invaders about; and the older men and watchmen had finally rescued the aggressors and sent them back with no worse handling than they would have got anywhere for the like misconduct.

One can imagine what would have happened to the man, prisoner or advocate, who should have dared to tell the truth in this fashion. The prisoners knew better than to attempt it. On the scaffold, Darweesh turned to his house as he stood on the trap, and exclaimed 'May God compensate us well for this world of meanness, for this world of injustice, for this world of cruelty.' If he had dared in court thus to compare God with the tribunal to the disadvantage of the latter, he would no doubt have had fifty lashes before his hanging, to teach him the greatness of the Empire. As it was, he kept his views to himself until it was too late to do anything worse to him than hang him. In court, he did as all the rest did. They lied; they denied; they set up desperate alibis; they protested they had been in the next village, or tending cattle a mile off, or threshing, or what not. One of them, when identified, said 'All men are alike.' He had only one eye. Darweesh, who had secured one of the officers' guns, declared that his enemies had come in the night and buried it in his house, where his mother sat on it, like Rachel on Laban's stolen teraphim, until she was dragged off. A pitiable business, yet not so pitiable as the virtuous indignation with which Judge Lynch, himself provable by his own judgment to be a prevaricator, hypocrite, tyrant, and coward of the first water, preened himself at its expense. When Lord Cromer, in his official apology for Judge Lynch, says that 'the prisoners had a perfectly fair trial' – not, observe, a trial as little unfair as human frailty could make it, which is the most that can be said for any trial on earth, but 'a *perfectly* fair trial' – he no doubt believes what he says; but his opinion is interesting mainly as an example of the state of his mind, and of the extent to which, after thirty years of official life in Egypt, one loses the plain sense of English words.

Lord Cromer recalls how, in the eighties, a man threatened with the courbash by a Moudir in the presence of Sir Claude MacDonald, said 'You dare not flog me now that the British are here.' 'So bold an answer,' says Lord Cromer, 'was probably due to the presence of a British officer.' What would that man say now? What does Lord Cromer say now? He deprecates 'premature endeavors to thrust Western ideas on an Eastern people', by which he means that when you are in Egypt you must do as the Egyptians do: terrorize by the lash and the scaffold. Thus does the East conquer its conquerors. In 1883 Lord Dufferin was abolishing the bastinado as 'a horrible and infamous punishment'. In 1906 Lord Cromer guarantees ferocious sentences of flogging as 'just and necessary', and can see 'nothing reprehensible in the manner in which they were carried out'. 'I have,' he adds, 'passed nearly thirty years of my life in an earnest endeavor to raise the moral and material condition of the people of Egypt. I have been assisted by a number of very capable officials, all of whom, I may say, have been animated by the same spirit as myself.' Egypt may well shudder as she reads those words. If the first thirty years have been crowned by the Denshawai incident, what will Egypt be like at the end of another thirty years of moral elevation 'animated by the same spirit'?

It is pleasanter to return to Lord Cromer's first letter on Denshawai, written to Sir Edward Grey the day after the shooting party. It says that 'orders will shortly be issued by the General prohibiting officers in the army from shooting pigeons in the future under any circumstances whatever'. But pray why this prohibition, if, as the tribunal declared, the officers were 'guests [actually *guests!*] who had done nothing to deserve blame'?

Mr Findlay is another interesting official correspondent of Sir Edward. Even after the trial, at which it had been impossible to push the medical evidence further than to say that the officer who died of sunstroke had been predisposed to it by the knocking about he had suffered and by his flight under the Egyptian sun, whilst the officers who had remained defenceless in the hands of the villagers were in court, alive and well, Mr Findlay writes that the four hanged men were 'convicted of a brutal and premeditated murder', and complains that 'the native press disregards the fact' and 'is being conducted with such an absolute disregard for the truth as to make it evident that large sums of money have been expended'. Mr Findlay is also a bit of a philosopher. 'The Egyptian, being a fatalist,' he says, 'does not greatly fear death, and there is therefore much to be said for flogging as a judicial punishment in Egypt.' Logically, then, the four hanged men ought to have been flogged instead. But Mr Findlay does not draw that conclusion. Logic is not his strong point: he is a man of feeling, and a very nervous one at that. 'I do not believe that this brutal attack on British officers had anything directly to do with political animosity. It

is, however, due to the insubordinate spirit which has been sedulously
fostered during the last year by unscrupulous and interested agitators.'
Again, 'it is my duty to warn you of the deplorable effect which is being
produced in Egypt by the fact that Members of Parliament have seriously
called in question the unanimous sentence passed by a legally constituted
Court, of which the best English and the best native Judge were members.
This fact will, moreover, supply the lever which has, up to the present,
been lacking to the venal agitators who are at the head of the so-called
patriotic party.' I find Mr Findlay irresistible, so exquisitely does he give
us the measure and flavor of officialism. 'A few days after the Denshawai
affray some native stoned and severely injured an irrigation inspector.
Two days ago three natives knocked a soldier off his donkey and kicked
him in the stomach: his injuries are serious. In the latter case theft appears
to have been the motive. My object in mentioning these instances is to
shew the results to be expected if once respect for the law is shaken. Should
the present state of things continue, and, still more, should the agitation
in this country find support at home, the date is not far distant when the
necessity will arise for bringing in a press law and for considerably
increasing the army of occupation.' Just think of it! In a population of
nearly ten million, one irrigation inspector is stoned. The Denshawai
executions are then carried out to make the law respected. The result is
that three natives knock a soldier off his donkey and rob him. Thereupon
Mr Findlay, appalled at the bankruptcy of civilization, sees nothing for it
now but suppression of the native newspapers and a considerable increase
in the army of occupation! And Lord Cromer writes 'All I need say is that
I concur generally in Mr Findlay's remarks, and that, had I remained in
Egypt, I should in every respect have adopted the same course as that
which he pursued.'

But I must resolutely shut this rich parliamentary paper. I have
extracted enough to paint the picture, and enforce my warning to England
that if her Empire means ruling the world as Denshawai has been ruled
in 1906 – and that, I am afraid, is what the Empire does mean to the main
body of our aristocratic-military caste and to our Jingo plutocrats – then
there can be no more sacred and urgent political duty on earth than the
disruption, defeat, and suppression of the Empire, and, incidentally, the
humanization of its supporters by the sternest lessons of that adversity
which comes finally to institutions which make themselves abhorred by

the aspiring will of humanity towards divinity. As for the Egyptians, any man cradled by the Nile who, after the Denshawai incident, will ever voluntarily submit to British rule, or accept any bond with us except the bond of a Federation of free and equal states, will deserve the worst that Lord Cromer can consider 'just and necessary' for him. That is what you get by attempting to prove your supremacy by the excesses of frightened soldiers and denaturalized officials instead of by courageous helpfulness and moral superiority.

In any case let no Englishman who is content to leave Abd-el-Nebi and his twenty-year-old neighbor in penal servitude for life, and to plume himself on the power to do it, pretend to be fit to govern either my country or his own. The responsibility cannot be confined to the tribunal and to the demoralized officials of the Occupation. The House of Commons had twentyfour hours clear notice, with the telegraph under the hand of Sir Edward Grey, to enable it to declare that England was a civilized Power and would not stand these barbarous lashings and vindictive hangings. Yet Mr Dillon, representing the Irish party, which well knows what British Occupation and Findlay 'loyalism' mean, protested in vain. Sir Edward, on behalf of the new Liberal Government (still simmering with virtuous indignation at the flogging of Chinamen and the military executions in South Africa in the forced presence of the victims' families under the late Imperialist Government), not only permitted and defended the Denshawai executions, but appealed to the House almost passionately not to criticize or repudiate them, on the ground – how incredible it now appears! – that Abd-el-Nebi and Hassan Mahfouz and Darweesh and the rest were the fuglemen of a gigantic Moslem plot to rise against Christendom in the name of the Prophet and sweep Christendom out of Africa and Asia by a colossal second edition of the Indian Mutiny. That this idiotic romance, gross and ridiculous as the lies of Falstaff, should have imposed on any intelligent and politically experienced human being, is strange enough – though the secret shame of revolted humanity will make cabinet ministers snatch at fantastic excuses – but what humanity will not forgive our foreign secretary for is his failure to see that even if such a conspiracy really existed, England should have faced it and fought it bravely by honorable means, instead of wildly lashing and strangling a handful of poor peasants to scare Islam into terrified submission. Were I abject enough to grant to Sir Edward Grey as valid that main asset of 'thinking Imperially', the conviction that we are all going to be murdered, I should still suggest to him that we can at least die like gentlemen? Might I even be so personal as to say that the reason for giving him a social position and political opportunities that are denied to his tradesmen is that he is supposed to understand better than they that honor is worth its danger and its cost, and that life is worthless without honor? It is true that Sir John Falstaff did not think so; but Sir John is hardly a model for Sir Edward. Yet even Sir John would have had enough gumption to see that the Denshawai panic was more dangerous to the Empire than the loss of ten pitched battles.

As cowardice is highly infectious, would it not be desirable to supersede officials who, after years of oriental service, have lost the familiar art of concealing their terrors? I am myself a sedentary literary civilian, constitutionally timid; but I find it possible to keep up appearances, and can even face the risk of being run over, or garotted, or burnt out in London without shrieking for martial law, suppression of the newspapers, exemplary flogging and hanging of motor-bus drivers, and compulsory police service. Why are soldiers and officials on foreign service so much more cowardly than citizens? Is it not clearly because the whole Imperial military system of coercion and terrorism is unnatural, and that the truth formulated by William Morris that 'no man is good enough to be another man's master' is true also of nations, and very specially true of those plutocrat-ridden Powers which have of late stumbled into an enormous increase of material wealth without having made any intelligent provision for its proper distribution and administration?

However, the economic reform of the Empire is a long business, whereas the release of Abd-el-Nebi and his neighbors is a matter of the stroke of a pen, once public opinion is shamed into activity. I fear I have stated their case very unfairly and inadequately, because I am hampered, as an Irishman, by my implacable hostility to English domination. Mistrusting my own prejudices, I have taken the story from the two parliamentary papers in which our officials have done their utmost to whitewash the tribunals and the pigeon-shooting party, and to blackwash the villagers. Those who wish to have it told to them by an Englishman of unquestionable personal and social credentials, and an intimate knowledge of Egypt and the Egyptians, can find it in Mr Wilfrid Scawen Blunt's pamphlet entitled 'Atrocities of British Rule in Egypt'. When they have read it they will appreciate my forbearance; and when I add that English rule in Ireland has been 'animated by the same spirit' (I thank Lord Cromer for the phrase) as English rule in Egypt, and that this is the inevitable spirit of all coercive military rule, they will perhaps begin to understand why Home Rule is a necessity not only for Ireland, but for all constituents of those Federations of Commonwealths which are now the only permanently practicable form of Empire.

POSTSCRIPT. These sheets had passed through the press when the news came of Lord Cromer's resignation. As he accuses himself of failing health, he will perhaps forgive me for accusing him of failing judgment, and for suggesting that his retirement from office might well be celebrated in Egypt by the retirement, at his intercession, of Abd-el-Nabi and the rest from penal servitude.

A YEAR LATER

It may be a relief to some of my readers to learn that very shortly after the publication of the above account of the Denshawai atrocity, I received a private assurance that Abd-el-Nebi and his fellow-prisoners would be released on the following New Year's Day, which is the customary occasion in Egypt for such acts of grace and clemency as the Occupation may allow the Khedive to perform, and that in the meantime their detention would not be rigorous. As the hanged men could not be un-hanged nor the flogged men unflogged, this was all that could be done. I am bound to add, in justice to the Government, that this was, as far as I could ascertain, an act of pure conscience on the part of the Cabinet; for there was no sign of any serious pressure of public opinion. One or two newspapers seemed to be amused at my calling the Denshawai villagers Denshavians; but they shewed no other interest in the matter: another illustration of how hopeless it is to induce one modern nation, pre-occupied as it necessarily is with its own affairs, to take any real interest in the welfare of another, even when it professes to govern that other in a superior manner for its good. Sir Edward Grey's reputation as a great Minister for Foreign Affairs was not shaken in the least: the eulogies which were heaped on him by both parties increased in volume; and an attempt which I made to call attention to the real character of the Anglo-Russian agreement as to Persia, which was held up as a masterpiece of his diplomacy (I was apparently the only person who had taken the trouble to read it) had no effect. Not until Sir Edward ventured to threaten a really formidable European Power in 1911, and threatened it successfully from his point of view, did a sudden and violent agitation against him spring up. Until then, men of both parties idolized him without knowing why, just as they had formerly idolized Lord Cromer and Lord Milner without knowing why. They will now very possibly turn on him and rend him, also without knowing why. The one thing they will not do is to blame themselves, which is the only blaming that can be of any profit to them.

Preface to the
Home Rule Edition of
1912

[When Shaw reprinted this Preface in the Collected Edition of his works in 1930, he placed it before the original Preface and added an explanatory note. The text has now been placed in its proper chronological order. The prefatory note has been retained without editorial revision.]

(I reprint this interim preface after much hesitation. It is based on two confident political assumptions that have since been not merely disproved but catastrophically shattered.

The first was that Parliament in 1912 was still what it had been in the heyday of Gladstonian Liberalism, when it was utterly inconceivable that an Act of constitutional reform which had been duly passed and assented-to by the Crown could be dropped into the waste paper basket because a handful of ladies and gentlemen objected to it, and the army officers' messes blustered mutinously against it.

The second assumption was that Ireland was politically one and indivisible, and, consequently, that when Home Rule came, as it was evident it must come, the Protestants of Ireland must stand together and make the best of it. The possibility of a Partition by which Belfast Protestantism should accept Home Rule for itself in a concentration camp and thus abandon its co-religionists outside the camp to what must then inevitably become a Roman Catholic Home Rule Government of the rest of Ireland, was undreamt of.

How both these things nevertheless happened I have described in a postscript to the original preface which will be found on a later page. Readers who skip to that preface will lose nothing by missing this one except a possibly instructive example of how our eternal march into the future must always be a blindfold march. I guessed ahead, and guessed wrongly, whilst stupider and more ignorant fellow-pilgrims guessed rightly.)

John Bull's Other Island was written when a Unionist Government was in power, and had been in power with one brief interval for twenty years. The reason for this apparent eclipse of Home Rule was that the Liberal Party had during that period persisted in assuring the English people anxiously that it had no intention of doing anything for England (its object being to shew its abhorrence of Socialism) and that it cared for nothing but Home Rule in Ireland. Now as the English electors, being mostly worse off than the Irish, were anxious to have something done to alleviate their own wretched condition, they steadily voted for the Unionist Party (not because it was Unionist, but because it cared more for England than for Ireland), except on one occasion in 1893, when the Liberals put all their Home Rule tracts in the fire, and fought on a program of English Social Reform, known as the Newcastle Program, drawn up by my friend and Fabian colleague, Mr Sidney Webb, and ingeniously foisted on the Liberals by myself and other Fabians disguised as artless Gladstonian members of certain little local caucuses which called themselves Liberal and Radical Associations, and were open to any passer-by who might astonish them by seeming to take an interest in their routine of bleeding candidates for registration expenses and local subscriptions. The program won the election for the Home Rulers. It was a close thing; but it won it. The Liberals then dropped it; and Lord Rosebery made his famous discovery that programs are a mistake, a view which, though supported with deep conviction by his Party, which still had no desire to do or mean or understand anything that could conceivably benefit anyone in England, had the immediate effect of extinguishing its noble author politically, and sending his party back into opposition for another ten years, at the end of which the Unionists, quite as ignorant of what the people of England were thinking about as Lord Rosebery, entered upon an impassioned defence of the employment of Chinese labor in South Africa without considering the fact that every one of their arguments was equally valid for the introduction of Chinese labor into Lancashire. And as the people of Lancashire were concerned about Lancashire and not at all about South Africa, the Unionist Party followed Lord Rosebery into the shades.

One consequence of this political swing of the pendulum was that John Bull's Other Island, which had up to that moment been a topical play, immediately became a historical one. Broadbent is no longer up-to-date. His *bête noir*, Mr Joseph Chamberlain, has retired from public life. The controversies about Tariff Reform, the Education and Licensing Bills, and the South African war, have given way to the far more vital questions raised by Mr Lloyd George's first unskilful essays in Collectivism, and to the agitation for Votes for Women. Broadbent is still strong on the question of Persia: stronger than he was on that of Armenia (probably because Persia is further off); but there is little left of the subjects that excited him in 1904 except Home Rule. And Home Rule is to be disposed of this year.

The Government will no doubt be glad to get rid of it. The English people, with prices up and wages down, care less, if possible, than they ever did about it. Even the governing classes are feeling the pressure of the Home Rule agitations in Egypt and India more than in Ireland; for the Irish, now confident that their battle is won, are keeping comparatively quiet, whilst in the East the question is in the acute stage in which the Government has to explain that really very few people have had confessions extorted by torture in the police stations, and that if the natives would only be reasonable and recognize the advantages of British rule, and their own utter unfitness for self-government, there would be no need to imprison nationalists either in India or Egypt; so that, in effect, the natives have themselves to thank for whatever unpleasantness may happen to them.

The only considerable body of Englishmen really concerned about Home Rule except as a Party question, are those members of the Free Churches, vulgarly called Dissenters or Nonconformists, who believe that the effect of Home Rule would be to deliver Ireland into the hands of the Roman Catholic Church, which they regard as The Scarlet Woman. It is clearly not a very deeply considered apprehension, because there is not a country in the world, not even Spain, where the people are so completely in the hands of the Roman Catholic Church as they are in Ireland under English rule and because of English rule. In the non-Protestant Christian countries which are politically independent, the clericals are struggling, not to regain their lost supremacy (that survives only in Ireland), but for their houses, their property, their right to live in the country they were born in, and to have the political weight due to their merits; for they have merits: the priest is not so black as he is painted in all free countries nowadays. But our Free Churchmen are too much afraid of the Pope, and of the confessional, and of the priest in the house, to see how weak these forces are in the face of democracy. Also, they are not all well off enough to buy plays in six-shilling, or even in eighteenpenny volumes. Therefore, I think it opportune to issue this cheap edition of John Bull's Other Island this Home Rule Year, because its preface was written by an Irishman of Protestant family and Protestant prejudices, and shews that the one way in which the power of the priest can be kept within its proper limits in Ireland is by setting the Irish people free to take it in hand themselves without seeming to be treacherously taking the side of England against their own country.

Still more needed is this cheap edition in Ireland, where nobody can well afford to pay more than sixpence for anything, since, if I may put it elliptically, the only people in Ireland who can afford more than sixpence are those who live in England. I should like to call the attention of my nervous fellow Protestants in Ireland to the fact that in Italy, the centre of Roman Catholicism, the Pope is in a position closely resembling what that of Louis XVI would have been during the first years of the French Revolution if he, like the Pope, had had no wife to bring him to the scaffold by tempting him to betray his country to a foreign foe. Also that in France, in spite of the revocation of the Edict of Nantes by the Roman Catholic Church at the height of its power, the Huguenots have always wielded, and still wield today, a power that is out of all proportion to their comparative numbers, and even, I am afraid I must add, to their merits. The Huguenot of Ulster is a coward only when he breaks his own backbone by taking the part of a foreign country against his own. Shut him up in Derry with an English King besieging him, and he does not shriek for the Germans to come and help him as if the thumbscrews of the Spanish Armada were already on his hands; he chalks up No Surrender merrily, and puts up one of the famous fights of history. After all, what is the use of protesting that you will not be governed from Rome if the alternative is to be governed from London? The great Protestant Irishmen have been all the more powerful because they loved Ireland better, not only than Rome, but than England. Why was it that the priests had no power to impose a Roman Catholic Leader on the Home Rule movement instead of Parnell? Simply because Parnell was so proud of his Irish birthright that he would rather have been one of even a persecuted minority in an Irish parliament than the Premier of an English Cabinet. He was not afraid of his countrymen: he knew that Protestantism could hold its own only too well in a free Ireland; and even if he had not known it he would have taken his chance rather than sell his birthright and his country. It is the essential dishonor of acting as a foreign garrison in a land where they are not foreigners that makes the position of the Orangemen so impossible, and breaks in them the spirit that animates every man in Europe who is fighting for a minority; and what man of any dignity today is not one of a minority that cries in the wilderness against one or other of the manifold iniquities and falsehoods of our civilization? I think if I as a Home Ruler (and many other less orthodox things) can live in England and hold my own in a minority which on some very sensitive points reaches the odds of about 1 to 48,000,000, an Ulster Orangeman should be able to face Home Rule without his knees knocking shamefully in the face of a contemptuous England which despises him none the less because his cowardice seems to serve her own turn.

There are, I know, men and women who are political perverts by nature. The supreme misfortune of being born with one's natural instincts turned against nature by a freak of nature is a phenomenon that occurs politically as well as physiologically. There are Poles who are devoted with all their soul to Russia and the maintenance of Russian rule in Poland, Persians who are risking their lives to introduce it in Persia, Indians and Egyptians who are ready to sacrifice all they possess for England and English rule. And it is not to be denied that among these are persons of high character and remarkable ability, comparing very favorably with the dregs of the nationalist movements, which, just because they are national and normal, are made up of all sorts, and consequently have dregs: pretty nasty ones too. For that matter, if ever a Book of Spies be written, it will include examples of courage, conviction, perseverance, and ability, that will almost persuade shallow people that spies are the real heroes of military history. Even in more personal relations, natural passion cannot pretend to inspire more intense devotion than perverted passion. But when all is said, the pervert, however magnificently he may conduct his campaign against nature, remains abhorrent. When Napoleon, though he boasted of having made peers and marshals of peasants and ostlers, drew the line at promoting a spy, he followed a universal instinct and a sound one. When the Irish Catholic who, feeling bitterly that the domination of the priest is making his own lot hopeless, nevertheless stands shoulder to shoulder with the priest for Home Rule against Dublin Castle, he is behaving naturally and rightly. When the Orangeman sacrifices his nationality to his hatred of the priest, and fights against his own country for its conqueror, he is doing something for which, no matter how bravely he fights, history and humanity will never forgive him: English history and humanity, to their credit be it said, least of all.

Please do not suppose for a moment that I propose that the Irish Protestant should submit to the Irish Roman Catholic. I reproach the Irish Roman Catholic for his submission to Rome exactly as I reproach the Orangeman for his submission to England. If Catholicism is to be limited in Ireland by any geographical expression (in which case it ceases to be Catholic) let it be Irish Catholicism, not Italian Catholicism. Let us maintain our partnership with Rome as carefully as our partnership with England; but let it be, in the one case as in the other, a free partnership. But the Irish Catholics are not Italian in their politics. They do not oppose Home Rule; and that gives them the right to the support of every Irish Protestant until Home Rule is achieved. After that, let us by all means begin a civil war next day if we are fools enough. A war for an idea may be a folly; but it is not a dishonor. Both parties would be fighting for Ireland; and though the slaying of an Irishman by an Irishman for Ireland may be a tragedy – may be even a crime to those who think that all war is crime – at least it is not unnatural crime, like the slaying of an Irishman by an Irishman for England's sake. There will, of course, be no war of religion: I have shewn in this book that the Protestant under Home Rule will be far safer and stronger than he is today; but even if there were, that is the way to look at it.

The question is still more important for England than for Ireland, in spite of England's indifference to it. In Ireland we are still sane: we do not sneer at our country as 'Little Ireland', and cheer for a doubtful commercial speculation called The Empire which we could not point out accurately on the map, and which is populated by such an overwhelming majority of what an Irish peasant would call 'black heathens', that they force us to punish our own missionaries for asking them to buy and read The Bible, and compel the Protestant Passive Resisters, who will be sold up rather than pay a rate to maintain a Church school, to pay without a murmur for the establishment of the Roman Catholic Church in Malta. Formerly 'Little England', the 'right little, tight little Island', despised Spain for her imperial policy, and saw her lose her place, not only among the empires, but even among the nations, with self-satisfied superiority. Today England is letting herself be dragged into the path of Spain. She dreams of nothing but the old beginning: an Invincible Armada. Spain reckoned without the Lord of Hosts, who scattered that Invincible Armada for Little England. The modern Imperialist does not believe in the Lord of Hosts; but the Armada was defeated for all that, though England's fleet was far more inferior to it than the German fleet will ever again be to the English fleet. The Lord of Hosts may not be quite the sort of power that Philip of Spain conceived it to be: many of us are dropping the personal pronoun, as I have just dropped it lest I should be prosecuted for superstition by the Society for the Encouragement of Cruelty to Animals; but it can still send bigger fleets to the bottom than England can build, and exalt smaller nations than England ever was above drifting congeries of derelict regions held desperately together by terrified soldiers trying to wave half a dozen flags all at once in the name of Empire: a name that every man who has ever felt the sacredness of his own native soil to him, and thus learnt to regard that feeling in other men as something holy and inviolable, spits out of his mouth with enormous contempt.

Not that I have any delusions about Drake and his Elizabethan comrades: they were pirates and slave-traders, not a whit better than the Algerine corsair who shared with them what modern idiots call 'the command of the sea' (much the sea cares about their command!); but it is better to be a pirate trading in slaves out of sheer natural wickedness than a bankrupt in a cocked hat, doing the same things, and worse, against your own conscience, because you are paid for it and are afraid to do anything else. Drake thought nothing of burning a Spanish city; but he was not such a fool as to suppose that if he told off some of his crew to stay and govern that Spanish city by force when it was rebuilt, all the reasonable inhabitants of that town would recognize the arrangement as an enormous improvement, and be very much obliged to him, which is the modern Imperial idea. To singe the King of Spain's beard; pick his pocket; and run away, was, in the absence of any international police, a profitable bit of sport, if a rascally one; but if Drake had put a chain round the King's neck and led him round a prisoner for the rest of his life, he would have suffered as much by such a folly as the King, and probably died sooner of worry, anxiety, expense, and loss through the neglect of his own proper affairs, than the King would have died of captivity. Bermondsey goes to the dogs whilst those whose business it is to govern it are sitting on Bengal;

and the more Bengal kicks, the more Bermondsey is neglected, except by the tax collector. The notion that the way to prosper is to insist on managing everybody else's affairs is, on the face of it, a fool's notion. It is at bottom the folly of the ignorant simpletons who long to be kings and chiefs because they imagine that a king or chief is an idle voluptuary with lots of money, leisure, and power over others, to use irresponsibly for his own amusement.

In short, then, the future is not to the empires, but to federations of self-governing nations, exactly as, within these nations, the future is not to Capitalist Oligarchies, but to Collectivist organizations of free and equal citizens. In short, to Commonwealths.

In expressing this irresistible sentiment of nationality with all the rhetoric to which it lends itself, I am not forgetting that there are international rights as well as national ones. We are not only natives within our own frontiers but inheritors of the earth. England has rights in Ireland as Ireland has rights in England. I demand of every nation right of ingress and egress, roads, police, an efficient post office, and, in reason, freedom of conscience. I am prepared to steam-roller Tibet if Tibet persist in refusing me my international rights. If the Moors and Arabs cannot or will not secure these common human conditions for me in North Africa, I am quite prepared to co-operate with the French, the Italians, and the Spaniards in Morocco, Algeria, Tunisia, and Tripoli, with the Russians in Siberia, with all three and the English and Germans as well in Africa, or with the Americans in the hunting grounds of the red man, to civilize these places; though I know as well as anyone that there are many detestable features in our civilization, many virtues in village and tribal communities, and a very large alloy indeed of brigandage in our explorations and colonizations.

I know also that what compels us to push our frontiers farther and farther into regions we call barbarous is the necessity of policing, not the barbarians, but the European dregs and riffraff who set up little hells of anarchy and infamy just beyond the border, and thus compel us to advance and rope them in, step by step, no matter how much we are adding to that 'white man's burden', which is none the less a real thing because it is not specially a white man's burden any more than it is specially an Englishman's burden, as most of Mr Kipling's readers seem to interpret it. Tribes must make themselves into nations before they can claim the rights of nations; and this they can do only by civilization.

Also I cannot deny that the exclusion of the Chinese from America and Australia is a violation of international right which the Chinese will be perfectly justified in resisting by arms as soon as they feel strong enough. If nations are to limit immigration, inter-marriage with foreigners, and even international trade by tariffs, it had better be done by international law than by arbitrary national force as at present. It will be seen that I am under no delusion as to the freedom of Nationalism from abuse. I know that there are abuses in England which would not exist if she were governed by Germany, and that there will no doubt be abuses in Ireland under Home Rule which do not exist under English rule, just as things have been done under the Irish Local Government Act that the old oligarchical grand juries would not have tolerated. There are, indeed, a hundred horses on which I could ride off if I wished to shirk the main issue. But when all is said, it is so certain that in the long run all civilized nations must at the same time become more dependent one on another and do their own governing work themselves, that if Ireland refused Home Rule now, it would sooner or later be forced on her by England because England will need all her time and political energy for her own affairs when once she realizes that the day for letting them slide and muddling through is past.

LONDON
19th January 1912

TWENTYFOUR YEARS LATER

The sequel to these events confirmed my unheeded warning with a sanguinary completeness of which I had no prevision. At Easter 1916 a handful of Irishmen seized the Dublin Post Office and proclaimed an Irish Republic, with one of their number, a schoolmaster named Pearse, as President. If all Ireland had risen at this gesture it would have been a serious matter for England, then up to her neck in the war against the Central Empires. But there was no response: the gesture was a complete failure. All that was necessary was to blockade the Post Office until its microscopic republic was starved out and made ridiculous. What actually happened would be incredible if there were not so many living witnesses of it. From a battery planted at Trinity College (the Irish equivalent of Oxford University), and from a warship in the river Liffey, a bombardment was poured on the centre of the city which reduced more than a square mile of it to such a condition that when, in the following year, I was taken through Arras and Ypres to shew me what the German artillery had done to these cities in two and a half years, I laughed and said, 'You should see what the British artillery did to my native city in a week.' It would not be true to say that not one stone was left upon another; for the marksmanship was so bad that the Post Office itself was left standing amid a waste of rubbish heaps; and enough scraps of wall were left for the British Army, which needed recruits, to cover with appeals to the Irish to remember Belgium lest the fate of Louvain should befall their own hearths and homes.

Having thus worked up a harebrained romantic adventure into a heroic episode in the struggle for Irish freedom, the victorious artillerists proceeded to kill their prisoners of war in a drawn-out string of executions. Those who were executed accordingly became not only national heroes, but the martyrs whose blood was the seed of the present Irish Free State. Among those who escaped was its first President. Nothing more blindly savage, stupid, and terror-mad could have been devised by England's worst enemies. It was a very characteristic example of the mentality produced by the conventional gentleman-militarist education at Marlborough and Sandhurst and the conventional gentleman-diplomatist education at Eton and Oxford, Harrow and Cambridge. Is it surprising that the Russian Soviet Government, though fanatically credulous as to the need for popular education, absolutely refused to employ as teachers anyone who had been touched by the equivalent public school and university routine in Russia, and stuck to its resolution even at the cost of carrying on for some years with teachers who were hardly a day ahead of their pupils?

But the Post Office episode was eclipsed by an event which was much more than an episode, as it shattered the whole case for parliamentary government throughout the world. The Irish Nationalists, after thirty years of constitutional procedure in the British Parliament, had carried an Act to establish Irish Home Rule, as it was then called, which duly received the royal assent and became a statute of the realm. Immediately the British officers on service in Ireland mutinied, refusing to enforce the

Act or operate against the northern Orangemen who were openly arming themselves to resist it. They were assured of support by their fellow-officers at home. The Act was suspended after prominent English statesmen had taken part in the military manoeuvres of the Orangemen. The Prime Minister publicly pledged himself that Belfast, the Orange capital, would not in any case be coerced. In short, the Act was shelved under a threat of civil war; and the Clan na Gael, which in America had steadfastly maintained that the constitutional movement was useless, as England would in the last resort repudiate the constitution and hold Ireland against the Irish by physical force, and had been rebuked, lectured, and repudiated by the parliamentary Home Rulers for a whole generation for saying so, was justified. The Catholic Irish accordingly armed themselves and drilled as Volunteers in spite of the hostility of the Government, which meanwhile gave every possible assistance to the parallel preparations of the Orangemen. An Irish parliament (or Dail) sat in Dublin and claimed to be the national government. Irish courts were set up for the administration of Irish justice; Irish order was kept by Irish police; Irish taxes were collected by Irish officials; and British courts were boycotted. Upon this interesting but hopeless attempt to ignore British rule the Government let loose a specially recruited force (known to history as the Black and Tans) with *carte blanche* to kill, burn, and destroy, save only that they must stop short of rapine. They wrecked the Irish courts and produced a state of anarchy. They struck at the Irish through the popular co-operative stores and creameries, which they burnt. The people found a civil leader in Arthur Griffiths and a military one in Michael Collins. The Black and Tans had the British Government at their back: Collins had the people at his back. He threatened that for every creamery or co-operative store or cabin or cottage burnt by the Black and Tans he would burn two country houses of the Protestant gentry. The country houses that were not burnt were raided at night and laid under contribution for needed supplies. If the occupants reported the raid, the house was burnt. The Black and Tans and the ordinary constabulary were treated as enemies in uniform: that is, they were shot at sight and their stations burnt; or they were ambushed and killed in petty battles. Those who gave warnings or information of any helpful kind to them were mercilessly executed without privilege of sex or benefit of clergy. Collins, with allies in every street and hamlet, proved able to carry out his threat.

He won the crown of the Reign of Terror; and the position of the Protestant gentry became unbearable.

Thus by fire and bullet, murder and torture and devastation, a situation was produced in which the British Government had either to capitulate at the cost of a far more complete concession of self-government to Ireland than that decreed by the repudiated Home Rule Act, or to let loose the military strength of England in a Cromwellian reconquest, massacre, and replantation which it knew that public opinion in England and America would not tolerate; for some of the most conspicuous English champions of Ulster warned the Government that they could stand no more of the Black and Tan terrorism. And so we settled the Irish Question, not as civilized and reasonable men should have settled it, but as dogs settle a dispute over a bone.

Future historians will probably see in these catastrophes a ritual of human sacrifice without which the savages of the twentieth century could not effect any redistribution of political power or wealth. Nothing was learnt from Denshawai or the Black and Tan terror. In India, which is still struggling for self-government, and obviously must finally have it, a military panic led to the cannonading of a forbidden public meeting at Amritsar, the crowd being dealt with precisely as if it were a body of German shocktroops rushing the British trenches in Flanders. In London the police would have broken a score or two of heads and dragged a handful of ringleaders to the police courts. And there was the usual combination of mean spite with hyperbolical violence. Indians were forced to crawl past official buildings on their hands and knees. The effect was to make British imperial rule ridiculous in Europe, and implacably resented in India.

In Egypt the British domination died of Denshawai; but at its deathbed the British Sirdar was assassinated, whereupon the British Government, just then rather drunk after a sweeping election victory secured by an anti-Russian scare, announced to an amazed world that it was going to cut off the Nile at its source and destroy Egypt by stopping its water supply. Of course nothing happened but an ignominious climb down; but the incident illustrates my contention that our authority, when it is too far flung (as our patriotic rhapsodists put it), goes stark mad at the periphery if a pin drops. As to what further panics and atrocities will ensue before India is left to govern itself as much as Ireland and Egypt now are I am in the dark until the event enlightens me. But on the folly of allowing military counsels to prevail in political settlements I may point to the frontiers established by the victors after the war of 1914–18. Almost every one of these frontiers has a new war implicit in it, because the soldier recognizes no ethnographical, linguistic, or moral boundaries: he demands a line that he can defend, or rather that Napoleon or Wellington could have defended; for he has not yet learnt to think of offence and defence in terms of airplanes which ignore his Waterloo ridges. And the inevitable nationalist rebellions against these military frontiers, and the atrocities by which they are countered, are in full swing as I write.

Meanwhile, John Bull's Other Island, though its freedom has destroyed all the romantic interest that used to attach to it, has become at last highly interesting to the student of political science as an experiment in political structure. Protestant Ulster, which armed against the rest of Ireland and defied the British Parliament to the cry of 'We wont have it,' meaning that they would die in the last ditch singing 'O God, our help in ages past' rather than suffer or tolerate Home Rule, is now suffering and indeed hugging Home Rule on a much more homely scale than the Home Rulers ever demanded or dreamt of; for it has a Belfast Home Rule Parliament instead of an Irish one. And it has allowed Catholic Ireland to secure the Irish parliament. Thus, of the two regional parliaments which have been established on a sectarian basis, Protestant Ulster has been left with the smaller. Now it happens that Protestant Ulster is industrial Ireland and Catholic Ireland agricultural Ireland. And throughout the world for a century past the farmer, the peasant, and the Catholic have been the bulwark of the industrial capitalists against the growing political power of the industrial proletariat organized in trade unions, Labor parties, and the ubiquitous sodalities of that new ultra-Catholic Church called Socialism.

From this defensive alliance the Ulster employers, blinded by an obsolete bigotry and snobbery, have deliberately cut themselves off. In my preface of 1906, and again in my 1912 preface to a sixpenny edition of this play called the Home Rule edition, I exhorted the Protestants to take their chance, trust their grit, and play their part in a single parliament ruling an undivided Ireland. They did not take my advice. Probably they did not even read it, being too deeply absorbed in the History of Maria Monk, or the latest demonstration that all the evil in the world is the work of an underground conspiracy entitled by them 'the Jesuits'. It is a pity they did not begin their political education, as I began mine, by reading Karl Marx. It is true that I had occasion to point out that Marx was not infallible; but he left me with a very strong disposition to back the economic situation to control all the other situations, religious, nationalist, or romantic, in the long run. And so I do not despair of seeing Protestant Ulster seeking the alliance it repudiated. The Northern Parliament will not merge into the Oireachtas; for until both of them are superseded by a completely modernized central government, made for action and not for obstruction, they will remain more effective as regional parliaments than they would be as national ones; but they will soon have to take counsel together through conferences which will recur until they become a permanent institution and finally develop into what the Americans call Congress, or Federal Government of the whole island. No doubt this will be received in Belfast (if noticed at all) with shouts of 'We wont have it.' But I have heard that cry before, and regard it as a very hopeful sign that they will have it gladly enough when they have the luck to get it.

AYOT ST LAWRENCE,
    November 1929

John Bull's Other Island

Composition begun 17 June 1904; completed 23 August 1904. Published in *John Bull's Other Island, How He Lied to Her Husband, Major Barbara*, 1907. Revised text in Collected Edition, 1930. First presented at the Royal Court Theatre, London, on 1 November 1904, for six matinées.

Broadbent	*Louis Calvert*
Larry Doyle	*J. L. Shine*
Tim Haffigan	*Percival Stevens*
Hodson	*Nigel Playfair*
Peter Keegan	*Granville Barker*
Patsy Farrell	*Graham Browne*
Father Dempsey	*Charles Daly*
Corney Doyle	*F. Cremlin*
Barney Doran	*Wilfred Shine*
Matthew Haffigan	*A. E. George*
Aunt Judy	*Agnes Thomas*
Nora	*Ellen O'Malley*

Period – The Present. London and Ireland

ACT I *Office of Broadbent and Doyle, Civil Engineers, Great George Street, Westminster*

ACT II Scene 1: *Roscullen Hill*
Scene 2: *The Round Tower*

ACT III *The Grass Plot before Corney Doyle's House*

ACT IV Scene 1: *The Parlor at Corney Doyle's*
Scene 2: *Roscullen Hill*

ACT I

Great George Street, Westminster, is the address of Doyle and Broadbent, civil engineers. On the threshold one reads that the firm consists of Mr Laurence Doyle and Mr Thomas Broadbent, and that their rooms are on the first floor. Most of these rooms are private; for the partners, being bachelors and bosom friends, live there; and the door marked Private, next the clerks' office, is their domestic sitting room as well as their reception room for clients. Let me describe it briefly from the point of view of a sparrow on the window sill. The outer door is in the opposite wall, close to the right hand corner. Between this door and the left hand corner is a hatstand and a table consisting of large drawing boards on trestles, with plans, rolls of tracing paper, mathematical instruments, and other draughtsman's accessories on it. In the left hand wall is the fireplace, and the door of an inner room between the fireplace and our observant sparrow. Against the right hand wall is a filing cabinet, with a cupboard on it, and, nearer, a tall office desk and stool for one person. In the middle of the room a large double writing table is set across, with a chair at each end for the two partners. It is a room which no woman would tolerate, smelling of tobacco, and much in need of repapering, repainting, and recarpeting; but this is the effect of bachelor untidiness and indifference, not want of means; for nothing that Doyle and Broadbent themselves have purchased is cheap; nor is anything they want lacking. On the walls hang a large map of South America, a pictorial advertisement of a steamship company, an impressive portrait of Gladstone, and several caricatures of Mr Balfour as a rabbit and Mr Chamberlain as a fox by Francis Carruthers Gould.

At twenty minutes to five o'clock on a summer afternoon in 1904, the room is empty. Presently the outer door is opened, and a valet comes in laden with a large Gladstone bag and a strap of rugs. He carries them into the inner room. He is a respectable valet, old enough to have lost all alacrity and acquired an air of putting up patiently with a great deal of trouble and indifferent health. The luggage belongs to Broadbent, who enters after the valet. He pulls off his overcoat and hangs it with his hat on the stand. Then he comes to the writing table and looks through the letters waiting there for him. He is a robust, full-blooded, energetic man in the prime of life, sometimes eager and credulous, sometimes shrewd and roguish, sometimes portentously solemn, sometimes jolly and impetuous, always buoyant and irresistible, mostly likeable, and enormously absurd in his most earnest moments. He bursts open his letters with his thumb, and glances through them, flinging the envelopes about the floor with reckless untidiness whilst he talks to the valet.

BROADBENT [*calling*] Hodson.

HODSON [*in the bedroom*] Yes sir.

BROADBENT. Dont unpack. Just take out the things Ive worn; and put in clean things.

HODSON [*appearing at the bedroom door*] Yes sir. [*He turns to go back into the bedroom*].

BROADBENT. And look here! [*Hodson turns again*]. Do you remember where I put my revolver?

HODSON. Revolver, sir! Yes sir. Mr Doyle uses it as a paperweight, sir, when he's drawing.

BROADBENT. Well, I want it packed. Theres a packet of cartridges somewhere, I think. Find it and pack it as well.

HODSON. Yes sir.

BROADBENT. By the way, pack your own traps too. I shall take you with me this time.

HODSON [*hesitant*] Is it a dangerous part youre going to, sir? Should I be expected to carry a revolver, sir?

BROADBENT. Perhaps it might be as well. I'm going to Ireland.

HODSON [*reassured*] Yes sir.

BROADBENT. You dont feel nervous about it, I suppose?

HODSON. Not at all, sir. I'll risk it, sir.

BROADBENT. Ever been in Ireland?

HODSON. No sir. I understand it's a very wet climate, sir. I'd better pack your india-rubber overalls.

BROADBENT. Do. Wheres Mr Doyle?

HODSON. I'm expecting him at five, sir. He went out after lunch.

BROADBENT. Anybody been looking for me?

HODSON. A person giving the name of Haffigan has called twice today, sir.

BROADBENT. Oh, I'm sorry. Why didnt he wait? I told him to wait if I wasnt in.

HODSON. Well sir, I didnt know you expected him; so I thought it best to — to — not to encourage him, sir.

BROADBENT. Oh, he's all right. He's an Irishman, and not very particular about his appearance.

HODSON. Yes sir: I noticed that he was rather Irish.

BROADBENT. If he calls again let him come up.

HODSON. I think I saw him waiting about, sir, when you drove up. Shall I fetch him, sir?

BROADBENT. Do, Hodson.

HODSON. Yes sir [*He makes for the outer door*].

BROADBENT. He'll want tea. Let us have some.

HODSON [*stopping*] I shouldnt think he drank tea, sir.

BROADBENT. Well, bring whatever you think he'd like.

HODSON. Yes sir [*An electric bell rings*]. Here he is, sir. Saw you arrive, sir.

BROADBENT. Right. Shew him in. [*Hodson goes out. Broadbent gets through the rest of his letters before Hodson returns with the visitor*].

HODSON. Mr Affigan.

Haffigan is a stunted, shortnecked, smallheaded man of about 30, with a small bullet head, a red nose, and furtive eyes. He is dressed in seedy black, almost clerically, and might be a tenth-rate schoolmaster ruined by drink. He hastens to shake Broadbent's hand with a show of reckless geniality and high spirits, helped out by a rollicking stage brogue. This is perhaps a comfort to himself, as he is secretly pursued by the horrors of incipient delirium tremens.

HAFFIGAN. Tim Haffigan, sir, at your service. The top o the mornin to you, Misther Broadbent.

BROADBENT [*delighted with his Irish visitor*] Good afternoon, Mr Haffigan.

TIM. An is it the afthernoon it is already? Begorra, what I call the mornin is all the time a man fasts afther breakfast.

BROADBENT. Havnt you lunched?

TIM. Divil a lunch!

BROADBENT. I'm sorry I couldnt get back from Brighton in time to offer you some; but –

TIM. Not a word, sir, not a word. Sure itll do tomorrow. Besides, I'm Irish, sir: a poor aither, but a powerful dhrinker.

BROADBENT. I was just about to ring for tea when you came. Sit down, Mr Haffigan.

TIM. Tay is a good dhrink if your nerves can stand it. Mine cant.

Haffigan sits down at the writing table, with his back to the filing cabinet. Broadbent sits opposite him. Hodson enters empty-handed; takes two glasses, a siphon, and a tantalus from the cupboard: places them before Broadbent on the writing table; looks ruthlessly at Haffigan, who cannot meet his eye; and retires.

BROADBENT. Try a whisky and soda.

TIM [*sobered*] There you touch the national wakeness, sir. [*Piously*] Not that I share it meself. Ive seen too much of the mischief of it.

BROADBENT [*pouring the whisky*] Say when.

TIM. Not too sthrong. [*Broadbent stops and looks inquiringly at him*]. Say half-an-half. [*Broadbent, somewhat startled by this demand, pours a little more, and again stops and looks*]. Just a dhrain more: the lower half o the tumber doesnt hold a fair half. Thankya.

BROADBENT [*laughing*] You Irishmen certainly know how to drink. [*Pouring some whisky for himself*] Now thats my poor English idea of a whisky and soda.

TIM. An a very good idea it is too. Dhrink is the curse o me unhappy counthry. I take it meself because Ive a wake heart and a poor digestion; but in principle I'm a teetoatler.

BROADBENT [*suddenly solemn and strenuous*] So am I, of course. I'm a Local Optionist to the backbone. You have no idea, Mr Haffigan, of the ruin that is wrought in this country by the unholy alliance of the publicans, the bishops, the Tories, and The Times. We must close the public-houses at all costs [*he drinks*].

TIM. Sure I know. It's awful [*he drinks*]. I see youre a good Liberal like meself, sir.

BROADBENT. I am a lover of liberty, like every true Englishman, Mr Haffigan. My name is Broadbent. If my name were Breitstein, and I had a hooked nose and a house in Park Lane, I should carry a Union Jack handkerchief and a penny trumpet, and tax the food of the people to support the Navy League, and clamor for the destruction of the last remnants of national liberty –

TIM. Not another word. Shake hands.

BROADBENT. But I should like to explain –

TIM. Sure I know every word youre goin to say before yev said it. *I* know the sort o man yar. An so youre thinkin o comin to Ireland for a bit?

BROADBENT. Where else can I go? I am an Englishman and a Liberal; and now that South Africa has been enslaved and destroyed, there is no country left to me to take an interest in but Ireland. Mind: I dont say that an Englishman has not other duties. He has a duty to Finland and a duty to Macedonia. But what sane man can deny that an Englishman's first duty is his duty to Ireland? Unfortunately, we have politicians here more unscrupulous than Bobrikoff, more bloodthirsty than Abdul the Damned; and it is under their heel that Ireland is now writhing.

TIM. Faith, theyve reckoned up with poor oul Bobrikoff anyhow.

BROADBENT. Not that I defend assassination: God forbid! However strongly we may feel that the unfortunate and patriotic young man who avenged the wrongs of Finland on the Russian tyrant was perfectly right from his own point of view, yet every civilized man must regard murder with abhorrence. Not even in defence of Free Trade would I lift my hand against a political opponent, however richly he might deserve it.

TIM. I'm sure you wouldnt; and I honor you for it. Youre goin to Ireland, then, out o sympithy: is it?

BROADBENT. I'm going to develop an estate there for the Land Development Syndicate, in which I am interested. I am convinced that all it needs to make it pay is to handle it properly, as estates are handled in England. You know the English plan, Mr Haffigan, dont you?

TIM. Bedad I do, sir. Take all you can out of Ireland and spend it in England: thats it.

BROADBENT [not quite liking this] My plan, sir, will be to take a little money out of England and spend it in Ireland.

TIM. More power to your elbow! an may your shadda never be less! for youre the broth of a boy entirely. An how can I help you? Command me to the last dhrop o me blood.

BROADBENT. Have you ever heard of Garden City?

TIM [doubtfully] D'ye mane heavn?

BROADBENT. Heaven! No: it's near Hitchin. If you can spare half an hour I'll go into it with you.

TIM. I tell you hwat. Gimme a prospectus. Lemmy take it home and reflect on it.

BROADBENT. Youre quite right: I will [He gives him a copy of Ebenezer Howard's book, and several pamphlets]. You understand that the map of the city – the circular construction – is only a suggestion.

TIM. I'll make a careful note o that [looking dazedly at the map].

BROADBENT. What I say is, why not start a Garden City in Ireland?

TIM [*with enthusiasm*] Thats just what was on the tip o me tongue to ask you. Why not? [*Defiantly*] Tell me why not.

BROADBENT. There are difficulties. I shall overcome them; but there are difficulties. When I first arrive in Ireland I shall be hated as an Englishman. As a Protestant, I shall be denounced from every altar. My life may be in danger. Well, I am prepared to face that.

TIM. Never fear, sir. We know how to respict a brave innimy.

BROADBENT. What I really dread is misunderstanding. I think you could help me to avoid that. When I heard you speak the other evening in Bermondsey at the meeting of the National League, I saw at once that you were – You wont mind my speaking frankly?

TIM. Tell me all me faults as man to man. I can stand anything but flatthery.

BROADBENT. May I put it in this way? that I saw at once that you are a thorough Irishman, with all the faults and all the qualities of your race: rash and improvident but brave and goodnatured; not likely to succeed in business on your own account perhaps, but eloquent, humorous, a lover of freedom, and a true follower of that great Englishman Gladstone.

TIM. Spare me blushes. I mustnt sit here to be praised to me face. But I confess to the goodnature: it's an Irish wakeness. I'd share me last shillin with a friend.

BROADBENT. I feel sure you would, Mr Haffigan.

TIM [*impulsively*] Damn it! call me Tim. A man that talks about Ireland as you do may call me anything. Gimmy a howlt o that whisky bottle [*he replenishes*].

BROADBENT [*smiling indulgently*] Well, Tim, will you come with me and help to break the ice between me and your warmhearted, impulsive countrymen?

TIM. Will I come to Madagascar or Cochin China wid you? Bedad I'll come to the North Pole wid you if yll pay me fare; for the divil a shillin I have to buy a third class ticket.

BROADBENT. Ive not forgotten that, Tim. We must put that little matter on a solid English footing, though the rest can be as Irish as you please. You must come as my – my – well, I hardly know what to call it. If we call you my agent, theyll shoot you. If we call you a bailiff, theyll duck you in the horsepond. I have a secretary already; and –

TIM. Then we'll call him the Home Secretary and me the Irish Secretary. Eh?

BROADBENT [*laughing industriously*] Capital. Your Irish wit has settled the first difficulty. Now about your salary –

TIM. A salary, is it? Sure I'd do it for nothin, only me cloes ud disgrace you; and I'd be dhriven to borra money from your friends: a thing thats agin me nacher. But I wont take a penny more than a hundherd a year. [*He looks with restless cunning at Broadbent, trying to guess how far he may go*].

BROADBENT. If that will satisfy you –

TIM [*more than reassured*] Why shouldnt it satisfy me? A hundherd a year is twelve pound a month, isnt it?

BROADBENT. No. Eight pound six and eightpence.

TIM. Oh murdher! An I'll have to sind five timmy poor oul mother in Ireland. But no matther: I said a hundherd; and what I said I'll stick to, if I have to starve for it.

BROADBENT [*with business caution*] Well, let us say twelve pounds for the first month. Afterwards, we shall see how we get on.

TIM. Youre a gentleman, sir. Whin me mother turns up her toes, you shall take the five pounds off; for your expinses must be kep down wid a sthrong hand; an – [*He is interrupted by the arrival of Broadbent's partner*].

Mr Laurence Doyle is a man of 36, with cold grey eyes, strained nose, fine fastidious lips, critical brows, clever head, rather refined and goodlooking on the whole, but with a suggestion of thinskinnedness and dissatisfaction that contrasts strongly with Broadbent's eupeptic jollity.

He comes in as a man at home there, but on seeing the stranger shrinks at once, and is about to withdraw when Broadbent reassures him. He then comes forward to the table, between the two others.

DOYLE [*retreating*] Youre engaged.

BROADBENT. Not at all, not at all. Come in. [*to Tim*] This gentleman is a friend who lives with me here: my partner, Mr Doyle. [*To Doyle*] This is a new Irish friend of mine, Mr Tim Haffigan.

TIM [*rising with effusion*] Sure it's meself thats proud to meet any friend o Misther Broadbent's. The top o the mornin to you, sir! Me heart goes out teeye both. It's not often I meet two such splendid speciments iv the Anglo-Saxon race.

BROADBENT [*chuckling*] Wrong for once, Tim. My friend Mr Doyle is a countryman of yours.

Tim is noticeably dashed by this announcement. He draws in his horns at once, and scowls suspiciously at Doyle under a vanishing mask of good-fellowship: cringing a little, too, in mere nerveless fear of him.

DOYLE [*with cool disgust*] Good evening. [*He retires to the fireplace, and says to Broadbent in a tone which conveys the strongest possible hint to Haffigan that he is unwelcome*] Will you soon be disengaged?

TIM [*his brogue decaying into a common would-be genteel accent with an unexpected strain of Glasgow in it*] I must be going. Avnmpoartnt engeegement in the west end.

BROADBENT [*rising*] It's settled, then, that you come with me.

TIM. Ashll be verra pleased to accompany ye, sir.

BROADBENT. But how soon? Can you start tonight? from Paddington? We go by Milford Haven.

TIM [*hesitating*] Well – A'm afraid – A [*Doyle goes abruptly into the bedroom, slamming the door and shattering the last remnant of Tim's nerve. The poor wretch saves himself from bursting into tears by plunging again into his role of daredevil Irishman. He rushes to Broadbent; plucks at his sleeve with trembling fingers; and pours forth his entreaty with all the brogue he can muster, subduing his voice lest Doyle should hear and return*]. Misther Broadbent: dont humiliate me before a fella counthryman. Look here: me cloes is up the spout. Gimmy a fypounnote – I'll pay ya nex Choosda whin me ship comes home – or you can stop it out o me month's sallery. I'll be on the platform at Paddnton punctial an ready. Gimmy it quick, before he comes back. You wont mind me axin, will ye?

BROADBENT. Not at all. I was about to offer you an advance for travelling expenses. [*He gives him a bank note*].

TIM [*pocketing it*] Thank you. I'll be there half an hour before the thrain starts. [*Larry is heard at the bedroom door, returning*]. Whisht: he's comin back. Goodbye and God bless ye. [*He hurries out almost crying, the £5 note and all the drink it means to him being too much for his empty stomach and overstrained nerves*].

DOYLE [*returning*] Where the devil did you pick up that seedy swindler? What was he doing here? [*He goes up to the table where the plans are, and makes a note on one of them, referring to his pocket book as he does so*].

BROADBENT. There you go! Why are you so down on every Irishman you meet, especially if he's a bit shabby? poor devil! Surely a fellow-countryman may pass you the top of the morning without offence, even if his coat is a bit shiny at the seams.

DOYLE [*contemptuously*] The top of the morning! Did he call you the broth of a boy? [*He comes to the writing table*].

BROADBENT [*triumphantly*] Yes.

DOYLE. And wished you more power to your elbow?

BROADBENT. He did.

DOYLE. And that your shadow might never be less?

BROADBENT. Certainly.

DOYLE [*taking up the depleted whisky bottle and shaking his head at it*] And he got about half a pint of whisky out of you.

BROADBENT. It did him no harm. He never turned a hair.

DOYLE. How much money did he borrow?

BROADBENT. It was not borrowing exactly. He shewed a very honorable spirit about money. I believe he would share his last shilling with a friend.

DOYLE. No doubt he would share his friend's last shilling if his friend was fool enough to let him. How much did he touch you for?

BROADBENT. Oh, nothing. An advance on his salary – for travelling expenses.

DOYLE. Salary! In Heaven's name, what for?

BROADBENT. For being my Home Secretary, as he very wittily called it.

DOYLE. I dont see the joke.

BROADBENT. You can spoil any joke by being cold blooded about it. I saw it all right when he said it. It was something – something really very amusing – about the Home Secretary and the Irish Secretary. At all events, he's evidently the very man to take with me to Ireland to break the ice for me. He can gain the confidence of the people there, and make them friendly to me. Eh? [*He seats himself on the office stool, and tilts it back so that the edge of the standing desk supports his back and prevents his toppling over*].

DOYLE. A nice introduction, by George! Do you suppose the whole population of Ireland consists of drunken begging letter writers, or that even if it did, they would accept one another as references?

BROADBENT. Pooh! nonsense! he's only an Irishman. Besides, you dont seriously suppose that Haffigan can humbug me, do you?

DOYLE. No: he's too lazy to take the trouble. All he has to do is to sit there and drink your whisky while you humbug yourself. However, we neednt argue about Haffigan, for two reasons. First, with your money in his pocket he will never reach Paddington: there are too many public houses on the way. Second, he's not an Irishman at all.

BROADBENT. Not an Irishman! [*He is so amazed by the statement that he straightens himself and brings the stool bolt upright*].

DOYLE. Born in Glasgow. Never was in Ireland in his life. I know all about him.

BROADBENT. But he spoke – he behaved just like an Irishman.

DOYLE. Like an Irishman!! Man alive, dont you know that all this top-o-the-morning and broth-of-a-boy and more-power-to-your-elbow business is got up in England to fool you, like the Albert Hall concerts of Irish music? No Irishman ever talks like that in Ireland, or ever did, or ever will. But when a thoroughly worthless Irishman comes to England, and finds the whole place full of romantic duffers like you, who will let him loaf and drink and sponge and brag as long as he flatters your sense of moral superiority by playing the fool and degrading himself and his country, he soon learns the antics that take you in. He picks them up at the theatre or the music hall. Haffigan learnt the rudiments from his father, who came from my part of Ireland. I knew his uncles, Matt and Andy Haffigan of Rosscullen.

BROADBENT [*still incredulous*] But his brogue?

DOYLE. His brogue! A fat lot you know about brogues! Ive heard you call a Dublin accent that you could hang your hat on, a brogue. Heaven help you! you dont know the difference between Connemara and Rathmines. [*With violent irritation*] Oh, damn Tim Haffigan! lets drop the subject: he's not worth wrangling about.

BROADBENT. Whats wrong with you today, Larry? Why are you so bitter? *Doyle looks at him perplexedly; comes slowly to the writing table; and sits down at the end next the fireplace before replying.*

DOYLE. Well: your letter completely upset me, for one thing.

BROADBENT. Why?

DOYLE. Your foreclosing this Rosscullen mortgage and turning poor Nick

Lestrange out of house and home has rather taken me aback; for I liked the old rascal when I was a boy and had the run of his park to play in. I was brought up on the property.

BROADBENT. But he wouldnt pay the interest. I had to foreclose on behalf of the Syndicate. So now I'm off to Rosscullen to look after the property myself. [*He sits down at the writing table opposite Larry, and adds, casually, but with an anxious glance at his partner*] Youre coming with me, of course?

DOYLE [*rising nervously and recommencing his restless movements*] Thats it. Thats what I dread. Thats what has upset me.

BROADBENT. But dont you want to see your country again after 18 years absence? to see your people? to be in the old home again? to –

DOYLE [*interrupting him very impatiently*] Yes, yes: I know all that as well as you do.

BROADBENT. Oh well, of course [*with a shrug*] if you take it in that way, I'm sorry.

DOYLE. Never you mind my temper: it's not meant for you, as you ought to know by this time. [*He sits down again, a little ashamed of his petulance; reflects a moment bitterly; then bursts out*] I have an instinct against going back to Ireland: an instinct so strong that I'd rather go with you to the South Pole than to Rosscullen.

BROADBENT. What! Here you are, belonging to a nation with the strongest patriotism! the most inveterate homing instinct in the world! and you pretend youd rather go anywhere than back to Ireland. You dont suppose I believe you, do you? In your heart –

DOYLE. Never mind my heart: an Irishman's heart is nothing but his imagination. How many of all those millions that have left Ireland have ever come back or wanted to come back? But whats the use of talking to you? Three verses of twaddle about the Irish emigrant 'sitting on the stile, Mary', or three hours of Irish patriotism in Bermondsey or the Scotland Division of Liverpool, go further with you than all the facts that stare you in the face. Why, man alive, look at me! You know the way I nag, and worry, and carp, and cavil, and disparage, and am never satisfied and never quiet, and try the patience of my best friends.

BROADBENT. Oh, come, Larry! do yourself justice. Youre very amusing and agreeable to strangers.

DOYLE. Yes, to strangers. Perhaps if I was a bit stiffer to strangers, and a bit easier at home, like an Englishman, I'd be better company for you.

BROADBENT. We get on well enough. Of course you have the melancholy of the Keltic race —

DOYLE [*bounding out of his chair*] Good God!!!

BROADBENT [*slyly*] — and also its habit of using strong language when theres nothing the matter.

DOYLE. Nothing the matter! When people talk about the Celtic race, I feel as if I could burn down London. That sort of rot does more harm than ten Coercion Acts. Do you suppose a man need be a Celt to feel melancholy in Rosscullen? Why, man, Ireland was peopled just as England was; and its breed was crossed by just the same invaders.

BROADBENT. True. All the capable people in Ireland are of English extraction. It has often struck me as a most remarkable circumstance that the only party in parliament which shews the genuine old English character and spirit is the Irish party. Look at its independence, its determination, its defiance of bad Governments, its sympathy with oppressed nationalities all the world over! How English!

DOYLE. Not to mention the solemnity with which it talks old fashioned nonsense which it knows perfectly well to be a century behind the times. Thats English, if you like.

BROADBENT. No, Larry, no. You are thinking of the modern hybrids that now monopolize England. Hypocrites, humbugs, Germans, Jews, Yankees, foreigners, Park Laners, cosmopolitan riffraff. Dont call them English. They dont belong to the dear old island, but to their confounded new empire; and by George! theyre worthy of it; and I wish them joy of it.

DOYLE [*unmoved by this outburst*] There! You feel better now, dont you?

BROADBENT [*defiantly*] I do. Much better.

DOYLE. My dear Tom, you only need a touch of the Irish climate to be as big a fool as I am myself. If all my Irish blood were poured into your veins, you wouldnt turn a hair of your constitution and character. Go and marry the most English Englishwoman you can find, and then bring up your son in Rosscullen; and that son's character will be so like mine and so unlike yours that everybody will accuse me of being the father. [*With sudden anguish*] Rosscullen! oh, good Lord, Rosscullen! The dullness! The hopelessness! the ignorance! the bigotry!

BROADBENT [*matter-of-factly*] The usual thing in the country, Larry. Just the same here.

DOYLE [*hastily*] No, no: the climate is different. Here, if the life is dull, you can be dull too, and no great harm done. [*Going off into a passionate dream*] But your wits cant thicken in that soft moist air, on those white springy roads, in those misty rushes and brown bogs, on those hillsides of granite rocks and magenta heather. Youve no such colors in the sky, no such lure in the distances, no such sadness in the evenings. Oh, the dreaming! the dreaming! the torturing, heart-scalding, never satisfying dreaming, dreaming, dreaming, dreaming! [*Savagely*] No debauchery that ever coarsened and brutalized an Englishman can take the worth and usefulness out of him like that dreaming. An Irishman's imagination never lets him alone, never convinces him, never satisfies him; but it makes him that he cant face reality nor deal with it nor handle it nor conquer it: he can only sneer at them that do, and [*bitterly, at Broadbent*] be 'agreeable to strangers', like a good-for-nothing woman on the streets. [*Gabbling at Broadbent across the table*] It's all dreaming, all imagination. He cant be religious. The inspired Churchman that teaches him the sanctity of life and the importance of conduct is sent away empty; while the poor village priest that gives him a miracle or a sentimental story of a saint, has cathedrals built for him out of the pennies of the poor. He cant be intelligently political: he dreams of what the Shan Van Vocht said in ninetyeight. If you want to interest him in Ireland youve got to call the unfortunate island Kathleen ni Hoolihan and pretend she's a little old woman. It saves thinking. It saves working. It saves everything except imagination, imagination, imagination; and imagination's such a torture that you cant bear it without whisky. [*With fierce shivering self-contempt*] At last you get that you can bear nothing real at all: youd rather starve than cook a meal; youd rather go shabby and dirty than set your mind to take care of your clothes and wash yourself; you nag and squabble at home because your wife isnt an angel, and she despises you because youre not a hero; and you hate the whole lot round you because theyre only poor slovenly useless devils like yourself. [*Dropping his voice like a man making some shameful confidence*] And all the while there goes on a horrible, senseless, mischievous laughter. When youre young, you exchange vile stories with them; and as youre too futile to be able to help or cheer them, you chaff and sneer and taunt them for not doing the things you darent do yourself. And all the time you laugh! laugh! laugh! eternal derision, eternal envy, eternal folly, eternal fouling and staining and degrading, until, when you come at last to a country where men take a question seriously and give a serious answer to it, you deride them for having no sense of humor, and plume yourself on your own worthlessness as if it made you better than them.

BROADBENT [*roused to intense earnestness by Doyle's eloquence*] Never despair, Larry. There are great possibilities for Ireland. Home Rule will work wonders under English guidance.

DOYLE [*pulled up short, his face twitching with a reluctant smile*] Tom: why do you select my most tragic moments for your most irresistible strokes of humor?

BROADBENT. Humor! I was perfectly serious. What do you mean? Do you doubt my seriousness about Home Rule?

DOYLE. I am sure you are serious, Tom, about the English guidance.

BROADBENT [*quite reassured*] Of course I am. Our guidance is the important thing. We English must place our capacity for government without stint at the service of nations who are less fortunately endowed in that respect; so as to allow them to develop in perfect freedom to the English level of self-government, you know. You understand me?

DOYLE. Perfectly. And Rosscullen will understand you too.

BROADBENT [*cheerfully*] Of course it will. So thats all right. [*He pulls up his chair and settles himself comfortably to lecture Doyle*]. Now Larry, Ive listened carefully to all youve said about Ireland; and I can see nothing whatever to prevent your coming with me. What does it all come to? Simply that you were only a young fellow when you were in Ireland. Youll find all that chaffing and drinking and not knowing what to be at in Peckham just the same as in Donnybrook. You looked at Ireland with a boy's eyes and saw only boyish things. Come back with me and look at it with a man's; and get a better opinion of your country.

DOYLE. I daresay youre partly right in that: at all events I know very well that if I had been the son of a laborer instead of the son of a country landagent, I should have struck more grit than I did. Unfortunately I'm not going back to visit the Irish nation, but to visit my father and Aunt Judy and Nora Reilly and Father Dempsey and the rest of them.

BROADBENT. Well, why not? Theyll be delighted to see you, now that England has made a man of you.

DOYLE [*struck by this*] Ah! you hit the mark there, Tom, with true British inspiration.

BROADBENT. Common sense, you mean.

DOYLE [*quickly*] No I dont: youve no more common sense than a gander. No Englishman has any common sense, or ever had, or ever will have. Youre going on a sentimental expedition for perfectly ridiculous reasons with your head full of political nonsense that would not take in any ordinarily intelligent donkey; but you can hit me in the eye with the simple truth about myself and my father.

BROADBENT [*amazed*] I never mentioned your father.

DOYLE [*not heeding the interruption*] There he is in Rosscullen, a landagent who's always been in a small way because he's a Catholic, and the landlords are mostly Protestants. What with land courts reducing rents and Land Purchase Acts turning big estates into little holdings, he'd be a beggar if he hadnt taken to collecting the new purchase instalments instead of the old rents. I doubt if he's been further from home than Athenmullet for twenty years. And here am I, made a man of, as you say, by England.

BROADBENT [*apologetically*] I assure you I never meant –

DOYLE. Oh, dont apologize: it's quite true. I daresay Ive learnt something in America and a few other remote and inferior spots; but in the main it is by living with you and working in double harness with you that I have learnt to live in a real world and not in an imaginary one. I owe more to you than to any Irishman.

BROADBENT [*shaking his head with a twinkle in his eye*] Very friendly of you, Larry, old man, but all blarney. I like blarney; but it's rot, all the same.

DOYLE. No it's not. I should never have done anything without you; though I never stop wondering at that blessed old head of yours with all its ideas in watertight compartments, and all the compartments warranted impervious to anything it doesnt suit you to understand.

BROADBENT [*invincible*] Unmitigated rot, Larry, I assure you.

DOYLE. Well, at any rate you will admit that all my friends are either Englishmen or men of the big world that belongs to the big Powers. All the serious part of my life has been lived in that atmosphere: all the

serious part of my work has been done with men of that sort. Just think
of me as I am now going back to Rosscullen! to that hell of littleness
and monotony! How am I to get on with a little country landagent that
ekes out his 5 per cent with a little farming and a scrap of house property
in the nearest country town? What am I to say to him? What is he to
say to me?

BROADBENT [*scandalized*] But youre father and son, man!

DOYLE. What difference does that make? What would you say if I proposed
a visit to your father?

BROADBENT [*with filial rectitude*] I always made a point of going to see my
father regularly until his mind gave way.

DOYLE [*concerned*] Has he gone mad? You never told me.

BROADBENT. He has joined the Tariff Reform League. He would never
have done that if his mind had not been weakened. [*Beginning
to declaim*] He has fallen a victim to the arts of a political charlatan
who –

DOYLE [*interrupting him*] You mean that you keep clear of your father
because he differs from you about Free Trade, and you dont want to
quarrel with him. Well, think of me and my father! He's a Nationalist
and a Separatist. I'm a metallurgical chemist turned civil engineer. Now
whatever else metallurgical chemistry may be, it's not national. It's
international. And my business and yours as civil engineers is to join
countries, not to separate them. The one real political conviction that
our business has rubbed into us is that frontiers are hindrances and flags
confounded nuisances.

BROADBENT [*still smarting under Mr Chamberlain's economic heresy*] Only
when there is a protective tariff –

DOYLE [*firmly*] Now look here, Tom: you want to get in a speech on Free
Trade; and youre not going to do it: I wont stand it. My father wants
to make St George's Channel a frontier and hoist a green flag on College
Green; and I want to bring Galway within 3 hours of Colchester and
24 of New York. I want Ireland to be the brains and imagination of a
big Commonwealth, not a Robinson Crusoe island. Then theres the
religious difficulty. My Catholicism is the Catholicism of Charlemagne
or Dante, qualified by a great deal of modern science and folklore which
Father Dempsey would call the ravings of an Atheist. Well, my father's
Catholicism is the Catholicism of Father Dempsey.

BROADBENT [*shrewdly*] I dont want to interrupt you, Larry; but you know this is all gammon. These differences exist in all families; but the members rub on together all right. [*Suddenly relapsing into portentousness*] Of course there are some questions which touch the very foundations of morals; and on these I grant you even the closest relationships cannot excuse any compromise or laxity. For instance –

DOYLE [*impatiently springing up and walking about*] For instance, Home Rule, South Africa, Free Trade, and putting the Church schools on the Education Rate. Well, I should differ from my father on every one of them, probably, just as I differ from you about them.

BROADBENT. Yes; but you are an Irishman; and these things are not serious to you as they are to an Englishman.

DOYLE. What! not even Home Rule!

BROADBENT [*steadfastly*] Not even Home Rule. We owe Home Rule not to the Irish, but to our English Gladstone. No, Larry: I cant help thinking that theres something behind all this.

DOYLE [*hotly*] What is there behind it? Do you think I'm humbugging you?

BROADBENT. Dont fly out, old chap. I only thought –

DOYLE. What did you think?

BROADBENT. Well, a moment ago I caught a name which is new to me: a Miss Nora Reilly, I think. [*Doyle stops dead and stares at him with something like awe*]. I dont wish to be impertinent, as you know, Larry; but are you sure she has nothing to do with your reluctance to come to Ireland with me?

DOYLE [*sitting down again, vanquished*] Thomas Broadbent: I surrender. The poor silly-clever Irishman takes off his hat to God's Englishman. The man who could in all seriousness make that recent remark of yours about Home Rule and Gladstone must be simply the champion idiot of all the world. Yet the man who could in the very next sentence sweep away all my special pleading and go straight to the heart of my motives must be a man of genius. But that the idiot and the genius should be the same man! how is that possible? [*Springing to his feet*] By Jove, I see it all now. I'll write an article about it, and send it to Nature.

BROADBENT [*staring at him*] What on earth –

DOYLE. It's quite simple. You know that a caterpillar –

BROADBENT. A caterpillar!!!

DOYLE. Yes, a caterpillar. Now give your mind to what I am going to say; for it's a new and important scientific theory of the English national character. A caterpillar –

BROADBENT. Look here, Larry: dont be an ass.

DOYLE [*insisting*] I say a caterpillar and I mean a caterpillar. Youll understand presently. A caterpillar [*Broadbent mutters a slight protest, but does not press it*] when it gets into a tree, instinctively makes itself look exactly like a leaf; so that both its enemies and its prey may mistake it for one and think it not worth bothering about.

BROADBENT. Whats that got to do with our English national character?

DOYLE. I'll tell you. The world is as full of fools as a tree is full of leaves. Well, the Englishman does what the caterpillar does. He instinctively makes himself look like a fool, and eats up all the real fools at his ease while his enemies let him alone and laugh at him for being a fool like the rest. Oh, nature is cunning! cunning! [*He sits down, lost in contemplation of his word-picture*].

BROADBENT [*with hearty admiration*] Now you know, Larry, that would never have occurred to me. You Irish people are amazingly clever. Of course it's all tommy rot; but it's so brilliant, you know! How the dickens do you think of such things! You really must write an article about it: they'll pay you something for it. If Nature wont have it, I can get it into Engineering for you: I know the editor.

DOYLE. Lets get back to business. I'd better tell you about Nora Reilly.

BROADBENT. No: never mind. I shouldnt have alluded to her.

DOYLE. I'd rather. Nora has a fortune.

BROADBENT [*keenly interested*] Eh? How much?

DOYLE. Forty per annum.

BROADBENT. Forty thousand?

DOYLE. No forty. Forty pounds.

BROADBENT [*much dashed*] Thats what you call a fortune in Rosscullen, is it?

DOYLE. A girl with a dowry of five pounds calls it a fortune in Rosscullen. Whats more, £40 a year is a fortune there; and Nora Reilly enjoys a good deal of social consideration as an heiress on the strength of it. It has helped my father's household through many a tight place. My father was her father's agent. She came on a visit to us when he died, and has lived with us ever since.

BROADBENT [*attentively, beginning to suspect Larry of misconduct with Nora, and resolving to get to the bottom of it*] Since when? I mean how old were you when she came?

DOYLE. I was seventeen. So was she: if she'd been older she'd have had more sense than to stay with us. We were together for 18 months before I went up to Dublin to study. When I went home for Christmas and Easter, she was there. I suppose it used to be something of an event for her; though of course I never thought of that then.

BROADBENT. Were you at all hard hit?

DOYLE. Not really. I had only two ideas at that time: first, to learn to do something; and then to get out of Ireland and have a chance of doing it. She didnt count. I was romantic about her, just as I was romantic about Byron's heroines or the old Round Tower of Rosscullen; but she didnt count any more than they did. Ive never crossed St George's Channel since for her sake – never even landed at Queenstown and come back to London through Ireland.

BROADBENT. But did you ever say anything that would justify her in waiting for you?

DOYLE. No, never. But she is waiting for me.

BROADBENT. How do you know?

DOYLE. She writes to me – on her birthday. She used to write on mine, and send me little things as presents; but I stopped that by pretending that it was no use when I was travelling, as they got lost in the foreign post-offices. [*He pronounces post-offices with the stress on offices, instead of on post*].

BROADBENT. You answer the letters?

DOYLE. Not very punctually. But they get acknowledged at one time or another.

BROADBENT. How do you feel when you see her handwriting?

DOYLE. Uneasy. I'd give £50 to escape a letter.

BROADBENT [*looking grave, and throwing himself back in his chair to intimate that the cross-examination is over, and the result very damaging to the witness*] Hm!

DOYLE. What d'ye mean by Hm!

BROADBENT. Of course I know that the moral code is different in Ireland. But in England it's not considered fair to trifle with a woman's affections.

DOYLE. You mean that an Englishman would get engaged to another woman and return Nora her letters and presents with a letter to say he was unworthy of her and wished her every happiness?

BROADBENT. Well, even that would set the poor girl's mind at rest.

DOYLE. Would it? I wonder! One thing I can tell you; and that is that Nora would wait until she died of old age sooner than ask my intentions or condescend to hint at the possibility of my having any. You dont know what Irish pride is. England may have knocked a good deal of it out of me; but she's never been in England; and if I had to choose between wounding that delicacy in her and hitting her in the face, I'd hit her in the face without a moment's hesitation.

BROADBENT [who has been nursing his knee and reflecting, apparently rather agreeably] You know, all this sounds rather interesting. Theres the Irish charm about it. Thats the worst of you: the Irish charm doesnt exist for you.

DOYLE. Oh yes it does. But it's the charm of a dream. Live in contact with dreams and you will get something of their charm: live in contact with facts and you will get something of their brutality. I wish I could find a country to live in where the facts were not brutal and the dreams not unreal.

BROADBENT [changing his attitude and responding to Doyle's earnestness with deep conviction: his elbows on the table and his hands clenched] Dont despair, Larry, old boy: things may look black; but there will be a great change after the next election.

DOYLE [jumping up] Oh, get out, you idiot!

BROADBENT [rising also, not a bit snubbed] Ha! Ha! you may laugh; but we shall see. However, dont let us argue about that. Come now! you ask my advice about Miss Reilly?

DOYLE [reddening] No I dont. Damn your advice! [Softening] Lets have it, all the same.

BROADBENT. Well, everything you tell me about her impresses me favorably. She seems to have the feelings of a lady; and though we must face the fact that in England her income would hardly maintain her in the lower middle class —

DOYLE [interrupting] Now look here, Tom. That reminds me. When you go to Ireland, just drop talking about the middle class and bragging of belonging to it. In Ireland youre either a gentleman or youre not. If you want to be particularly offensive to Nora, you can call her a Papist; but if you call her a middle-class woman, Heaven help you!

BROADBENT [*irrepressible*] Never fear. Youre all descended from the ancient kings: I know that. [*Complacently*] I'm not so tactless as you think, my boy. [*Earnest again*] I expect to find Miss Reilly a perfect lady; and I strongly advise you to come and have another look at her before you make up your mind about her. By the way, have you a photograph of her?

DOYLE. Her photographs stopped at twenty-five.

BROADBENT [*saddened*] Ah yes, I suppose so. [*With feeling, severely*] Larry: youve treated that poor girl disgracefully.

DOYLE. By George, if she only knew that two men were talking about her like this –!

BROADBENT. She wouldnt like it, would she? Of course not. We ought to be ashamed of ourselves, Larry. [*More and more carried away by his new fancy*]. You know, I have a sort of presentiment that Miss Reilly is a very superior woman.

DOYLE [*staring hard at him*] Oh! you have, have you?

BROADBENT. Yes I have. There is something very touching about the history of this beautiful girl.

DOYLE. Beau –! Oho! Heres a chance for Nora! and for me! [*Calling*] Hodson.

HODSON [*appearing at the bedroom door*] Did you call, sir?

DOYLE. Pack for me too. I'm going to Ireland with Mr Broadbent.

HODSON. Right sir. [*He retires into the bedroom*].

BROADBENT [*clapping Doyle on the shoulder*] Thank you, old chap. Thank you.

ACT II

Rosscullen. Westward a hillside of granite rock and heather slopes upward across the prospect from south to north. A huge stone stands on it in a naturally impossible place, as if it had been tossed up there by a giant. Over the brow, in the desolate valley beyond, is a round tower. A lonely white high road trending away westward past the tower loses itself at the foot of the far mountains. It is evening; and there are great breadths of silken green in the Irish sky. The sun is setting.

A man with the face of a young saint, yet with white hair and perhaps 50 years on his back, is standing near the stone in a trance of intense melancholy, looking over the hills as if by mere intensity of gaze he could pierce the glories of the sunset and see into the streets of heaven. He is dressed in black, and is rather more clerical in appearances than most English curates are nowadays; but he does not wear the collar and waistcoat of a parish priest. He is roused from his trance by the chirp of an insect from a tuft of grass in a crevice of the stone. His face relaxes; he turns quietly, and gravely takes off his hat to the tuft, addressing the insect in a brogue which is the jocular assumption of a gentleman and not the natural speech of a peasant.

THE MAN. An is that yourself, Misther Grasshopper? I hope I see you well this fine evenin.

THE GRASSHOPPER [*prompt and shrill in answer*] X.X.

THE MAN [*encouragingly*] Thats right. I suppose now youve come out to make yourself miserable be admyerin the sunset?

THE GRASSHOPPER [*sadly*] X.X.

THE MAN. Aye, youre a thrue Irish grasshopper.

THE GRASSHOPPER [*loudly*] X.X.X.

THE MAN. Three cheers for ould Ireland, is it? That helps you to face out the misery and the poverty and the torment, doesnt it?

THE GRASSHOPPER [*plaintively*] X.X.

THE MAN. Ah, it's no use, me poor little friend. If you could jump as far as a kangaroo you couldnt jump away from your own heart an its punishment. You can only look at Heaven from here: you cant reach it. There! [*pointing with his stick to the sunset*] thats the gate o' glory, isnt it?

THE GRASSHOPPER [*assenting*] X.X.

THE MAN. Sure it's the wise grasshopper yar to know that. But tell me this, Misther Unworldly Wiseman: why does the sight of Heaven wring your heart an mine as the sight of holy wather wrings the heart o the divil? What wickedness have you done to bring that curse on you? Here! where are you jumpin to? Wheres your manners to go skyrocketing like that out o the box in the middle o your confession [*he threatens it with his stick*]?

THE GRASSHOPPER [*penitently*] X.

THE MAN. [*lowering the stick*] I accept your apology; but dont do it again. And now tell me one thing before I let you go home to bed. Which would you say this country was: hell or purgatory?

THE GRASSHOPPER. X.

THE MAN. Hell! Faith I'm afraid youre right. I wondher what you and me did when we were alive to get sent here.

THE GRASSHOPPER [*shrilly*] X.X.

THE MAN [*nodding*] Well, as you say, it's a delicate subject; and I wont press it on you. Now off widja.

THE GRASSHOPPER. X.X. [*It springs away*].

THE MAN [*waving his stick*] God speed you! [*He walks away past the stone towards the brow of the hill. Immediately a young laborer, his face distorted with terror, slips round from behind the stone*].

THE LABORER [*crossing himself repeatedly*] Oh glory be to God! glory be to God! Oh Holy Mother an all the saints! Oh murdher! murdher! [*Beside himself, calling*] Fadher Keegan! Fadher Keegan!

THE MAN [*turning*] Who's there? What's that? [*He comes back and finds the laborer, who clasps his knees*] Patsy Farrell! What are you doing here?

PATSY. Oh for the love o God dont lave me here wi dhe grasshopper. I hard it spakin to you. Dont let it do me any harm, Father darlint.

KEEGAN. Get up, you foolish man, get up. Are you afraid of a poor insect because I pretended it was talking to me?

PATSY. Oh, it was no pretendin, Fadher dear. Didnt it give three cheers n say it was a divil out o hell? Oh say youll see me safe home, Fadher; n put a blessin on me or somethin [*he moans with terror*].

KEEGAN. What were you doin there, Patsy, listnin? Were you spyin on me?

PATSY. No, Fadher: on me oath an soul I wasnt: I was waitn to meet

Masther Larry n carry his luggage from the car; n I fell asleep on the grass; n you woke me talking to the grasshopper; n I hard its wicked little voice. Oh, d'ye think I'll die before year's out, Fadher?

KEEGAN. For shame, Patsy! Is that your religion, to be afraid of a little deeshy grasshopper? Suppose it was a divil, what call have you to fear it? If I could ketch it, I'd make you take it home widja in your hat for a penance.

PATSY. Sure, if you wont let it harm me, I'm not afraid, your riverence. [*He gets up, a little reassured. He is a callow, flaxen polled, smoothfaced, downy chinned lad, fully grown but not yet fully filled out, with blue eyes and an instinctively acquired air of helplessness and silliness, indicating, not his real character, but a cunning developed by his constant dread of a hostile dominance, which he habitually tries to disarm and tempt into unmasking by pretending to be a much greater fool than he really is. Englishmen think him half-witted, which is exactly what he intends them to think. He is clad in corduroy trousers, unbuttoned waistcoat, and coarse blue striped shirt*].

KEEGAN [*admonitorily*] Patsy: what did I tell you about callin me Father Keegan an your reverence? What did Father Dempsey tell you about it?

PATSY. Yis, Fadher.

KEEGAN. Father!

PATSY [*desperately*] Arra, hwat am I to call you? Fadher Dempsey sez youre not a priest; n we all know youre not a man: n how do we know what ud happen to us if we shewed any disrespect to you? N sure they say wanse a priest always a priest.

KEEGAN [*sternly*] It's not for the like of you, Patsy, to go behind the instruction of your parish priest and set yourself up to judge whether your Church is right or wrong.

PATSY. Sure I know that, sir.

KEEGAN. The Church let me be its priest as long as it thought me fit for its work. When it took away my papers it meant you to know that I was only a poor madman, unfit and unworthy to take charge of the souls of the people.

PATSY. But wasnt it only because you knew more Latn than Father Dempsey that he was jealous of you?

KEEGAN [*scolding him to keep himself from smiling*] How dar you, Patsy

Farrell, put your own wicked little spites and foolishnesses into the heart of your priest? For two pins I'd tell him what you just said.

PATSY [*coaxing*] Sure you wouldnt –

KEEGAN. Wouldnt I? God forgive you! youre little better than a heathen.

PATSY. Deedn I am, Fadher: it's me bruddher the tinsmith in Dublin youre thinkin of. Sure he had to be a free-thinker when he larnt a thrade and went to live in the town.

KEEGAN. Well, he'll get to Heaven before you if youre not careful, Patsy. And now you listen to me, once and for all. Youll talk to me and pray for me by the name of Pether Keegan, so you will. And when youre angry and tempted to lift your hand agen the donkey or stamp your foot on the little grasshopper, remember that the donkey's Pether Keegan's brother, and the grasshopper Pether Keegan's friend. And when youre tempted to throw a stone at a sinner or a curse at a beggar, remember that Pether Keegan is a worse sinner and a worse beggar, and keep the stone and the curse for him the next time you meet him. Now say God bless you, Pether, to me before I go, just to practise you a bit.

PATSY. Sure it wouldnt be right, Fadher, I cant –

KEEGAN. Yes you can. Now out with it; or I'll put this stick into your hand an make you hit me with it.

PATSY [*throwing himself on his knees in an ecstasy of adoration*] Sure it's your blessin I want, Fadher Keegan. I'll have no luck widhout it.

KEEGAN [*shocked*] Get up out o that, man. Dont kneel to me: I'm not a saint.

PATSY [*with intense conviction*] Oh in throth yar, sir. [*The grasshopper chirps. Patsy, terrified, clutches at Keegan's hands*] Dont set it on me, Fadher: I'll do anythin you bid me.

KEEGAN [*pulling him up*] You bosthoon, you! Dont you see that it only whistled to tell me Miss Reilly's comin? There! Look at her and pull yourself together for shame. Off widja to the road: youll be late for the car if you dont make haste [*bustling him down the hill*]. I can see the dust of it in the gap already.

PATSY. The Lord save us! [*He goes down the hill towards the road like a haunted man*].

Nora Reilly comes down the hill. A slight weak woman in a pretty muslin print gown (her best), she is a figure commonplace enough to Irish eyes; but on the inhabitants of fatter-fed, (crowded, hustling and bustling modern

countries she makes a very different impression. The absence of any symptoms
of coarseness or hardness or appetite in her, her comparative delicacy of
manner and sensibility of apprehension, her fine hands and frail figure, her
novel accent, with the caressing plaintive Irish melody of her speech, give her
a charm which is all the more effective because, being untravelled, she is
unconscious of it, and never dreams of deliberately dramatizing and exploiting
it, as the Irishwomen in England do. For Tom Broadbent therefore, an
attractive woman, whom he would even call ethereal. To Larry Doyle, an
everyday woman fit only for the eighteenth century, helpless, useless, almost
sexless, an invalid without the excuse of disease, an incarnation of everything
in Ireland that drove him out of it. These judgments have little value and
no finality; but they are the judgments on which her fate hangs just at present.
Keegan touches his hat to her: he does not take it off.

NORA. Mr Keegan: I want to speak to you a minute if you dont mind.

KEEGAN [*dropping the broad Irish vernacular of his speech to Patsy*] An hour
if you like, Miss Reilly: youre always welcome. Shall we sit down?

NORA. Thank you. [*They sit on the heather. She is shy and anxious; but she
comes to the point promptly because she can think of nothing else*]. They
say you did a gradle o travelling at one time.

KEEGAN. Well, you see I'm not a Mnooth man [*he means that he was not a
student at Maynooth College*]. When I was young I admired the older
generation of priests that had been educated in Salamanca. So when I
felt sure of my vocation I went to Salamanca. Then I walked from
Salamanca to Rome, an sted in a monastery there for a year. My
pilgrimage to Rome taught me that walking is a better way of travelling
than the train; so I walked from Rome to the Sorbonne in Paris; and
I wish I could have walked from Paris to Oxford; for I was very sick
on the sea. After a year of Oxford I had to walk to Jerusalem to walk
the Oxford feeling off me. From Jerusalem I came back to Patmos, and
spent six months at the monastery of Mount Athos. From that I came
to Ireland and settled down as a parish priest until I went mad.

NORA [*startled*] Oh dont say that.

KEEGAN. Why not? Dont you know the story? how I confessed a black man
and gave him absolution? and how he put a spell on me and drove me
mad?

NORA. How can you talk such nonsense about yourself? For shame!

KEEGAN. It's not nonsense at all: it's true – in a way. But never mind the black man. Now that you know what a travelled man I am, what can I do for you? [*She hesitates and plucks nervously at the heather. He stays her hand gently*]. Dear Miss Nora: dont pluck the little flower. If it was a pretty baby you wouldnt want to pull its head off and stick it in a vawse o water to look at. [*The grasshopper chirps: Keegan turns his head and addresses it in the vernacular*]. Be aisy, me son: she wont spoil the swing-swong in your little three. [*To Nora, resuming his urbane style*] You see I'm quite cracked; but never mind: I'm harmless. Now what is it?

NORA [*embarrassed*] Oh, only idle curiosity. I wanted to know whether you found Ireland – I mean the country part of Ireland, of course – very small and backwardlike when you came back to it from Rome and Oxford and all the great cities.

KEEGAN. When I went to those great cities I saw wonders I had never seen in Ireland. But when I came back to Ireland I found all the wonders there waiting for me. You see they had been there all the time; but my eyes had never been opened to them. I did not know what my own house was like, because I had never been outside it.

NORA. D'ye think thats the same with everybody?

KEEGAN. With everybody who has eyes in his soul as well as in his head.

NORA. But really and truly now, werent the people rather disappointing? I should think the girls must have seemed rather coarse and dowdy after the foreign princesses and people? But I suppose a priest wouldnt notice that.

KEEGAN. It's a priest's business to notice everything. I wont tell you all I noticed about women; but I'll tell you this. The more a man knows, and the farther he travels, the more likely he is to marry a country girl afterwards.

NORA [*blushing with delight*] Youre joking, Mr Keegan: I'm sure yar.

KEEGAN. My way of joking is to tell the truth. It's the funniest joke in the world.

NORA [*incredulous*] Galong with you!

KEEGAN [*springing up actively*] Shall we go down to the road and meet the car? [*She gives him her hand and he helps her up*]. Patsy Farrell told me you were expecting young Doyle.

NORA [*tossing her chin up at once*] Oh, I'm not expecting him particularly. It's a wonder he's come back at all. After staying away eighteen years he can harly expect us to be very anxious to see him: can he now?

KEEGAN. Well, not anxious perhaps; but you will be curious to see how much he's changed in all these years.

NORA [*with a sudden bitter flush*] I suppose thats all that brings him back to look at us just to see how much weve changed. Well, he can wait and see me by candlelight: I didnt come out to meet him: I'm going to walk to the Round Tower [*going west across the hill*].

KEEGAN. You couldnt do better this fine evening. [*Gravely*] I'll tell him where youve gone. [*She turns as if to forbid him; but the deep understanding in his eyes makes that impossible; and she only looks at him earnestly and goes. He watches her disappear on the other side of the hill; then says*] Aye, he's come to torment you; and youre driven already to torment him. [*He shakes his head, and goes slowly away across the hill in the opposite direction, lost in thought*].

By this time the car has arrived, and dropped three of its passengers on the high road at the foot of the hill. It is a monster jaunting car, black and dilapidated, one of the last survivors of the public vehicles known to earlier generations as Beeyankiny cars, the Irish having laid violent tongues on the name of their projector, one Bianconi, an enterprising Italian. The three passengers are the parish priest, Father Dempsey; Cornelius Doyle, Larry's father; and Broadbent, all in overcoats and as stiff as only an Irish car could make them.

The priest, stout and fatherly, falls far short of that finest type of countryside pastor which represents the genius of priesthood; but he is equally far above the base type in which a strongminded unscrupulous peasant uses the Church to extort money, power, and privilege. He is a priest neither by vocation nor ambition, but because the life suits him. He has boundless authority over his flock, and taxes them stiffly enough to be a rich man. The old Protestant ascendency is now too broken to gall him. On the whole, an easygoing, amiable, even modest man as long as his dues are paid and his authority and dignity fully admitted.

Cornelius Doyle is an elder of the small wiry type, with a hardskinned, rather worried face, clean shaven except for sandy whiskers blanching into a lustreless pale yellow and quite white at the roots. His dress is that of a country-town man of business: that is, an oldish shooting suit, with elastic sided boots quite unconnected with shooting. Feeling shy with Broadbent, he is hasty, which is his way of trying to appear genial.

Broadbent, for reasons which will appear later, has no luggage except a field glass and a guide book. The other two have left theirs to the unfortunate Patsy Farrell, who struggles up the hill after them, loaded with a sack of potatoes, a hamper, a fat goose, a colossal salmon, and several paper parcels.

Cornelius leads the way up the hill, with Broadbent at his heels. The priest follows. Patsy lags laboriously behind.

CORNELIUS. This is a bit of a climb, Mr Broadbent; but it's shorter than goin round be the road.

BROADBENT [*stopping to examine the great stone*] Just a moment, Mr Doyle: I want to look at this stone. It must be Finian's die-cast.

CORNELIUS [*in blank bewilderment*] Hwat?

BROADBENT. Murray describes it. One of your great national heroes – I cant pronounce the name – Finian Somebody, I think.

FATHER DEMPSEY [*also perplexed, and rather scandalized*] Is it Fin McCool you mean?

BROADBENT. I daresay it is. [*Referring to the guide book*] Murray says that a huge stone, probably of Druidic origin, is still pointed out as the die cast by Fin in his celebrated match with the devil.

CORNELIUS [*dubiously*] Jeuce a word I ever heard of it!

FATHER DEMPSEY [*very seriously indeed, and even a little severely*] Dont believe any such nonsense, sir. There never was any such thing. When people talk to you about Fin McCool and the like, take no notice of them. It's all idle stories and superstition.

BROADBENT [*somewhat indignantly; for to be rebuked by an Irish priest for superstition is more than he can stand*] You dont suppose I believe it, do you?

FATHER DEMPSEY. Oh, I thought you did. D'ye see the top of the Roun Tower there? thats an antiquity worth lookin at.

BROADBENT [*deeply interested*] Have you any theory as to what the Round Towers were for?

FATHER DEMPSEY [*a little offended*] A theory? Me! [*Theories are connected in his mind with the late Professor Tyndall, and with scientific scepticism generally: also perhaps with the view that the Round Towers are phallic symbols*].

CORNELIUS [*remonstrating*] Father Dempsey is the priest of the parish, Mr Broadbent. What would he be doing with a theory?

FATHER DEMPSEY [*with gentle emphasis*] I have a knowledge of what

the Round Towers were, if thats what you mean. They are the fore-
fingers of the early Church, pointing us all to God.

*Patsy, intolerably overburdened, loses his balance, and sits down involun-
tarily. His burdens are scattered over the hillside. Cornelius and Father
Dempsey turn furiously on him, leaving Broadbent beaming at the stone and
the tower with fatuous interest.*

CORNELIUS. Oh, be the hokey, the sammin's broke in two! You schoopid
ass, what d'ye mean?

FATHER DEMPSEY. Are you drunk, Patsy Farrell? Did I tell you to carry
that hamper carefully or did I not?

PATSY [*rubbing the back of his head, which has almost dinted a slab of granite*]
Sure me fut slipt. Howkn I carry three men's luggage at wanst?

FATHER DEMPSEY. You were told to leave behind what you couldnt
carry, an go back for it.

PATSY. An whose things was I to lave behind? Hwat would your reverence
think if I left your hamper behind in the wet grass; n hwat would the
masther say if I left the sammin and the goose be the side o the road
for annywan to pick up?

CORNELIUS. Oh, youve a dale to say for yourself, you butther-
fingered omadhaun. Waitll Ant Judy sees the state o that sammin:
she'll talk to you. Here! gimmy that birdn that fish there; an take
Father Dempsey's hamper to his house for him; n then come back for the
rest.

FATHER DEMPSEY. Do, Patsy. And mind you dont fall down again.

PATSY. Sure I –

CORNELIUS [*bustling him up the hill*] Whisht! heres Ant Judy. [*Patsy goes
grumbling in disgrace, with Father Dempsey's hamper*].

*Aunt Judy comes down the hill, a woman of 50, in no way remarkable, lively
and busy without energy or grip, placid without tranquillity, kindly without
concern for others: indeed without much concern for herself: a contented
product of a narrow, strainless life. She wears her hair parted in the middle
and quite smooth, with a flattened bun at the back. Her dress is a plain brown
frock, with a woollen pelerine of black and aniline mauve over her shoulders,
all very trim in honor of the occasion. She looks round for Larry; is puzzled;
then stares incredulously at Broadbent.*

AUNT JUDY. Surely to goodness thats not you, Larry!

CORNELIUS. Arra how could he be Larry, woman alive? Larry's in no hurry home, it seems. I havnt set eyes on him. This is his friend, Mr Broadbent. Mr Broadbent: me sister Judy.

AUNT JUDY [*hospitably: going to Broadbent and shaking hands heartily*] Mr Broadbent! Fancy me takin you for Larry! Sure we havn't seen a sight of him for eighteen years, n he ony a lad when he left us.

BROADBENT. It's not Larry's fault: he was to have been here before me. He started in our motor an hour before Mr Doyle arrived, to meet us at Athenmullet, intending to get here long before me.

AUNT JUDY. Lord save us! do you think he's had n axidnt?

BROADBENT. No: he's wired to say he's had a breakdown and will come on as soon as he can. He expects to be here at about ten.

AUNT JUDY. There now! Fancy him trustn himself in a motor and we all expectn him! Just like him! he'd never do anything like anybody else. Well, what cant be cured must be injoored. Come on in, all of you. You must be dyin for your tea, Mr Broadbent.

BROADBENT [*with a slight start*] Oh, I'm afraid it's too late for tea [*he looks at his watch*].

AUNT JUDY. Not a bit: we never have it airlier than this. I hope they gave you a good dinner at Athenmullet.

BROADBENT [*trying to conceal his consternation as he realizes that he is not going to get any dinner after his drive*] Oh – er – excellent, excellent. By the way, hadnt I better see about a room at the hotel? [*They stare at him*].

CORNELIUS. The hotel!

FATHER DEMPSEY. Hwat hotel?

AUNT JUDY. Indeedn youre not going to a hotel. Youll stay with us. I'd have put you into Larry's room, ony the boy's pallyass is too short for you; but we'll make a comfortable bed for you on the sofa in the parlor.

BROADBENT. Youre very kind, Miss Doyle; but really I'm ashamed to give you so much trouble unnecessarily. I shant mind the hotel in the least.

FATHER DEMPSEY. Man alive! theres no hotel in Rosscullen.

BROADBENT. No hotel! Why, the driver told me there was the finest hotel in Ireland here. [*They regard him joylessly*].

AUNT JUDY. Arra would you mind what the like of him would tell you? Sure he'd say hwatever was the least trouble to himself and the pleasantest to you, thinkin you might give him a thruppeny bit for himself or the like.

BROADBENT. Perhaps theres a public house.

FATHER DEMPSEY [*grimly*] Theres seventeen.

AUNT JUDY. Ah then, how could you stay at a public house? theyd have no place to put you even if it was a right place for you to go. Come! is it the sofa youre afraid of? If it is, you can have me own bed. I can sleep with Nora.

BROADBENT. Not at all: I should be only too delighted. But to upset your arrangements in this way —

CORNELIUS [*anxious to cut short the discussion, which makes him ashamed of his house; for he guesses Broadbent's standard of comfort a little more accurately than his sister does*] Thats all right; itll be no trouble at all. Hweres Nora?

AUNT JUDY. Oh, how do I know? She slipped out a little while ago: I thought she was going to meet the car.

CORNELIUS [*dissatisfied*] It's a queer thing of her to run out o the way at such a time.

AUNT JUDY. Sure she's a queer girl altogether. Come. Come in: come in.

FATHER DEMPSEY. I'll say good night, Mr Broadbent. If theres anything I can do for you in this parish, let me know. [*He shakes hands with Broadbent*].

BROADBENT [*effusively cordial*] Thank you, Father Dempsey. Delighted to have met you, sir.

FATHER DEMPSEY [*passing on to Aunt Judy*] Good night, Miss Doyle.

AUNT JUDY. Wont you stay to tea?

FATHER DEMPSEY. Not tonight, thank you kindly: I have business to do at home. [*He turns to go, and meets Patsy Farrell returning unloaded*]. Have you left that hamper for me?

PATSY. Yis, your reverence.

FATHER DEMPSEY. Thats a good lad [*going*].

PATSY [*to Aunt Judy*] Fadher Keegan sez —

FATHER DEMPSEY [*turning sharply on him*] Whats that you say?

PATSY [*frightened*] Fadher Keegan —

FATHER DEMPSEY. How often have you heard me bid you call Mister Keegan in his proper name, the same as I do? Father Keegan indeed! Cant you tell the difference between your priest and any ole madman in a black coat?

PATSY. Sure I'm afraid he might put a spell on me.

FATHER DEMPSEY [*wrathfully*] You mind what I tell you or I'll put a spell on you thatll make you lep. D'ye mind that now? [*He goes home*].

Patsy goes down the hill to retrieve the fish, the bird, and the sack.

AUNT JUDY. Ah, hwy cant you hold your tongue, Patsy, before Father Dempsey?

PATSY. Well, hwat was I to do? Father Keegan bid me tell you Miss Nora was gone to the Roun Tower.

AUNT JUDY. An hwy couldnt you wait to tell us until Father Dempsey was gone?

PATSY. I was afeerd o forgetn it; and then may be he'd a sent the grasshopper or the little dark looker into me at night to remind me of it. [*The dark looker is the common grey lizard, which is supposed to walk down the throats of incautious sleepers and cause them to perish in a slow decline*].

CORNELIUS. Yah, you great gaum, you! Widjer grasshoppers and dark lookers! Here: take up them things and let me hear no more o your foolish lip. [*Patsy obeys*]. You can take the sammin under your oxther. [*He wedges the salmon into Patsy's axilla*].

PATSY. I can take the goose too, sir. Put it on me back n gimmy the neck of it in me mouth. [*Cornelius is about to comply thoughtlessly*].

AUNT JUDY [*feeling that Broadbent's presence demands special punctilious-ness*] For shame, Patsy! to offer to take the goose in your mouth that we have to eat after you! The masterll bring it in for you.

PATSY. Arra what would a dead goose care for me mouth? [*He takes his load up the hill*].

CORNELIUS. Hwats Nora doin at the Roun Tower?

AUNT JUDY. Oh, the Lord knows! Romancin, I suppose. Praps she thinks Larry would go there to look for her and see her safe home.

BROADBENT. Miss Reilly must not be left to wait and walk home alone at night. Shall I go for her?

AUNT JUDY [*contemptuously*] Arra hwat ud happen to her? Hurry in now, Corny. Come, Mr Broadbent: I left the tea on the hob to draw; and itll be black if we dont go in and drink it.

They go up the hill. It is dusk by this time.

Broadbent does not fare so badly after all at Aunt Judy's board. He gets not only tea and bread-and-butter, but more mutton chops than he has ever conceived it possible to eat at one sitting. There is also a most filling substance called potato cake. Hardly have his fears of being starved been replaced by his first misgiving that he is eating too much and will be sorry for it tomorrow, when his appetite is revived by the production of a bottle of illicitly distilled whisky, called potcheen, which he has read and dreamed of (he calls it pottine) and is now at last to taste. His goodhumor rises almost to excitement before Cornelius shows signs of sleepiness. The contrast between Aunt Judy's table service and that of the south and east coast hotels at which he spends his Fridays-to-Tuesdays when he is in London, seems to him delightfully Irish. The almost total atrophy of any sense of enjoyment in Cornelius, or even any desire for it or toleration of the possibility of life being something better than a round of sordid worries, relieved by tobacco, punch, fine mornings, and petty successes in buying and selling, passes with his guest as the whimsical affectation of a shrewd Irish humorist and incorrigible spendthrift. Aunt Judy seems to him an incarnate joke. The likelihood that the joke will pall after a month or so, and is probably not apparent at any time to born Rossculleners, or that he himself unconsciously entertains Aunt Judy by his fantastic English personality and English mispronunciations, does not occur to him for a moment. In the end he is so charmed, and so loth to go to bed and perhaps dream of prosaic England, that he insists on going out to smoke a cigar and look for Nora Reilly at the Round Tower. Not that any special insistence is needed; for the English inhibitive instinct does not seem to exist in Rosscullen. Just as Nora's liking to miss a meal and stay out at the Round Tower is accepted as a sufficient reason for her doing it, and for the family going to bed and leaving the door open for her, so Broadbent's whim to go out for a late stroll provokes neither hospitable remonstrance nor surprise. Indeed Aunt Judy wants to get rid of him whilst she makes a bed for him on the sofa. So off he goes, full fed, happy and enthusiastic, to explore the valley by moonlight.

The Round Tower stands about half an Irish mile from Rosscullen, some fifty yards south of the road on a knoll with a circle of wild greensward on it. The road once ran over this knoll; but modern engineering has tempered the level to the Beeyankiny car by carrying the road partly round the knoll and partly through a cutting; so that the way from the road to the tower is a footpath up the embankment through furze and brambles.

On the edge of this slope, at the top of the path, Nora is straining her eyes in the moonlight, watching for Larry. At last she gives it up with a sob of impatience, and retreats to the hoary foot of the tower, where she sits down discouraged and cries a little. Then she settles herself resignedly to wait, and hums a song – not an Irish melody, but a hackneyed English drawing room

ballad of the season before last — until some slight noise suggests a footstep,
when she springs up eagerly and runs to the edge of the slope again. Some
moments of silence and suspense follow, broken by unmistakable footsteps. She
gives a little gasp as she sees a man approaching.

NORA. Is that you, Larry? [*Frightened a little*] Who's that?

BROADBENT'S *voice from below her on the path.* Dont be alarmed.

NORA. Oh, what an English accent youve got!

BROADBENT [*rising into view*] I must introduce myself —

NORA [*violently startled, retreating*] It's not you! Who are you? What do you want?

BROADBENT [*Advancing*] I'm really so sorry to have alarmed you, Miss Reilly. My name is Broadbent. Larry's friend, you know.

NORA [*chilled*] And has Mr Doyle not come with you?

BROADBENT. No. Ive come instead. I hope I am not unwelcome.

NORA [*deeply mortified*] I'm sorry Mr Doyle should have given you the trouble, I'm sure.

BROADBENT. You see, as a stranger and an Englishman, I thought it would be interesting to see the Round Tower by moonlight.

NORA. Oh, you came to see the tower. I thought — [*confused, trying to recover her manners*] Oh, of course. I was so startled. It's a beautiful night, isnt it?

BROADBENT. Lovely. I must explain why Larry has not come himself.

NORA. Why should he come? He's seen the tower often enough: it's no attraction to him [*Genteelly*] An what do you think of Ireland, Mr Broadbent? Have you ever been here before?

BROADBENT. Never.

NORA. An how do you like it?

BROADBENT [*suddenly betraying a condition of extreme sentimentality*] I can hardly trust myself to say how much I like it. The magic of this Irish scene, and — I really dont want to be personal, Miss Reilly; but the charm of your Irish voice —

NORA [*quite accustomed to gallantry, and attaching no seriousness whatever to it*] Oh, get along with you, Mr Broadbent! Youre breaking your heart about me already, I daresay, after seeing me for two minutes in the dark.

BROADBENT. The voice is just as beautiful in the dark you know. Besides, Ive heard a great deal about you from Larry.

NORA [*with bitter indifference*] Have you now? Well, thats a great honor, I'm sure.

BROADBENT. I have looked forward to meeting you more than to anything else in Ireland.

NORA [*ironically*] Dear me! did you now?

BROADBENT. I did really. I wish you had taken half as much interest in me.

NORA. Oh, I was dying to see you, of course. I daresay you can imagine the sensation an Englishman like you would make among us poor Irish people.

BROADBENT. Ah, now youre chaffing me, Miss Reilly: you know you are. You mustnt chaff me. I'm very much in earnest about Ireland and everything Irish. I'm very much in earnest about you and about Larry.

NORA. Larry has nothing to do with me, Mr Broadbent.

BROADBENT. If I really thought that, Miss Reilly, I should – well, I should let myself feel that charm of which I spoke just now more deeply than I – than I –

NORA. Is it making love to me you are?

BROADBENT [*scared and much upset*] On my word I believe I am, Miss Reilly. If you say that to me again I shant answer for myself: all the harps of Ireland are in your voice. [*She laughs at him. He suddenly loses his head and seizes her arms, to her great indignation*]. Stop laughing: do you hear? I am in earnest: in English earnest. When I say a thing like that to a woman, I mean it. [*Releasing her and trying to recover his ordinary manner in spite of his bewildering emotion*] I beg your pardon.

NORA. How dare you touch me?

BROADBENT. There are not many things I would not dare for you. That does not sound right perhaps; but I really – [*he stops and passes his hand over his forehead, rather lost*].

NORA. I think you ought to be ashamed. I think if you were a gentleman, and me alone with you in this place at night, you would die rather than do such a thing.

BROADBENT. You mean that it's an act of treachery to Larry?

NORA. Deed I dont. What has Larry to do with it? It's an act of disrespect and rudeness to me: it shews what you take me for. You can go your way now; and I'll go mine. Good night, Mr Broadbent.

BROADBENT. No, please, Miss Reilly. One moment. Listen to me. I'm serious: I'm desperately serious. Tell me that I'm interfering with

Larry; and I'll go straight from this spot back to London and never see you again. Thats on my honor: I will. Am I interfering with him?

NORA [*answering in spite of herself in a sudden spring of bitterness*] I should think you ought to know better than me whether youre interfering with him. Youve seen him oftener than I have. You know him better than I do, by this time. Youve come to me quicker than he has, havnt you?

BROADBENT. I'm bound to tell you, Miss Reilly, that Larry has not arrived in Rosscullen yet. He meant to get here before me; but his car broke down; and he may not arrive until tomorrow.

NORA [*her face lighting up*] Is that the truth?

BROADBENT. Yes: thats the truth. [*She gives a sigh of relief*]. Youre glad of that?

NORA [*up in arms at once*] Glad indeed! Why should I be glad? As weve waited eighteen years for him we can afford to wait a day longer, I should think.

BROADBENT. If you really feel like that about him, there may be a chance for another man yet. Eh?

NORA [*deeply offended*] I suppose people are different in England, Mr Broadbent; so perhaps you dont mean any harm. In Ireland nobody'd mind what a man'd say in fun, nor take advantage of what a woman might say in answer to it. If a woman couldnt talk to a man for two minutes at their first meeting without being treated the way youre treating me, no decent woman would ever talk to a man at all.

BROADBENT. I dont understand that. I dont admit that. I am sincere; and my intentions are perfectly honorable. I think you will accept the fact that I'm an Englishman as a guarantee that I am not a man to act hastily or romantically; though I confess that your voice had such an extraordinary effect on me just now when you asked me so quaintly whether I was making love to you –

NORA [*flushing*] I never thought –

BROADBENT [*quickly*] Of course you didnt: I'm not so stupid as that. But I couldnt bear your laughing at the feeling it gave me. You – [*again struggling with a surge of emotion*] you dont know what I – [*he chokes for a moment and then blurts out with unnatural steadiness*] Will you be my wife?

NORA [*promptly*] Deed I wont. The idea! [*Looking at him more carefully*] Arra, come home, Mr Broadbent; and get your senses back again. I think youre not accustomed to potcheen punch in the evening after your tea.

BROADBENT [*horrified*] Do you mean to say that I – I – I – my God! that I appear drunk to you, Miss Reilly?

NORA [*compassionately*] How many tumblers had you?

BROADBENT [*helplessly*] Two.

NORA. The flavor of the turf prevented you noticing the strength of it. Youd better come home to bed.

BROADBENT [*fearfully agitated*] But this is such a horrible doubt to put into my mind – to – to – For Heaven's sake, Miss Reilly, am I really drunk?

NORA [*soothingly*] Youll be able to judge better in the morning. Come on now back with me, an think no more about it. [*She takes his arm with motherly solicitude and urges him gently towards the path*].

BROADBENT [*yielding in despair*] I must be drunk: frightfully drunk; for your voice drove me out of my senses – [*he stumbles over a stone*]. No: on my word, on my most sacred word of honor, Miss Reilly, I tripped over that stone. It was an accident: it was indeed.

NORA. Yes, of course it was. Just take my arm, Mr Broadbent, while we're going down the path to the road. Youll be all right then.

BROADBENT [*submissively taking it*] I cant sufficiently apologize, Miss Reilly, or express my sense of your kindness when I am in such a disgusting state. How could I be such a bea – [*he trips again*] damn the heather! my foot caught in it.

NORA. Steady now, steady. Come along: come. [*He is led down to the road in the character of a convicted drunkard. To him there is something divine in the sympathetic indulgence she substitutes for the angry disgust with which one of his own countrywomen would resent his supposed condition. And he has no suspicion of the fact, or of her ignorance of it, that when an Englishman is sentimental he behaves very much as an Irishman does when he is drunk*].

ACT III

*Next morning Broadbent and Larry are sitting at the ends of a breakfast
table in the middle of a small grass plot before Cornelius Doyle's house. They
have finished their meal, and are buried in newspapers. Most of the crockery
is crowded upon a large square black tray of japanned metal. The teapot
is of brown delft ware. There is no silver; and the butter, on a dinner plate,
is en bloc. The background to this breakfast is the house, a small white slated
building, accessible by a half-glazed door. A person coming out into the garden
by this door would find the table straight in front of him, and a gate leading
to the road half-way down the garden on his right; or, if he turned sharp
to his left, he could pass round the end of the house through an unkempt
shrubbery. The mutilated remnant of a huge plaster statue, nearly dissolved
by the rains of a century, and vaguely resembling a majestic female in Roman
draperies, with a wreath in her hand, stands neglected amid the laurels. Such
statues, though apparently works of art, grow naturally in Irish gardens.
Their germination is a mystery to the oldest inhabitants, to whose means
and tastes they are totally foreign.*

*There is a rustic bench, much soiled by the birds, and decorticated and
split by the weather, near the little gate. At the opposite side, a basket lies
unmolested because it might as well be there as anywhere else. An empty
chair at the table was lately occupied by Cornelius, who has finished his
breakfast and gone into the room in which he receives rents and keeps his
books and cash, known in the household as 'the office'. This chair, like the
two occupied by Larry and Broadbent, has a mahogany frame and is up-
holstered in black horsehair.*

*Larry rises and goes off through the shrubbery with his newspaper. Hodson
comes in through the garden gate, disconsolate. Broadbent, who sits facing
the gate, augurs the worst from his expression.*

BROADBENT. Have you been to the village?

HODSON. No use, sir. We'll have to get everything from London by
parcel post.

BROADBENT. I hope they made you comfortable last night.

HODSON. I was no worse than you were on that sofa, sir. One expects to rough it here, sir.

BROADBENT. We shall have to look out for some other arrangement. [*Cheering up irrepressibly*] Still, it's no end of a joke. How do you like the Irish, Hodson?

HODSON. Well, sir, theyre all right anywhere but in their own country. Ive known lots of em in England, and generally liked em. But here, sir, I seem simply to hate em. The feeling come over me the moment we landed at Cork, sir. It's no use my pretendin, sir: I cant bear em. My mind rises up agin their ways, somehow: they rub me the wrong way all over.

BROADBENT. Oh, their faults are on the surface: at heart they are one of the finest races on earth. [*Hodson turns away, without affecting to respond to his enthusiasm*]. By the way, Hodson —

HODSON [*turning*] Yes, sir.

BROADBENT. Did you notice anything about me last night when I came in with that lady?

HODSON [*surprised*] No, sir.

BROADBENT. Not any — er —? You may speak frankly.

HODSON. I didnt notice nothing, sir. What sort of thing did you mean, sir?

BROADBENT. Well — er — er — well, to put it plainly, was I drunk?

HODSON [*amazed*] No, sir.

BROADBENT. Quite sure?

HODSON. Well, I should a said rather the opposite, sir. Usually when youve been enjoying yourself, youre a bit hearty like. Last night you seemed rather low, if anything.

BROADBENT. I certainly have no headache. Did you try the pottine, Hodson?

HODSON. I just took a mouthful, sir. It tasted of peat: oh! something horrid, sir. The people here call peat turf. Potcheen and strong porter is what they like, sir. I'm sure I dont know how they can stand it. Give me beer, I say.

BROADBENT. By the way, you told me I couldnt have porridge for breakfast; but Mr Doyle had some.

HODSON. Yes, sir. Very sorry, sir. They call it stirabout, sir: thats how it was. They know no better, sir.

BROADBENT. All right: I'll have some tomorrow.

Hodson goes to the house. When he opens the door he finds Nora and Aunt Judy on the threshold. He stands aside to let them pass, with the air of a well trained servant oppressed by heavy trials. Then he goes in. Broadbent rises. Aunt Judy goes to the table and collects the plates and cups on the tray. Nora goes to the back of the rustic seat and looks out at the gate with the air of a woman accustomed to have nothing to do. Larry returns from the shrubbery.

BROADBENT. Good morning, Miss Doyle.

AUNT JUDY [*thinking it absurdly late in the day for such a salutation*] Oh, good morning. [*Before moving his plate*] Have you done?

BROADBENT. Quite, thank you. You must excuse us for not waiting for you. The country air tempted us to get up early.

AUNT JUDY. N d'ye call this airly, God help you?

LARRY. Aunt Judy probably breakfasted about half past six.

AUNT JUDY. Whisht, you! draggin the parlor chairs out into the gardn n giving Mr Broadbent his death over his meals out here in the cold air. [*To Broadbent*] Why d'ye put up with his foolishness, Mr Broadbent?

BROADBENT. I assure you I like the open air.

AUNT JUDY. Ah galong! How can you like whats not natural? I hope you slept well.

NORA. Did anything wake yup with a thump at three o'clock? I thought the house was falling. But then I'm a very light sleeper.

LARRY. I seem to recollect that one of the legs of the sofa in the parlor had a way of coming out unexpectedly eighteen years ago. Was that it, Tom?

BROADBENT [*hastily*] Oh, it doesnt matter: I was not hurt – at least – er –

AUNT JUDY. Oh now what a shame! An I told Patsy Farrll to put a nail in it.

BROADBENT. He did, Miss Doyle. There was a nail, certainly.

AUNT JUDY. Dear oh dear!

An oldish peasant farmer, small, leathery, peat-faced, with a deep voice and a surliness that is meant to be aggressive, and is in effect pathetic – the voice of a man of hard life and many sorrows – comes in at the gate. He is old enough to have perhaps worn a long tailed frieze coat and knee breeches in his time; but now he is dressed respectably in a black frock coat, tall hat, and pollard colored trousers; and his face is as clean as washing can make it, though that is not saying much, as the habit is recently acquired and not yet congenial.

THE NEW-COMER [*at the gate*] God save all here! [*He comes a little way into the garden*].

LARRY [*patronizingly, speaking across the garden to him*] Is that yourself, Matt Haffigan? Do you remember me?

MATTHEW [*intentionally rude and blunt*] No. Who are you?

NORA. Oh, I'm sure you remember him, Mr Haffigan.

MATTHEW [*grudgingly admitting it*] I suppose he'll be young Larry Doyle that was.

LARRY. Yes

MATTHEW [*to Larry*] I hear you done well in America.

LARRY. Fairly well.

MATTHEW. I suppose you saw me brother Andy out dhere.

LARRY. No. It's such a big place that looking for a man there is like looking for a needle in a bundle of hay. They tell me he's a great man out there.

MATTHEW. So he is, God be praised. Wheres your father?

AUNT JUDY. He's inside, in the office, Mr Haffigan, with Barney Doarn n Father Dempsey.

Matthew, without wasting further words on the company, goes curtly into the house.

LARRY [*staring after him*] Is anything wrong with old Matt?

NORA. No. He's the same as ever. Why?

LARRY. He's not the same to me. He used to be very civil to Masther Larry: a deal too civil, I used to think. Now he's as surly and stand-off as a bear.

AUNT JUDY. Oh sure he's bought his farm in the Land Purchase. He's independent now.

NORA. It's made a great change, Larry. Youd harly know the old tenants now. Youd think it was a liberty to speak t'dhem — some o dhem. [*She goes to the table, and helps to take off the cloth, which she and Aunt Judy fold up between them*].

AUNT JUDY. I wonder what he wants to see Corny for. He hasnt been here since he paid the last of his old rent; and then he as good as threw it in Corny's face, I thought.

LARRY. No wonder! Of course they all hated us like the devil. Ugh! [*Moodily*] Ive seen them in that office, telling my father what a fine boy I was, and plastering him with compliments, with your honor here and your honor there, when all the time their fingers were itching to be at his throat.

AUNT JUDY. Deedn why should they want to hurt poor Corny? It was he that got Matt the lease of his farm, and stood up for him as an industrious decent man.

BROADBENT. Was he industrious? Thats remarkable, you know, in an Irishman.

LARRY. Industrious! That man's industry used to make me sick, even as a boy. I tell you, an Irish peasant's industry is not human: it's worse than the industry of a coral insect. An Englishman has some sense about working: he never does more than he can help — and hard enough to get him to do that without scamping it; but an Irishman will work as if he'd die the moment he stopped. That man Matthew Haffigan and his brother Andy made a farm out of a patch of stones on the hillside: cleared it and dug it with their own naked hands and bought their first spade out of their first crop of potatoes. Talk of making two blades of wheat grow where one grew before! those two men made a whole field of wheat grow where not even a furze bush had ever got its head up between the stones.

BROADBENT. That was magnificent, you know. Only a great race is capable of producing such men.

LARRY. Such fools, you mean! What good was it to them? The moment theyd done it, the landlord put a rent of £5 a year on them, and turned them out because they couldnt pay it.

AUNT JUDY. Why couldnt they pay as well as Billy Byrne that took it after them?

LARRY [*angrily*] You know very well that Billy Byrne never paid it. He only offered it to get possession. He never paid it.

AUNT JUDY. That was because Andy Haffigan hurt him with a brick so that he was never the same again. Andy had to run away to America for it.

BROADBENT [*glowing with indignation*] Who can blame him, Miss Doyle? Who can blame him?

LARRY [*impatiently*] Oh, rubbish! whats the good of the man thats starved

out of a farm murdering the man thats starved into it? Would you
have done such a thing?

BROADBENT. Yes. I – I – I – I – [*stammering with fury*] I should have
shot the confounded landlord, and wrung the neck of the damned agent,
and blown the farm up with dynamite, and Dublin Castle along with
it.

LARRY. Oh yes: youd have done great things; and a fat lot of good youd
have got out of it, too! Thats an Englishman all over! make bad laws
and give away all the land, and then, when your economic incompetence
produces its natural and inevitable results, get virtuously indignant
and kill the people that carry out your laws.

AUNT JUDY. Sure never mind him, Mr Broadbent. It doesnt matter,
anyhow, because theres harly any landlords left; and therll soon be
none at all.

LARRY. On the contrary, therll soon be nothing else; and the Lord help
Ireland then!

AUNT JUDY. Ah, youre never satisfied, Larry. [*To Nora*] Come on,
alanna, an make the paste for the pie. We can leave them to their
talk. They dont want us [*she takes up the tray and goes into the house*].

BROADBENT [*rising and gallantly protesting*] Oh, Miss Doyle! Really,
really –

*Nora, following Aunt Judy with the rolled-up cloth in her hands, looks
at him and strikes him dumb. He watches her until she disappears; then comes
to Larry and addresses him with sudden intensity.*

BROADBENT. Larry.

LARRY. What is it?

BROADBENT. I got drunk last night, and proposed to Miss Reilly.

LARRY. You hwat??? [*He screams with laughter in the falsetto Irish
register unused for that purpose in England*].

BROADBENT. What are you laughing at?

LARRY [*stopping dead*] I dont know. Thats the sort of thing an Irishman
laughs at. Has she accepted you?

BROADBENT. I shall never forget that with the chivalry of her nation,
though I was utterly at her mercy, she refused me.

LARRY. That was extremely improvident of her. [*Beginning to reflect*]
But look here: when were you drunk? You were sober enough when
you came back from the Round Tower with her.

BROADBENT. No, Larry, I was drunk, I am sorry to say. I had two tumblers of punch. She had to lead me home. You must have noticed it.

LARRY. I did not.

BROADBENT. She did.

LARRY. May I ask how long it took you to come to business? You can hardly have known her for more than a couple of hours.

BROADBENT. I am afraid it was hardly a couple of minutes. She was not here when I arrived; and I saw her for the first time at the tower.

LARRY. Well, you are a nice infant to be let loose in this country! Fancy the potcheen going to your head like that!

BROADBENT. Not to my head, I think. I have no headache; and I could speak distinctly. No: potcheen goes to the heart, not to the head. What ought I to do?

LARRY. Nothing. What need you do?

BROADBENT. There is rather a delicate moral question involved. The point is, was I drunk enough not to be morally responsible for my proposal? Or was I sober enough to be bound to repeat it now that I am undoubtedly sober?

LARRY. I should see a little more of her before deciding.

BROADBENT. No, no. That would not be right. That would not be fair. I am either under a moral obligation or I am not. I wish I knew how drunk I was.

LARRY. Well, you were evidently in a state of blithering sentimentality, anyhow.

BROADBENT. That is true, Larry: I admit it. Her voice has a most extraordinary effect on me. That Irish voice!

LARRY [sympathetically] Yes, I know. When I first went to London I very nearly proposed to walk out with a waitress in an Aerated Bread shop because her Whitechapel accent was so distinguished, so quaintly touching, so pretty –

BROADBENT [angrily] Miss Reilly is not a waitress, is she?

LARRY. Oh, come! The waitress was a very nice girl.

BROADBENT. You think every Englishwoman an angel. You really have coarse tastes in that way, Larry. Miss Reilly is one of the finer types: a type rare in England, except perhaps in the best of the aristocracy.

LARRY. Aristocracy be blowed! Do you know what Nora eats?

BROADBENT. Eats! what do you mean?

LARRY. Breakfast: tea and bread-and-butter, with an occasional rasher, and an egg on special occasions: say on her birthday. Dinner in the middle of the day, one course and nothing else. In the evening, tea and bread-and-butter again. You compare her with your English-women who wolf down from three to five meat meals a day; and naturally you find her a sylph. The difference is not a difference of type: it's the difference between the woman who eats not wisely but too well, and the woman who eats not wisely but too little.

BROADBENT [*furious*] Larry: you – you – you disgust me. You are a damned fool. [*He sits down angrily on the rustic seat, which sustains the shock with difficulty*].

LARRY. Steady! stead-eee! [*He laughs and seats himself on the table*].

Cornelius Doyle, Father Dempsey, Barney Doran, and Matthew Haffigan come from the house. Doran is a stout bodied, short armed, roundheaded, red haired man on the verge of middle age, of sanguine temperament, with an enormous capacity for derisive, obscene, blasphemous, or merely cruel and senseless fun, and a violent and impetuous intolerance of other temperaments and other opinions, all this representing energy and capacity wasted and demoralized by want of sufficient training and social pressure to force it into beneficent activity and build a character with it; for Barney is by no means either stupid or weak. He is recklessly untidy as to his person; but the worst effects of his neglect are mitigated by a powdering of flour and mill dust; and his unbrushed clothes, made of a fashionable tailor's sack-cloth, were evidently chosen regardless of expense for the sake of their appearance.

Matthew Haffigan, ill at ease, coasts the garden shyly on the shrubbery side until he anchors near the basket, where he feels least in the way. The priest comes to the table and slaps Larry on the shoulder. Larry, turning quickly, and recognizing Father Dempsey, alights from the table and shakes the priest's hand warmly. Doran comes down the garden between Father Dempsey and Matt; and Cornelius, on the other side of the table, turns to Broadbent, who rises genially.

CORNELIUS. I think we all met last night.

DORAN. I hadnt that pleasure.

CORNELIUS. To be sure, Barney: I forgot. [*To Broadbent, introducing Barney*] Mr Doran. He owns that fine mill you noticed from the car.

BROADBENT [*delighted with them all*] Most happy, Mr Doran. Very pleased indeed.

Doran, not quite sure whether he is being courted or patronized, nods independently.

DORAN. Hows yourself, Larry?

LARRY. Finely, thank you. No need to ask you [*Doran grins; and they shake hands*].

CORNELIUS. Give Father Dempsey a chair, Larry.

Matthew Haffigan runs to the nearest end of the table and takes the chair from it, placing it near the basket; but Larry has already taken the chair from the other end and placed it in front of the table. Father Dempsey accepts that more central position.

CORNELIUS. Sit down, Barney, will you; and you, Matt.

Doran takes the chair Matt is still offering to the priest; and poor Matthew, outfaced by the miller, humbly turns the basket upside down and sits on it. Cornelius brings his own breakfast chair from the table and sits down on Father Dempsey's right. Broadbent resumes his seat on the rustic bench. Larry crosses to the bench and is about to sit down beside him when Broadbent holds him off nervously.

BROADBENT. Do you think it will bear two, Larry?

LARRY. Perhaps not. Dont move. I'll stand. [*He posts himself behind the bench*].

They are all now seated, except Larry; and the session assumes a portentous air, as if something important were coming.

CORNELIUS. Praps youll explain, Father Dempsey.

FATHER DEMPSEY. No, no: go on, you: the Church has no politics.

CORNELIUS. Were yever thinkin o goin into parliament at all, Larry?

LARRY. Me!

FATHER DEMPSEY [*encouragingly*] Yes, you. Hwy not?

LARRY. I'm afraid my ideas would not be popular enough.

CORNELIUS. I dont know that. Do you, Barney?

DORAN. Theres too much blatherumskite in Irish politics: a dale too much.

LARRY. But what about your present member? Is he going to retire?

CORNELIUS. No: I dont know that he is.

LARRY [*interrogatively*] Well? then?

MATTHEW [*breaking out with surly bitterness*] Weve had enough of his foolish talk agen landlords. Hwat call has he to talk about the lan, that never was outside of a city office in his life?

CORNELIUS. We're tired of him. He doesnt know hwere to stop. Every man cant own land; and some men must own it to employ them. It was all very well when solid men like Doran an Matt were kep from ownin land. But hwat man in his senses ever wanted to give land to Patsy Farrll an dhe like o him?

BROADBENT. But surely Irish landlordism was accountable for what Mr Haffigan suffered.

MATTHEW. Never mind hwat I suffered. I know what I suffered adhout you tellin me. But did I ever ask for more dhan the farm I made wid me own hans? tell me that, Corny Doyle, and you that knows. Was I fit for the responsibility or was I not? [*Snarling angrily at Cornelius*] Am I to be compared to Patsy Farrll, that doesnt harly know his right hand from his left? What did he ever suffer, I'd like to know?

CORNELIUS. Thats just what I say. I wasnt comparin you to your disadvantage.

MATTHEW [*implacable*] Then hwat did you mane be talking about giving him lan?

DORAN. Aisy, Matt, aisy. Youre like a bear with a sore back.

MATTHEW [*trembling with rage*] An who are you, to offer to taitch me manners?

FATHER DEMPSEY [*admonitorily*] Now, now, now, Matt! none o dhat. How often have I told you youre too ready to take offence where none is meant? You dont understand: Corny Doyle is saying just what you want to have said. [*To Cornelius*] Go on, Mr Doyle; and never mind him.

MATTHEW [*rising*] Well, if me lan is to be given to Patsy and his like, I'm goin oura dhis. I —

DORAN [*with violent impatience*] Arra who's going to give your lan to Patsy, yowl fool ye?

FATHER DEMPSEY. Aisy, Barney, aisy. [*Sternly, to Matt*] I told you, Matthew Haffigan, that Corny Doyle was sayin nothin against you. I'm sorry your priest's word is not good enough for you. I'll go, sooner than stay to make you commit a sin against the Church. Good morning, gentlemen. [*He rises. They all rise, except Broadbent*].

DORAN [*to Matt*] There! Sarve you dam well right, you cantankerous oul noodle.

MATTHEW [*appalled*] Dont say dhat, Fadher Dempsey. I never had a thought agen you or the Holy Church. I know I'm a bit hasty when I think about the lan. I axe your pardon for it.

FATHER DEMPSEY [*resuming his seat with dignified reserve*] Very well: I'll overlook it this time. [*He sits down. The others sit down, except Matthew. Father Dempsey, about to ask Corny to proceed, remembers Matthew and turns to him, giving him just a crumb of graciousness*]. Sit down, Matt [*Matthew, crushed, sits down in disgrace, and is silent, his eyes shifting piteously from one speaker to another in an intensely mistrustful effort to understand them*]. Go on, Mr Doyle. We can make allowances. Go on.

CORNELIUS. Well, you see how it is, Larry. Round about here, weve got the land at last; and we want no more Government meddlin. We want a new class o man in parliament: one dhat knows dhat the farmer's the real backbone o the country, n doesnt care a snap of his fingers for the shoutn o the riff-raff in the towns, or for the foolishness of the laborers.

DORAN. Aye; and dhat can afford to live in London and pay his own way until Home Rule comes, instead of wantin subscriptions and the like.

FATHER DEMPSEY. Yes: thats a good point, Barney. When too much money goes to politics, it's the Church that has to starve for it. A member of parliament ought to be a help to the Church instead of a burden on it.

LARRY. Heres a chance for you, Tom. What do you say?

BROADBENT [*deprecatory, but important and smiling*] Oh, I have no claim whatever to the seat. Besides, I'm a Saxon.

DORAN. A hwat?

BROADBENT. A Saxon. An Englishman.

DORAN. An Englishman. Bedad I never heard it called that before.

MATTHEW [*cunningly*] If I might make so bould, Fadher, I wuldnt say but an English Prodestn mightnt have a more indepindent mind about the lan, an be less afeerd to spake out about it dhan an Irish Catholic.

CORNELIUS. But sure Larry's as good as English: arnt you, Larry?

LARRY. You may put me out of your head, father, once for all.

CORNELIUS. Arra why?

LARRY. I have strong opinions which wouldnt suit you.

DORAN [*rallying him blatantly*] Is it still Larry the bould Fenian?

LARRY. No: the bold Fenian is now an older and possibly foolisher man.

CORNELIUS. Hwat does it matter to us hwat your opinions are? You know that your father's bought his place here, just the same as Matt's farm n Barney's mill. All we ask now is to be let alone. Youve nothin against that, have you?

LARRY. Certainly I have. I dont believe in letting anybody or anything alone.

CORNELIUS [*losing his temper*] Arra what d'ye mean, you young fool? Here Ive got you the offer of a good seat in parliament; n you think yourself mighty smart to stand there and talk foolishness to me. Will you take it or leave it?

LARRY. Very well: I'll take it with pleasure if youll give it to me.

CORNELIUS [*subsiding sulkily*] Well, why couldnt you say so at once? It's a good job youve made up your mind at last.

DORAN [*suspiciously*] Stop a bit: stop a bit.

MATTHEW [*writhing between his dissatisfaction and his fear of the priest*] It's not because he's your son that he's to get the sate. Fadher Dempsey: wouldnt you think well to ask him what he manes about the lan?

LARRY [*coming down on Matt promptly*] I'll tell you, Matt. I always thought it was a stupid, lazy, good-for-nothing sort of thing to leave the land in the hands of the old landlords without calling them to a strict account for the use they made of it, and the condition of the people on it. I could see for myself that they thought of nothing but what they could get out of it to spend in England; and that they mortgaged and mortgaged until hardly one of them owned his own property or could have afforded to keep it up decently if he'd wanted to. But I tell you plump and plain, Matt, that if anybody thinks things will be any better now that the land is handed over to a lot of little men like you, without calling you to account either, theyre mistaken.

MATTHEW [*sullenly*] What call have you to look down on me? I suppose you think youre everybody because your father was a landagent.

LARRY. What call have you to look down on Patsy Farrell? I suppose you think youre everybody because you own a few fields.

MATTHEW. Was Patsy Farrll ever ill used as I was ill used? tell me dhat.

LARRY. He will be, if ever he gets into your power as you were in the power of your old landlord. Do you think, because youre poor and ignorant and half-crazy with toiling and moiling morning noon and night, that youll be any less greedy and oppressive to them that have no land at all than old Nick Lestrange, who was an educated travelled gentleman that would not have been tempted as hard by a hundred pounds as youd be by five shillings? Nick was too high above Patsy Farrell to be jealous of him; but you, that are only one little step above him, would die sooner than let him come up that step; and well you know it.

MATTHEW [*black with rage, in a low growl*] Lemmy oura dhis. [*He tries to rise; but Doran catches his coat and drags him down again*] I'm goin, I say. [*Raising his voice*] Leggo me coat, Barney Doran.

DORAN. Sit down, yowl omadhaun, you. [*Whispering*] Dont you want to stay an vote agen him?

FATHER DEMPSEY [*holding up his finger*] Matt! [*Matt subsides*]. Now, now, now! come, come! Hwats all dhis about Patsy Farrll? Hwy need you fall out about him?

LARRY. Because it was by using Patsy's poverty to undersell England in the markets of the world that we drove England to ruin Ireland. And she'll ruin us again the moment we lift our heads from the dust if we trade in cheap labor; and serve us right too! If I get into parliament, I'll try to get an Act to prevent any of you from giving Patsy less than a pound a week [*they all start, hardly able to believe their ears*] or working him harder than youd work a horse that cost you fifty guineas.

DORAN. Hwat!!!

CORNELIUS [*aghast*] A pound a — God save us! the boy's mad.

Matthew, feeling that here is something quite beyond his powers, turns openmouthed to the priest, as if looking for nothing less than the summary excommunication of Larry.

LARRY. How is the man to marry and live a decent life on less?

FATHER DEMPSEY. Man alive, hwere have you been living all these years? and hwat have you been dreaming of? Why, some o dhese honest men here cant make that much out o the land for dhemselves, much less give it to a laborer.

LARRY [*now thoroughly roused*] Then let them make room for those who can. Is Ireland never to have a chance? First she was given to the rich; and now that they have gorged on her flesh, her bones are to be flung to the poor, that can do nothing but suck the marrow out of her. If we cant have men of honor own the land, lets have men of ability. If we cant have men with ability, let us at least have men with capital. Anybody's better than Matt, who has neither honor, nor ability, nor capital, nor anything but mere brute labor and greed in him, Heaven help him!

DORAN. Well, we're not all foostherin oul doddherers like Matt. [*Pleasantly, to the subject of his description*] Are we, Matt?

LARRY. For modern industrial purposes you might just as well be, Barney. Youre all children: the big world that I belong to has gone past you and left you. Anyhow, we Irishmen were never made to be farmers; and we'll never do any good at it. We're like the Jews: the Almighty gave us brains, and bid us farm them and leave the clay and the worms alone.

FATHER DEMPSEY [*with gentle irony*] Oh! is it Jews you want to make of us? I must catechize you a bit meself, I think. The next thing youll be proposing is to repeal the disestablishment of the so-called Irish Church.

LARRY. Yes: why not? [*Sensation*].

MATTHEW [*rancorously*] He's a turncoat.

LARRY. St Peter, the rock on which our Church was built, was crucified head downwards for being a turncoat.

FATHER DEMPSEY [*with a quiet authoritative dignity which checks Doran, who is on the point of breaking out*] Thats true. You hold your tongue as befits your ignorance, Matthew Haffigan; and trust your priest to deal with this young man. Now, Larry Doyle, whatever the blessed St Peter was crucified for, it was not for being a Prodestan. Are you one?

LARRY. No. I am a Catholic intelligent enough to see that the Protestants are never more dangerous to us than when they are free from all alliances with the State. The so-called Irish Church is stronger today than ever it was.

MATTHEW. Fadher Dempsey: will you tell him dhat me mother's ant was shot and kilt dead in the sthreet o Rosscullen be a soljer in the tithe war? [*Frantically*] He wants to put the tithes on us again. He –

LARRY [*interrupting him with overbearing contempt*] Put the tithes on you

again! Did the tithes ever come off you? Was your land any dearer
when you paid the tithe to the parson than it was when you paid the
same money to Nick Lestrange as rent, and he handed it over to the
Church Sustentation Fund? Will you always be duped by Acts of
Parliament that change nothing but the necktie of the man that picks
your pocket? I'll tell you what I'd do with you, Matt Haffigan; I'd
make you pay tithes to your own Church. I want the Catholic Church
established in Ireland: thats what I want. Do you think that I, brought
up to regard myself as the son of a great and holy Church, can bear
to see her begging her bread from the ignorance and superstition of
men like you? I would have her as high above worldly want as I would
have her above worldly pride or ambition. Aye; and I would have
Ireland compete with Rome itself for the chair of St Peter and the
citadel of the Church; for Rome, in spite of all the blood of the martyrs,
is pagan at heart to this day, while in Ireland the people is the Church
and the Church the people.

FATHER DEMPSEY [*startled but not at all displeased*] Whisht, man!
youre worse than mad Pether Keegan himself.

BROADBENT [*who has listened in the greatest astonishment*] You amaze
me, Larry. Who would have thought of your coming out like this!
[*Solemnly*] But much as I appreciate your really brilliant eloquence,
I implore you not to desert the great Liberal principle of Disestablishment.

LARRY. I am not a Liberal: Heaven forbid! A disestablished Church
is the worst tyranny a nation can groan under.

BROADBENT [*making a wry face*] Dont be paradoxical, Larry. It really
gives me a pain in my stomach.

LARRY. Youll soon find out the truth of it here. Look at Father Dempsey!
he is disestablished: he has nothing to hope or fear from the State;
and the result is that he's the most powerful man in Rosscullen. The
member for Rosscullen would shake in his shoes if Father Dempsey
looked crooked at him. [*Father Dempsey smiles, by no means averse to
this acknowledgment of his authority*]. Look at yourself! you would
defy the established Archbishop of Canterbury ten times a day; but
catch you daring to say a word that would shock a Nonconformist!
not you. The Conservative party today is the only one thats not priest-
ridden – excuse the expression, Father [*Father Dempsey nods tolerantly*]

– because it's the only one that has established its Church and can prevent a clergyman becoming a bishop if he's not a Statesman as well as a Churchman.

He stops. They stare at him dumbfounded, and leave it to the priest to answer him.

FATHER DEMPSEY [*judicially*] Young man: youll not be the member for Rosscullen; but dheres more in your head than the comb will take out.

LARRY. I'm sorry to disappoint you, Father; but I told you it would be no use. And now I think the candidate had better retire and leave you to discuss his successor. [*He takes a newspaper from the table and goes away through the shrubbery amid dead silence, all turning to watch him until he passes out of sight round the corner of the house*].

DORAN [*dazed*] Hwat sort of a fella is he at all at all?

FATHER DEMPSEY. He's a clever lad: dheres the making of a man in him yet.

MATTHEW [*in consternation*] D'ye mane to say dhat yll put him into parliament to bring back Nick Lesthrange on me, and to put tithes on me, and to rob me for the like o Patsy Farrll, because he's Corny Doyle's son?

DORAN [*brutally*] Arra hould your whisht: who's going to send him into parliament? Maybe youd like us to send you dhere to thrate dhem to a little o your anxiety about dhat dirty little podato patch o yours.

MATTHEW [*plaintively*] Am I to be towld dhis afther all me sufferins?

DORAN. Och, I'm tired o your sufferins. Weve been hearin nothin else ever since we was childher but sufferins. Hwen it wasnt yours it was somebody else's; and hwen it was nobody else's it was ould Irelan's. How the divil are we to live on wan anodher's sufferins?

FATHER DEMPSEY. Thats a thrue word, Barney Doran; only your tongue's a little too familiar wi dhe divil. [*To Matt*] If youd think a little more o the sufferins of the blessed saints, Matt, an a little less o your own, youd find the way shorter from your farm to heaven [*Matt is about to reply*] Dhere now! dhats enough! we know you mean well; an I'm not angry with you.

BROADBENT. Surely, Mr Haffigan, you can see the simple explanation of all this. My friend Larry Doyle is a most brilliant speaker; but he's a Tory: an ingrained old-fashioned Tory.

CORNELIUS. N how d'ye make dhat out, if I might ask you, Mr Broadbent?

BROADBENT [*collecting himself for a political deliverance*] Well, you know, Mr Doyle, theres a strong dash of Toryism in the Irish character. Larry himself says that the great Duke of Wellington was the most typical Irishman that ever lived. Of course thats an absurd paradox; but still theres a great deal of truth in it. Now I am a Liberal. You know the great principles of the Liberal Party. Peace –

FATHER DEMPSEY [*piously*] Hear! hear!

BROADBENT [*encouraged*] Thank you. Retrenchment – [*he waits for further applause*].

MATTHEW [*timidly*] What might rethrenchment mane now?

BROADBENT. It means an immense reduction in the burden of the rates and taxes.

MATTHEW [*respectfully approving*] Dhats right. Dhats right, sir.

BROADBENT [*perfunctorily*] And, of course, Reform.

CORNELIUS
FATHER DEMPSEY   } [*conventionally*] Of course.
DORAN

MATTHEW [*still suspicious*] Hwat does Reform mane, sir? Does it mane altherin annythin dhats as it is now?

BROADBENT [*impressively*] It means, Mr Haffigan, maintaining those reforms which have already been conferred on humanity by the Liberal Party, and trusting for future developments to the free activity of a free people on the basis of those reforms.

DORAN. Dhats right. No more meddlin. We're all right now: all we want is to be let alone.

CORNELIUS. Hwat about Home Rule?

BROADBENT [*rising so as to address them more imposingly*] I really cannot tell you what I feel about Home Rule without using the language of hyperbole.

DORAN. Savin Fadher Dempsey's presence, eh?

BROADBENT [*not understanding him*] Quite so – er – oh yes. All I can say is that as an Englishman I blush for the Union. It is the blackest stain on our national history. I look forward to the time – and it cannot be far distant, gentlemen, because Humanity is looking forward to it too, and insisting on it with no uncertain voice – I look forward to the time when an Irish legislature shall arise once more on the emerald pasture of College Green, and the Union Jack — that detestable symbol of a decadent Imperialism — be replaced by a flag as green as the island over which it waves: a flag on which we shall ask for England only a modest quartering in memory of our great party and of the immortal name of our grand old leader.

DORAN [*enthusiastically*] Dhats the style, begob! [*He smites his knee, and winks at Matt*].

MATTHEW. More power to you, sir!

BROADBENT. I shall leave you now, gentlemen, to your deliberations. I should like to have enlarged on the services rendered by the Liberal Party to the religious faith of the great majority of the people of Ireland; but I shall content myself with saying that in my opinion you should choose no representative who — no matter what his personal creed may be — is not an ardent supporter of freedom of conscience, and is not prepared to prove it by contributions, as lavish as his means will allow, to the great and beneficent work which you, Father Dempsey [*Father Dempsey bows*], are doing for the people of Rosscullen. Nor should the lighter, but still most important question of the sports of the people be forgotten. The local cricket club —

CORNELIUS. The hwat!

DORAN. Nobody plays bat n ball here, if dhats what you mane.

BROADBENT. Well, let us say quoits. I saw two men, I think, last night — but after all, these are questions of detail. The main thing is that your candidate, whoever he may be, shall be a man of some means, able to help the locality instead of burdening it. And if he were a countryman of my own, the moral effect on the House of Commons would be immense! tremendous! Pardon my saying these few words: nobody feels their impertinence more than I do. Good morning, gentlemen.

He turns impressively to the gate, and trots away, congratulating himself, with a little twist of his head and cock of his eye, on having done a good stroke of political business.

MATTHEW [*awestruck*] Good morning, sir.

THE REST. Good morning. [*They watch him vacantly until he is out of earshot*].

CORNELIUS. Hwat d'ye think, Father Dempsey?

FATHER DEMPSEY [*indulgently*] Well, he hasnt much sense, God help him; but for the matter o that, neether has our present member.

DORAN. Arra musha he's good enough for parliament: what is there to do there but gas a bit, an chivy the Government, an vote wi dh Irish party?

CORNELIUS [*ruminatively*] He's the queerest Englishman *I* ever met. When he opened the paper dhis mornin the first thing he saw was that an English expedition had been bet in a battle in Inja somewhere; an he was as pleased as Punch! Larry told him that if he'd been alive when the news o Waterloo came, he'd a died o grief over it. Bedad I dont think he's quite right in his head.

DORAN. Divil a matther if he has plenty o money. He'll do for us right enough.

MATTHEW [*deeply impressed by Broadbent, and unable to understand their levity concerning him*] Did you mind what he said about rethrenchment? That was very good, I thought.

FATHER DEMPSEY. You might find out from Larry, Corny, what his means are. God forgive us all! it's poor work spoiling the Egyptians, though we have good warrant for it; so I'd like to know how much spoil there is before I commit meself. [*He rises. They all rise respectfully*].

CORNELIUS [*ruefully*] I'd set me mind on Larry himself for the seat; but I suppose it cant be helped.

FATHER DEMPSEY [*consoling him*] Well, the boy's young yet; an he has a head on him. Goodbye, all. [*He goes out through the gate*].

DORAN. I must be goin, too. [*He directs Cornelius's attention to what is passing in the road*]. Look at me bould Englishman shakin hans wid Fadher Dempsey for all the world like a candidate on election day. And look at Fadher Dempsey givin him a squeeze an a wink as much as to say It's all right, me boy. You watch him shakin hans with me too: he's waitn for me. I'll tell him he's as good as elected. [*He goes, chuckling mischievously*].

CORNELIUS. Come in with me, Matt. I think I'll sell you the pig after all. Come in an wet the bargain.

MATTHEW [*instantly dropping into the old whine of the tenant*] I'm afeerd I cant afford the price, sir. [*He follows Cornelius into the house*].

Larry, newspaper still in hand, comes back through the shrubbery. Broadbent returns through the gate.

LARRY. Well? What has happened?

BROADBENT [*hugely self-satisfied*] I think Ive done the trick this time. I just gave them a bit of straight talk; and it went home. They were greatly impressed: everyone of those men believes in me and will vote for me when the question of selecting a candidate comes up. After all, whatever you say, Larry, they like an Englishman. They feel they can trust him, I suppose.

LARRY. Oh! theyve transferred the honor to you, have they?

BROADBENT [*complacently*] Well, it was a pretty obvious move, I should think. You know, these fellows have plenty of shrewdness in spite of their Irish oddity. [*Hodson comes from the house. Larry sits in Doran's chair and reads*]. Oh, by the way, Hodson –

HODSON [*coming between Broadbent and Larry*] Yes, sir?

BROADBENT. I want you to be rather particular as to how you treat the people here.

HODSON. I havnt treated any of em yet, sir. If I was to accept all the treats they offer me I shouldnt be able to stand at this present moment, sir.

BROADBENT. Oh well, dont be too stand-offish, you know, Hodson. I should like you to be popular. If it costs anything I'll make it up to you. It doesnt matter if you get a bit upset at first: theyll like you all the better for it.

HODSON. I'm sure youre very kind, sir; but it dont seem to matter to me whether they like me or not. I'm not going to stand for parliament here, sir.

BROADBENT. Well, I am. Now do you understand?

HODSON [*waking up at once*] Oh, I beg your pardon, sir, I'm sure. I understand, sir.

CORNELIUS [*appearing at the house door with Matt*] Patsy'll drive the pig over this evenin, Matt. Goodbye. [*He goes back into the house. Matt makes for the gate. Broadbent stops him. Hodson, pained by the derelict basket, picks it up and carries it away behind the house*].

BROADBENT [*beaming candidatorially*] I must thank you very particularly, Mr Haffigan, for your support this morning. I value it because I know that the real heart of a nation is the class you represent, the yeomanry.

MATTHEW [*aghast*] The yeomanry!!!

LARRY [*looking up from his paper*] Take care, Tom! In Rosscullen a yeoman means a sort of Orange Bashi-Bazouk. In England, Matt, they call a freehold farmer a yeoman.

MATTHEW [*huffily*] I dont need to be insthructed be you, Larry Doyle. Some people think no one knows anythin but dhemselves. [*To Broadbent, deferentially*] Of course I know a gentleman like you would not compare me to the yeomanry. Me own granfather was flogged in the sthreets of Athenmullet be them when they put a gun in the thatch of his house and then went and found it there, bad cess to them!

BROADBENT [*with sympathetic interest*] Then you are not the first martyr of your family, Mr Haffigan?

MATTHEW. They turned me out o the farm I made out of the stones o Little Rosscullen hill wid me own hans.

BROADBENT. I have heard about it; and my blood still boils at the thought. [*Calling*] Hodson –

HODSON [*behind the corner of the house*] Yes, sir. [*He hurries forward*].

BROADBENT. Hodson: this gentleman's sufferings should make every Englishman think. It is want of thought rather than want of heart that allows such iniquities to disgrace society.

HODSON [*prosaically*] Yes, sir.

MATTHEW. Well, I'll be goin. Good mornin to you kindly, sir.

BROADBENT. You have some distance to go, Mr Haffigan: will you allow me to drive you home?

MATTHEW. Oh sure it'd be throublin your honor.

BROADBENT. I insist: it will give me the greatest pleasure, I assure you. My car is in the stable: I can get it round in five minutes.

MATTHEW. Well, sir, if you wouldnt mind, we could bring the pig Ive just bought from Corny –

BROADBENT [*with enthusiasm*] Certainly, Mr Haffigan: it will be quite delightful to drive with a pig in the car: I shall feel quite like an Irishman. Hodson: stay with Mr Haffigan; and give him a hand with the pig if necessary. Come, Larry; and help me. [*He rushes away through the shrubbery*].

LARRY [*throwing the paper ill-humoredly on the chair*] Look here, Tom! here, I say! confound it! – [*he runs after him*].

MATTHEW [*glowering disdainfully at Hodson, and sitting down on Cornelius's chair as an act of social self-assertion*] N are you the valley?

HODSON. The valley? Oh, I follow you: yes: I'm Mr Broadbent's valet.

MATTHEW. Ye have an aisy time of it: you look purty sleek. [*With suppressed ferocity*] Look at me! Do *I* look sleek?

HODSON [*sadly*] I wish I ad your ealth: you look as ard as nails. I suffer from an excess of uric acid.

MATTHEW. Musha what sort o disease is zhourag-assid? Didjever suffer from injustice and starvation? Dhats the Irish disease. It's aisy for you to talk o sufferin, and you livin on the fat o the land wid money wrung from us.

HODSON [*suddenly dropping the well-spoken valet, and breaking out in his native cockney*] Wots wrong with you, aold chep? Ez ennybody been doin ennythink to you?

MATTHEW. Anythin timmy! Didnt your English masther say that the blood biled in him to hear the way they put a rint on me for the farm I made wid me own hans, an turned me out of it to give it to Billy Byrne?

HODSON. Ow, Tom Broadbent's blad boils pretty easy over ennything that eppens aht of his aown cantry. Downt you be tiken in by my aowl men, Peddy.

MATTHEW [*indignantly*] Paddy yourself! How dar you call me Paddy?

HODSON [*unmoved*] You jast keep your air on and listen to me. You Awrish people are too well off: thets wots the metter with you. [*With sudden passion*] You talk of your rotten little fawm cause you mide it by chackin a few stowns dahn a ill! Well, wot prawce maw grenfawther, Oi should lawk to knaow, that fitted ap a fust clawss shop and built ap a fust clawss dripery business in Landon by sixty years work, and then was chacked aht of it on is ed at the end of is lease withaht a penny for his goodwill. You talk of evictions! you that cawnt be moved until youve ran ap ighteen months rent. Oi once ran ap four weeks in Lembeth wen Oi was aht of a job in winter. They took the door off its inges and the winder aht of its seshes on me, and gev maw wawf pnoomownia. Oi'm a widower nah. [*Between his teeth*] Gawd! when Oi think of the things we Englishmen as to pat ap with, and eah you Awrish ahlin abaht your silly little grievances, and see the wy you mike it worse for haz by the rotten wiges youll cam over and tike and the rotten plices youll sleep in, I jast feel that I could tike the aowl bloomin British awland and mike you a present of it, jast to let you fawnd aht wot reel awdship's lawk.

MATTHEW [*starting up, more in scandalized incredulity than in anger*] D'ye have the face to set up England agen Ireland for injustices an wrongs an disthress an sufferin?

HODSON [*with intense disgust and contempt*] Ow, chack it, Paddy. Cheese it. You danno wot awdship is owver eah: all you knaow is ah to ahl abaht it. You tike the biscuit at thet, you do. Oi'm a Owm Ruler, Oi em. Do you knaow woy?

MATTHEW [*equally contemptuous*] D'ye know, yourself?

HODSON. Yus Oi do. It's because Oi want a little attention pide to my aown cantry; and thetll never be as long as your cheps are ollerin at Westminster as if nowbody mettered but your own bloomin selves. Send em back to ell or C'naught, as good aowld English Cramwell said. I'm jast sick of Awrland. Let it gow. Cat the caible. Mike it a present to Germany to keep the aowl Kyzer busy for a wawl; and give poor aowld England a chawnce: thets wot Oi sy.

MATTHEW [*full of scorn for a man so ignorant as to be unable to pronounce the word Connaught, which practically rhymes with bonnet in Ireland, though in Hodson's dialect it rhymes with untaught*] Take care we dont cut the cable ourselves some day, bad scran to you! An tell me dhis: have yanny Coercion Acs in England? Have yanny Removable magisthruts? Have you Dublin Castle to suppress every newspaper dhat takes the part o your own counthry?

HODSON. We can beyive ahrselves withaht sich things.

MATTHEW. Bedad youre right. It'd ony be waste o time to muzzle a sheep. Here! wheres me pig? God forgimmy for talkin to a poor ignorant craycher like you!

HODSON [*grinning with good-humored malice, too convinced of his own superiority to feel his withers wrung*] Your pig'll ev a rare doin in that car, Peddy. Forty mawl an ahr dahn that rocky line will strawk it pretty pink, you bet.

MATTHEW [*scornfully*] Hwy cant you tell a raisonable lie when youre about it? What horse can go forty mile an hour?

HODSON. Orse! Wy, you silly aowl rotter, it's not a orse: it's a mowtor. Do you spowse Tom Broadbent ud gow himself to fetch a orse?

MATTHEW [*in consternation*] Holy Moses! dont tell me it's the ingine he wants to take me on.

HODSON. Wot else?

MATTHEW. Your sowl to Morris Kelly! why didnt you tell me that before? The divil an ingine he'll get me on this day. [*His ear catches an approaching teuf-teuf*]. Oh murdher! it's comin afther me: I hear the puff-puff of it. [*He runs away through the gate, much to Hodson's amusement. The noise of the motor ceases; and Hodson, anticipating Broadbent's return, throws off the cockney and recomposes himself as a valet. Broadbent and Larry come through the shrubbery. Hodson moves aside to the gate*].

BROADBENT. Where is Mr Haffigan? Has he gone for the pig?

HODSON. Bolted, sir. Afraid of the motor, sir.

BROADBENT [*much disappointed*] Oh, thats very tiresome. Did he leave any message?

HODSON. He was in too great a hurry, sir. Started to run home, sir, and left his pig behind him.

BROADBENT [*eagerly*] Left the pig! Then it's all right. The pig's the thing: the pig will win over every Irish heart to me. We'll take the pig home to Haffigan's farm in the motor: it will have a tremendous effect. Hodson!

HODSON. Yes, sir?

BROADBENT. Do you think you could collect a crowd to see the motor?

HODSON. Well, I'll try, sir.

BROADBENT. Thank you, Hodson: do.

Hodson goes out through the gate.

LARRY [*desperately*] Once more, Tom, will you listen to me?

BROADBENT. Rubbish! I tell you it will be all right.

LARRY. Only this morning you confessed how surprised you were to find that the people here shewed no sense of humor.

BROADBENT [*suddenly very solemn*] Yes: their sense of humor is in abeyance: I noticed it the moment we landed. Think of that in a country where every man is a born humorist! Think of what it means! [*Impressively*] Larry: we are in the presence of a great national grief.

LARRY. Whats to grieve them?

BROADBENT. I divined it, Larry: I saw it in their faces. Ireland has never smiled since her hopes were buried in the grave of Gladstone.

LARRY. Oh, whats the use of talking to such a man? Now look here, Tom. Be serious for a moment if you can.

BROADBENT [*stupent*] Serious! I!!!!

LARRY. Yes, you. You say the Irish sense of humor is in abeyance. Well, if you drive through Rosscullen in a motor car with Haffigan's pig, it wont stay in abeyance. Now I warn you.

BROADBENT [*breezily*] Why, so much the better! I shall enjoy the joke myself more than any of them. [*Shouting*] Hallo, Patsy Farrell, where are you?

PATSY [*appearing in the shrubbery*] Here I am, your honor.

BROADBENT. Go and catch the pig and put it into the car: we're going to take it to Mr Haffigan's. [*He gives Larry a slap on the shoulders that sends him staggering off through the gate, and follows him buoyantly, exclaiming*] Come on, you old croaker! I'll shew you how to win an Irish seat.

PATSY [*meditatively*] Bedad, if dhat pig gets a howlt o the handle o the machine – [*He shakes his head ominously and drifts away to the pigsty*].

ACT IV

The parlor in Cornelius Doyle's house. It communicates with the garden by a half glazed door. The fireplace is at the other side of the room, opposite the door and windows, the architect not having been sensitive to draughts. The table, rescued from the garden, is in the middle; and at it sits Keegan, the central figure in a rather crowded apartment. Nora, sitting with her back to the fire at the end of the table, is playing backgammon across its corner with him, on his left hand. Aunt Judy, a little further back, sits facing the fire knitting, with her feet on the fender. A little to Keegan's right, in front of the table, and almost sitting on it, is Barney Doran. Half a dozen friends of his, all men, are between him and the open door, supported by others outside. In the corner behind them is the sofa, of mahogany and horsehair, made up as a bed for Broadbent. Against the wall behind Keegan stands a mahogany sideboard. A door leading to the interior of the house is near the fireplace, behind Aunt Judy. There are chairs against the wall, one at each end of the sideboard. Keegan's hat is on the one nearest the inner door; and his stick is leaning against it. A third chair, also against the wall, is near the garden door.

There is a strong contrast of emotional atmosphere between the two sides of the room. Keegan is extraordinarily stern: no game of backgammon could possibly make a man's face so grim. Aunt Judy is quietly busy. Nora is trying to ignore Doran and attend to her game.

On the other hand Doran is reeling in an ecstasy of mischievous mirth which has infected all his friends. They are screaming with laughter, doubled up, leaning on the furniture and against the walls, shouting, screeching, crying.

AUNT JUDY [*as the noise lulls for a moment*] Arra hold your noise, Barney. What is there to laugh at?

DORAN. It got its fut into the little hweel – [*he is overcome afresh: and the rest collapse again*].

AUNT JUDY. Ah, have some sense: youre like a parcel o childher. Nora: hit him a thump on the back: he'll have a fit.

DORAN [*with squeezed eyes, exsufflicate with cachinnation*] Frens, he sez to dhem outside Doolan's: I'm takin the gintleman that pays the rint for a dhrive.

AUNT JUDY. Who did he mean be that?

DORAN. They call a pig that in England. Thats their notion of a joke.

AUNT JUDY. Musha God help them if they can joke no better than that!

DORAN [with renewed symptoms] Thin –

AUNT JUDY. Ah now dont be tellin it all over and settin yourself off again, Barney.

NORA. Youve told us three times, Mr Doran.

DORAN. Well but whin I think of it –!

AUNT JUDY. Then dont think of it, alanna.

DORAN. Dhere was Patsy Farrll in the back sate wi dhe pig between his knees, n me bould English boyoh in front at the machinery, n Larry Doyle in the road startin the injine wid a bed winch. At the first puff of it the pig lep out of its skin and bled Patsy's nose wi dhe ring in its snout. [Roars of laughter: Keegan glares at them]. Before Broadbint knew hwere he was, the pig was up his back and over into his lap; and bedad the poor baste did credit to Corny's thrainin of it; for it put in the fourth speed wid its right crubeen as if it was enthered for the Gordn Bennett.

NORA [reproachfully] And Larry in front of it and all! It's nothin to laugh at, Mr Doran.

DORAN. Bedad, Miss Reilly, Larry cleared six yards sideways at wan jump if he cleared an inch; and he'd a cleared seven if Doolan's granmother hadnt cotch him in her apern widhout intindin to. [Immense merriment].

AUNT JUDY. Ah, for shame, Barney! the poor old woman! An she was hurt before, too, when she slipped on the stairs.

DORAN. Bedad, maam, she's hurt behind now; for Larry bouled her over like a skittle. [General delight at this typical stroke of Irish Rabelaisianism].

NORA. It's well Mr Doyle wasnt killed.

DORAN. Faith it wasnt o Larry we were thinkin jus dhen, wi dhe pig takin the main sthreet o Rosscullen on market day at a mile a minnit. Dh ony thing Broadbint could get at wi dhe pig in front of him was a fut brake; n the pig's tail was undher dhat; so that whin he thought he was putn non the brake he was ony squeezin the life out o the pig's tail. The more he put the brake on the more the pig squealed n the fasther he dhruv.

AUNT JUDY. Why couldnt he throw the pig out into the road?

DORAN. Sure he couldnt stand up to it, because he was spanchelled-like between his seat and dhat thing like a wheel on top of a stick between his knees.

AUNT JUDY. Lord have mercy on us!

NORA. I dont know how you can laugh. Do you, Mr Keegan?

KEEGAN [grimly] Why not? There is danger, destruction, torment! What more do we need to make us merry? Go on, Barney: the last drops of joy are not squeezed from the story yet. Tell us again how our brother was torn asunder.

DORAN [puzzled] Whose bruddher?

KEEGAN. Mine.

NORA. He means the pig, Mr Doran. You know his way.

DORAN [rising gallantly to the occasion] Bedad I'm sorry for your poor bruddher, Misther Keegan; but I recommend you to thry him wid a couple o fried eggs for your breakfast tomorrow. It was a case of Excelsior wi dhat ambitious baste; for not content wid jumpin from the back seat into the front wan, he jumped from the front wan into the road in front of the car. And –

KEEGAN. And everybody laughed!

NORA. Dont go over that again, please, Mr Doran.

DORAN. Faith be the time the car went over the poor pig dhere was little left for me or anywan else to go over except wid a knife an fork.

AUNT JUDY. Why didnt Mr Broadbent stop the car when the pig was gone?

DORAN. Stop the car! He might as well ha tried to stop a mad bull. First it went wan way an made fireworks o Molly Ryan's crockery stall; an dhen it slewed round an ripped ten fut o wall out o the corner o the pound. [With enormous enjoyment] Begob, it just tore the town in two and sent the whole dam market to blazes. [Nora offended, rises].

KEEGAN [indignantly] Sir!

DORAN [quickly] Savin your presence, Miss Reilly, and Misther Keegan's. Dhere! I wont say anuddher word.

NORA. I'm surprised at you, Mr Doran. [She sits down again].

DORAN [reflectively] He has the divil's own luck, that Englishman, annyway; for hwen they picked him up he hadnt a scratch on him, barrn hwat the pig did to his cloes. Patsy had two fingers out o jynt; but the smith pulled them sthraight for him. Oh, you never heard such a hullaballoo as there was. There was Molly cryin Me chaney, me beautyful chaney! n oul Matt shoutin Me pig, me pig! n the polus takin the number o the car, n not a man in the town able to speak for laughin –

KEEGAN [*with intense emphasis*] It is hell: it is hell. Nowhere else could such a scene be a burst of happiness for the people.

Cornelius comes in hastily from the garden, pushing his way through the little crowd.

CORNELIUS. Whisht your laughin, boys! Here he is. [*He puts his hat on the sideboard, and goes to the fireplace, where he posts himself with his back to the chimneypiece*].

AUNT JUDY. Remember your behavior now.

Everybody becomes silent, solemn, concerned, sympathetic. Broadbent enters, soiled and disordered as to his motoring coat: immensely important and serious as to himself. He makes his way to the end of the table nearest the garden door, whilst Larry, who accompanies him, throws his motoring coat on the sofa bed, and sits down, watching the proceedings.

BROADBENT [*taking off his leather cap with dignity and placing it on the table*] I hope you have not been anxious about me.

AUNT JUDY. Deedn we have, Mr Broadbent. It's a mercy you werent killed.

DORAN. Kilt! It's a mercy dheres two bones of you left houldin together. How dijjescape at all at all? Well, I never thought I'd be so glad to see you safe and sound again. Not a man in the town would say less [*murmurs of kindly assent*]. Wont you come down to Doolan's and have a dhrop o brandy to take the shock off?

BROADBENT. Youre all really too kind; but the shock has quite passed off.

DORAN [*jovially*] Never mind. Come along all the same and tell us about it over a frenly glass.

BROADBENT. May I say how deeply I feel the kindness with which I have been overwhelmed since my accident? I can truthfully declare that I am glad it happened, because it has brought out the kindness and sympathy of the Irish character to an extent I had no conception of.

SEVERAL PRESENT { Oh, sure youre welcome!
Sure it's only natural.
Sure you might have been kilt.

A young man, feeling that he must laugh or burst, hurries out. Barney puts an iron constraint on his features.

BROADBENT. All I can say is that I wish I could drink the health of everyone of you.

DORAN. Dhen come an do it.`

BROADBENT [*very solemnly*] No: I am a teetotaller.

AUNT JUDY [*incredulously*] Arra since when?

BROADBENT. Since this morning, Miss Doyle. I have had a lesson [*he looks at Nora significantly*] that I shall not forget. It may be that total abstinence has already saved my life; for I was astonished at the steadiness of my nerves when death stared me in the face today. So I will ask you to excuse me. [*He collects himself for a speech*]. Gentlemen: I hope the gravity of the peril through which we have all passed – for I know that the danger to the bystanders was as great as to the occupants of the car – will prove an earnest of closer and more serious relations between us in the future. We have had a somewhat agitating day: a valuable and innocent animal has lost its life: a public building has been wrecked: an aged and infirm lady has suffered an impact for which I feel personally responsible, though my old friend Mr Laurence Doyle unfortunately incurred the first effects of her very natural resentment. I greatly regret the damage to Mr Patrick Farrell's fingers; and I have of course taken care that he shall not suffer pecuniarily by his mishap. [*Murmurs of admiration at his magnanimity, and A Voice* 'Youre a gentleman, sir']. I am glad to say that Patsy took it like an Irishman, and, far from expressing any vindictive feeling, declared his willingness to break all his fingers and toes for me on the same terms [*subdued applause, and* 'More power to Patsy!']. Gentlemen: I felt at home in Ireland from the first [*rising excitement among his hearers*]. In every Irish breast I have found that spirit of liberty [*A cheery voice* 'Hear hear'], that instinctive mistrust of the Government [*A small pious voice, with intense expression,* 'God bless you, sir!'], that love of independence [*A defiant voice,* 'Thats it! Independence!'], that indignant sympathy with the cause of oppressed nationalities abroad [*A threatening growl from all: the ground-swell of patriotic passion*] and with the resolute assertion of personal rights at home, which is all but extinct in my own country. If it were legally possible I should become a naturalized Irishman; and if ever it be my good fortune to represent an Irish constituency in parliament, it shall be my first care to introduce a Bill legalizing such an operation. I believe a large section of the Liberal party would avail themselves of it. [*Momentary scepticism*] I do. [*Convulsive cheering*]. Gentlemen: I have said enough. [*Cries of* 'Go on']. No: I have as yet no right to address you at all on political subjects; and we must not abuse the warm-hearted Irish hospitality of Miss Doyle by turning her sitting room into a public meeting.

DORAN [*energetically*] Three cheers for Tom Broadbent, the future member for Rosscullen!

AUNT JUDY [*waving a half knitted sock*] Hip hip hurray!

The cheers are given with great heartiness, as it is by this time, for the more humorous spirits present, a question of vociferation or internal rupture.

BROADBENT. Thank you from the bottom of my heart, friends.

NORA [*whispering to Doran*] Take them away, Mr Doran [*Doran nods*].

DORAN. Well, good evenin, Mr Broadbent; an may you never regret the day you wint dhrivin wid Haffigan's pig! [*They shake hands*]. Good evenin, Miss Doyle.

General handshaking, Broadbent shaking hands with everybody effusively. He accompanies them to the garden and can be heard outside saying Good night in every inflexion known to parliamentary candidates. Nora, Aunt Judy, Keegan, Larry, and Cornelius are left in the parlor. Larry goes to the threshold and watches the scene in the garden.

NORA. It's a shame to make game of him like that. He's a gradle more good in him than Barney Doran.

CORNELIUS. It's all up with his candidature. He'll be laughed out o the town.

LARRY [*turning quickly from the doorway*] Oh no he wont: he's not an Irishman. He'll never know theyre laughing at him; and while theyre laughing he'll win the seat.

CORNELIUS. But he cant prevent the story getting about.

LARRY. He wont want to. He'll tell it himself as one of the most providential episodes in the history of England and Ireland.

AUNT JUDY. Sure he wouldnt make a fool of himself like that.

LARRY. Are you sure he's such a fool after all, Aunt Judy? Suppose you had a vote! which would you rather give it to? the man that told the story of Haffigan's pig Barney Doran's way or Broadbent's way?

AUNT JUDY. Faith I wouldnt give it to a man at all. It's a few women they want in parliament to stop their foolish blather.

BROADBENT [*bustling into the room, and taking off his damaged motoring overcoat, which he puts down on the sofa*] Well thats over. I must apologize for making a speech, Miss Doyle; but they like it, you know. Everything helps in electioneering.

Larry takes the chair near the door; draws it near the table; and sits astride it, with his elbows folded on the back.

AUNT JUDY. I'd no notion you were such an orator, Mr Broadbent.

BROADBENT. Oh, it's only a knack. One picks it up on the platform. It stokes up their enthusiasm.

AUNT JUDY. Oh, I forgot. Youve not met Mr Keegan. Let me intro-joosha.

BROADBENT [*shaking hands effusively*] Most happy to meet you, Mr Keegan. I have heard of you, though I have not had the pleasure of shaking your hand before. And now may I ask you — for I value no man's opinion more — what you think of my chances here.

KEEGAN [*coldly*] Your chances, sir, are excellent. You will get into parliament.

BROADBENT [*delighted*] I hope so. I think so. [*Fluctuating*] You really think so? You are sure you are not allowing your enthusiasm for our principles to get the better of your judgment?

KEEGAN. I have no enthusiasm for your principles, sir. You will get into parliament because you want to get into it enough to be prepared to take the necessary steps to induce the people to vote for you. That is how people usually get into that fantastic assembly.

BROADBENT [*puzzled*] Of course. [*Pause*]. Quite so. [*Pause*]. Er — yes. [*Buoyant again*] I think they will vote for me. Eh? Yes?

AUNT JUDY. Arra why shouldnt they? Look at the people they do vote for!

BROADBENT [*encouraged*] Thats true: thats very true. When I see the windbags, the carpet-baggers, the charlatans, the — the — the fools and ignoramuses who corrupt the multitude by their wealth, or seduce them by spouting balderdash to them, I cannot help thinking that an Englishman with no humbug about him, who will talk straight common sense and take his stand on the solid ground of principle and public duty, must win his way with men of all classes.

KEEGAN [*quietly*] Sir: there was a time, in my ignorant youth, when I should have called you a hypocrite.

BROADBENT [*reddening*] A hypocrite!

NORA [*hastily*] Oh I'm sure you dont think anything of the sort, Mr Keegan.

BROADBENT [*emphatically*] Thank you, Miss Reilly: thank you.

CORNELIUS [*gloomily*] We all have to stretch it a bit in politics: hwats the use o pretendin we dont?

BROADBENT [*stiffly*] I hope I have said or done nothing that calls for any such observation, Mr Doyle. If there is a vice I detest – or against which my whole public life has been a protest – it is the vice of hypocrisy. I would almost rather be inconsistent than insincere.

KEEGAN. Do not be offended, sir: I know that you are quite sincere. There is a saying in the Scripture which runs – so far as the memory of an oldish man can carry the words – Let not the right side of your brain know what the left side doeth. I learnt at Oxford that this is the secret of the Englishman's strange power of making the best of both worlds.

BROADBENT. Surely the text refers to our right and left hands. I am somewhat surprised to hear a member of your Church quote so essentially Protestant a document as the Bible; but at least you might quote it accurately.

LARRY. Tom: with the best intentions youre making an ass of yourself. You dont understand Mr Keegan's peculiar vein of humor.

BROADBENT [*instantly recovering his confidence*] Ah! it was only your delightful Irish humor, Mr Keegan. Of course, of course. How stupid of me! I'm so sorry. [*He pats Keegan consolingly on the back*]. John Bull's wits are still slow, you see. Besides, calling me a hypocrite was too big a joke to swallow all at once, you know.

KEEGAN. You must also allow for the fact that I am mad.

NORA. Ah, dont talk like that, Mr Keegan.

BROADBENT [*encouragingly*] Not at all, not at all. Only a whimsical Irishman, eh?

LARRY. Are you really mad, Mr Keegan?

AUNT JUDY [*shocked*] Oh, Larry, how could you ask him such a thing?

LARRY. I dont think Mr Keegan minds. [*To Keegan*] Whats the true version of the story of that black man you confessed on his deathbed?

KEEGAN. What story have you heard about that?

LARRY. I am informed that when the devil came for the black heathen, he took off your head and turned it three times round before putting it on again; and that your head's been turned ever since.

NORA [*reproachfully*] Larry!

KEEGAN [*blandly*] That is not quite what occurred. [*He collects himself for a serious utterance: they attend involuntarily*]. I heard that a black man was dying, and that the people were afraid to go near him. When I went to the place I found an elderly Hindoo, who told me one of those tales of unmerited misfortune, of cruel ill luck, of relentless persecution by destiny, which sometimes wither the commonplaces of consolation on the lips of a priest. But this man did not complain of his misfortunes. They were brought upon him, he said, by sins committed in a former existence. Then without a word of comfort from me, he died with a clear-eyed resignation that my most earnest exhortations have rarely produced in a Christian, and left me sitting there by his bedside with the mystery of this world suddenly revealed to me.

BROADBENT. That is a remarkable tribute to the liberty of conscience enjoyed by the subjects of our Indian Empire.

LARRY. No doubt; but may we venture to ask what is the mystery of this world?

KEEGAN. This world, sir, is very clearly a place of torment and penance, a place where the fool flourishes and the good and wise are hated and persecuted, a place where men and women torture one another in the name of love; where children are scourged and enslaved in the name of parental duty and education; where the weak in body are poisoned and mutilated in the name of healing, and the weak in character are put to the horrible torture of imprisonment, not for hours but for years, in the name of justice. It is a place where the hardest toil is a welcome refuge from the horror and tedium of pleasure, and where charity and good works are done only for hire to ransom the souls of the spoiler and the sybarite. Now, sir, there is only one place of horror and torment known to my religion; and that place is hell. Therefore it is plain to me that this earth of ours must be hell, and that we are all here, as the Indian revealed to me – perhaps he was sent to reveal it to me – to expiate crimes committed by us in a former existence.

AUNT JUDY [*awestruck*] Heaven save us, what a thing to say!

CORNELIUS [*sighing*] It's a queer world: thats certain.

BROADBENT. Your idea is a very clever one, Mr Keegan: really most brilliant: *I* should never have thought of it. But it seems to me – if I may say so – that you are overlooking the fact that, of the evils you describe, some are absolutely necessary for the preservation of society, and others are encouraged only when the Tories are in office.

LARRY. I expect you were a Tory in a former existence; and that is why you are here.

BROADBENT [*with conviction*] Never, Larry, never. But leaving politics out of the question, I find the world quite good enough for me: rather a jolly place, in fact.

KEEGAN [*looking at him with quiet wonder*] You are satisfied?

BROADBENT. As a reasonable man, yes. I see no evils in the world – except, of course, natural evils – that cannot be remedied by freedom, self-government, and English institutions. I think so, not because I am an Englishman, but as a matter of common sense.

KEEGAN. You feel at home in the world, then?

BROADBENT. Of course. Dont you?

KEEGAN [*from the very depths of his nature*] No.

BROADBENT [*breezily*] Try phosphorus pills. I always take them when my brain is overworked. I'll give you the address in Oxford Street.

KEEGAN [*enigmatically: rising*] Miss Doyle: my wandering fit has come on me: will you excuse me?

AUNT JUDY. To be sure: you know you can come in n nout as you like.

KEEGAN. We can finish the game some other time, Miss Reilly. [*He goes for his hat and stick*].

NORA. No: I'm out with you [*she disarranges the pieces and rises*]. I was too wicked in a former existence to play backgammon with a good man like you.

AUNT JUDY [*whispering to her*] Whisht, whisht, child! Dont set him back on that again.

KEEGAN [*to Nora*] When I look at you, I think that perhaps Ireland is only purgatory, after all. [*He passes on to the garden door*].

NORA. Galong with you!

BROADBENT [*whispering to Cornelius*] Has he a vote?

CORNELIUS [*nodding*] Yes. An theres lotsle vote the way he tells them.

KEEGAN [*at the garden door, with gentle gravity*] Good evening, Mr Broadbent. You hae set me thinking. Thank you.

BROADBENT [*delighted, hurrying across to him to shake hands*] No, really? You find that contact with English ideas is stimulating, eh?

KEEGAN. I am never tired of hearing you talk, Mr Broadbent.

BROADBENT [*modestly remonstrating*] Oh come! come!

KEEGAN. Yes, I assure you. You are an extremely interesting man. [*He goes out*].

BROADBENT [*enthusiastically*] What a nice chap! What an intelligent, broadminded character, considering his cloth! By the way, I'd better have a wash [*He takes up his coat and cap, and leaves the room through the inner door*].

Nora returns to her chair and shuts up the backgammon board.

AUNT JUDY. Keegan's very queer today. He has his mad fit on him.

CORNELIUS [*worried and bitter*] I wouldnt say but he's right after all. It's a contrairy world. [*To Larry*] Why would you be such a fool as to let Broadbent take the seat in parliament from you?

LARRY [*glancing at Nora*] He will take more than that from me before he's done here.

CORNELIUS. I wish he'd never set foot in my house, bad luck to his fat face! D'ye think he'd lend me £300 on the farm, Larry? When I'm so hard up, it seems a waste o money not to mortgage it now it's me own.

LARRY. *I* can lend you £300 on it.

CORNELIUS. No, no; I wasnt putn in for that. When I die and leave you the farm I should like to be able to feel that it was all me own, and not half yours to start with. Now I'll take me oath Barney Doarn's going to ask Broadbent to lend him £500 on the mill to put in a new hweel; for the old one'll harly hol together. An Haffigan cant sleep with covetn that corner o land at the foot of his medda that belongs to Doolan. He'll have to mortgage to buy it. I may as well be first as last. D'ye think Broadbent'd len me a little?

LARRY. I'm quite sure he will.

CORNELIUS. Is he as ready as that? Would he len me five hunderd, d'ye think?

LARRY. He'll lend you more than the landll ever be worth to you; so for Heaven's sake be prudent.

CORNELIUS [*judicially*] All right, all right, me son: I'll be careful. I'm goin into the office for a bit. [*He withdraws through the inner door, obviously to prepare his application to Broadbent*].

AUNT JUDY [*indignantly*] As if he hadnt seen enough o borryin when he was an agent without beginning borryin himself! [*She rises*]. I'll borry him, so I will. [*She puts her knitting on the table and follows him out, with a resolute air that bodes trouble for Cornelius*].

Larry and Nora are left together for the first time since his arrival. She looks at him with a smile that perishes as she sees him aimlessly rocking his chair, and reflecting, evidently not about her, with his lips pursed as if he were whistling. With a catch in her throat she takes up Aunt Judy's knitting, and makes a pretence of going on with it.

NORA. I suppose it didnt seem very long to you.

LARRY [*starting*] Eh? What didnt?

NORA. The eighteen years youve been away.

LARRY. Oh, that! No: it seems hardly more than a week. I've been so busy – had so little time to think.

NORA. Ive had nothing else to do but think.

LARRY. That was very bad for you. Why didnt you give it up? Why did you stay here?

NORA. Because nobody sent for me to go anywhere else, I suppose. Thats why.

LARRY. Yes: one does stick frightfully in the same place, unless some external force comes and routs one out. [*He yawns slightly; but as she looks up quickly at him, he pulls himself together and rises with an air of waking up and setting to work cheerfully to make himself agreeable*]. And how have you been all this time?

NORA. Quite well, thank you.

LARRY. Thats right. [*Suddenly finding that he has nothing else to say, and being ill at ease in consequence, he strolls about the room humming distractedly*].

NORA [*struggling with her tears*] Is that all you have to say to me, Larry?

LARRY. Well, what is there to say? You see, we know each other so well.

NORA [*a little consoled*] Yes: of course we do. [*He does not reply*]. I wonder you came back at all.

LARRY. I couldnt help it. [*She looks up affectionately*]. Tom made me. [*She looks down again quickly to conceal the effect of this blow. He whistles another stave; then resumes*] I had a sort of dread of returning to Ireland. I felt somehow that my luck would turn if I came back. And now here I am, none the worse.

NORA. Praps it's a little dull for you.

LARRY. No: I havnt exhausted the interest of strolling about the old places and remembering and romancing about them.

NORA [*hopefully*] Oh! You do remember the places, then?

LARRY. Of course. They have associations.

NORA [*not doubting that the associations are with her*] I suppose so.

LARRY. M'yes. I can remember particular spots where I had long fits of thinking about the countries I meant to get to when I escaped from Ireland. America and London, and sometimes Rome and the east.

NORA [*deeply mortified*] Was that all you used to be thinking about?

LARRY. Well, there was precious little else to think about here, my dear Nora, except sometimes at sunset, when one got maudlin and called Ireland Erin, and imagined one was remembering the days of old, and so forth. [*He whistles Let Erin Remember*].

NORA. Did jever get a letter I wrote you last February?

LARRY. Oh yes; and I really intended to answer it. But I havnt had a moment; and I knew you wouldnt mind. You see, I am so afraid of boring you by writing about affairs you dont understand and people you dont know! And yet what else have I to write about? I begin a letter; and then I tear it up again. The fact is, fond as we are of one another, Nora, we have so little in common − I mean of course the things one can put in a letter − that correspondence is apt to become the hardest of hard work.

NORA. Yes: it's hard for me to know anything about you if you never tell me anything.

LARRY [*pettishly*] Nora: a man cant sit down and write his life day by day when he's tired enough with having lived it.

NORA. I'm not blaming you.

LARRY [*looking at her with some concern*] You seem rather out of spirits. [*Going closer to her, anxiously and tenderly*] You havnt got neuralgia, have you?

NORA. No.

LARRY [*reassured*] I get a touch of it sometimes when I am below par.

[*Absently, again strolling about*] Yes, yes. [*He gazes through the doorway at the Irish landscape, and sings, almost unconsciously, but very expressively, an air from Offenbach's Whittington*].

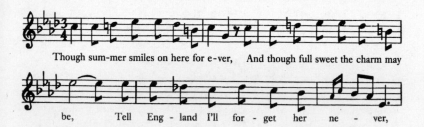

Though sum-mer smiles on here for e-ver, And though full sweet the charm may be, Tell Eng-land I'll for-get her ne-ver,

[*Nora, who has been at first touched by the tenderness of his singing, puts down her knitting at this very unexpected sentiment, and stares at him. He continues until the melody soars out of his range, when he trails off into whistling Let Erin Remember*].

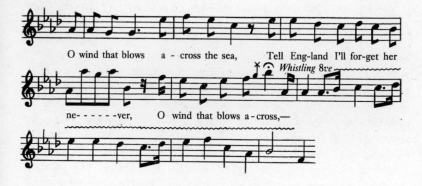

O wind that blows a-cross the sea, Tell Eng-land I'll for-get her ne------ver, O wind that blows a-cross,—

I'm afraid I'm boring you, Nora, though youre too kind to say so.

NORA. Are you wanting to get back to England already?

LARRY. Not at all. Not at all.

NORA. Thats a queer song to sing to me if youre not.

LARRY. The song! Oh, it doesnt mean anything: it's by a German Jew,

like most English patriotic sentiment. Never mind me, my dear: go
on with your work; and dont let me bore you.

NORA [*bitterly*] Rosscullen isnt such a lively place that I am likely to
be bored by you at our first talk together after eighteen years, though
you dont seem to have much to say to me after all.

LARRY. Eighteen years is a devilish long time, Nora. Now if it had been
eighteen minutes, or even eighteen months, we should be able to pick
up the interrupted thread, and chatter like two magpies. But as it is,
I have simply nothing to say; and you seem to have less.

NORA. I — [*her tears choke her; but she keeps up appearances desperately*].

LARRY [*quite unconscious of his cruelty*] In a week or so we shall be quite
old friends again. Meanwhile, as I feel that I am not making myself
particularly entertaining, I'll take myself off. Tell Tom Ive gone for
a stroll over the hill.

NORA. You seem very fond of Tom, as you call him.

LARRY [*the triviality going suddenly out of his voice*] Yes: I'm fond of
Tom.

NORA. Oh, well, dont let me keep you from him.

LARRY. I know quite well that my departure will be a relief. Rather
a failure, this first meeting after eighteen years, eh? Well, never mind:
these great sentimental events always are failures; and now the worst
of it's over anyhow. [*He goes out through the garden door*].

*Nora, left alone, struggles wildly to save herself from breaking down, and
then drops her face on the table and gives way to a convulsion of crying. Her
sobs shake her so that she can hear nothing; and she has no suspicion that she
is no longer alone until her head and breast are raised by Broadbent who,
returning newly washed and combed through the inner door, has seen her
condition, first with surprise and concern, and then with an emotional dis-
turbance that quite upsets him.*

BROADBENT. Miss Reilly. Miss Reilly. Whats the matter? Dont cry: I
cant stand it: you mustnt cry. [*She makes a choked effort to speak, so
painful that he continues with impulsive sympathy*] No: dont try to speak:
it's all right now. Have your cry out: never mind me: trust me.
[*Gathering her to him, and babbling consolatorily*] Cry on my chest: the
only really comfortable place for a woman to cry is a man's chest:
a real man, a real friend. A good broad chest, eh? not less than forty-
two inches — no: dont fuss: never mind the conventions: we're two

friends, arnt we? Come now, come, come! It's all right and comfortable and happy now, isnt it?

NORA [*through her tears*] Let me go. I want me hankerchief.

BROADBENT [*holding her with one arm and producing a large silk handkerchief from his breast pocket*] Heres a handkerchief. Let me [*he dabs her tears dry with it*]. Never mind your own: it's too small: it's one of those wretched little cambric handkerchiefs —

NORA [*sobbing*] Indeed it's a common cotton one.

BROADBENT. Of course it's a common cotton one — silly little cotton one — not good enough for the dear eyes of Nora Cryna —

NORA [*spluttering into a hysterical laugh and clutching him convulsively with her fingers while she tries to stifle her laughter against his collar bone*] Oh dont make me laugh: please dont make me laugh.

BROADBENT [*terrified*] I didnt mean to, on my soul. What is it? What is it?

NORA. Nora Creena, Nora Creena.

BROADBENT [*patting her*] Yes, yes, of course, Nora Creena, Nora acushla [*he makes cush rhyme to plush*] —

NORA. Acushla [*she makes cush rhyme to bush*].

BROADBENT. Oh, confound the language! Nora darling — my Nora — the Nora I love —

NORA [*shocked into propriety*] You mustnt talk like that to me.

BROADBENT [*suddenly becoming prodigiously solemn and letting her go*] No, of course not. I dont mean it. At least I do mean it, but I know it's premature. I had no right to take advantage of your being a little upset; but I lost my self-control for a moment.

NORA [*wondering at him*] I think youre a very kind-hearted man, Mr Broadbent; but you seem to me to have no self-control at all [*she turns her face away with a keen pang of shame and adds*] no more than myself.

BROADBENT [*resolutely*] Oh yes, I have: you should see me when I am really roused: then I have TREMENDOUS self-control. Remember: we have been alone together only once before; and then, I regret to say, I was in a disgusting state.

NORA. Ah no, Mr Broadbent: you wernt disgusting.

BROADBENT [*mercilessly*] Yes I was: nothing can excuse it: perfectly beastly. It must have made a most unfavorable impression on you.

NORA. Oh, sure it's all right. Say no more about that.

BROADBENT. I must, Miss Reilly: it is my duty. I shall not detain you long. May I ask you to sit down. [*He indicates her chair with oppressive solemnity. She sits down wondering. He then, with the same portentous gravity, places a chair for himself near her; sits down; and proceeds to explain*]. First, Miss Reilly, may I say that I have tasted nothing of an alcoholic nature today.

NORA. It doesnt seem to make as much difference in you as it would in an Irishman, somehow.

BROADBENT. Perhaps not. Perhaps not. I never quite lose myself.

NORA [*consolingly*] Well, anyhow, youre all right now.

BROADBENT [*fervently*] Thank you, Miss Reilly: I am. Now we shall get along. [*Tenderly, lowering his voice*] Nora: I was in earnest last night. [*Nora moves as if to rise*]. No: one moment. You must not think I am going to press you for an answer before you have known me for 24 hours. I am a reasonable man, I hope; and I am prepared to wait as long as you like, provided you will give me some small assurance that the answer will not be unfavorable.

NORA. How could I go back from it if I did? I sometimes think youre not quite right in your head, Mr Broadbent, you say such funny things.

BROADBENT. Yes: I know I have a strong sense of humor which sometimes makes people doubt whether I am quite serious. That is why I have always thought I should like to marry an Irishwoman. She would always understand my jokes. For instance, you would understand them, eh?

NORA [*uneasily*] Mr Broadbent: I couldnt.

BROADBENT [*soothingly*] Wait: let me break this to you gently, Miss Reilly: hear me out. I daresay you have noticed that in speaking to you I have been putting a very strong constraint on myself, so as to avoid wounding your delicacy by too abrupt an avowal of my feelings. Well, I feel now that the time has come to be open, to be frank, to be explicit. Miss Reilly: you have inspired in me a very strong attachment. Perhaps, with a woman's intuition, you have already guessed that.

NORA [*rising distractedly*] Why do you talk to me in that unfeeling nonsensical way?

BROADBENT [*rising also, much astonished*] Unfeeling! Nonsensical!

NORA. Dont you know that you have said things to me that no man ought to say unless – unless – [*she suddenly breaks down again and hides her face on the table as before*] Oh, go away from me: I wont get married at all: what is it but heartbreak and disappointment?

BROADBENT [*developing the most formidable symptoms of rage and grief*] Do you mean to say that you are going to refuse me? that you dont care for me?

NORA [*looking at him in consternation*] Oh, dont take it to heart, Mr Br—

BROADBENT [*flushed and almost choking*] I dont want to be petted and blarneyed. [*With childish rage*] I love you. I want you for my wife. [*In despair*] I cant help your refusing. I'm helpless: I can do nothing. You have no right to ruin my whole life. You – [*a hysterical convulsion stops him*].

NORA [*almost awestruck*] Youre not going to cry, are you? I never thought a man could cry. Dont.

BROADBENT. I'm not crying. I – I'– I leave that sort of thing to your damned sentimental Irishmen. You think I have no feeling because I am a plain unemotional Englishman, with no powers of expression.

NORA. I dont think you know the sort of man you are at all. Whatever may be the matter with you, it's not want of feeling.

BROADBENT [*hurt and petulant*] It's you who have no feeling. Youre as heartless as Larry.

NORA. What do you expect me to do? Is it to throw meself at your head the minute the word is out o your mouth?

BROADBENT [*striking his silly head with his fists*] Oh, what a fool! what a brute I am! It's only your Irish delicacy: of course, of course. You mean Yes. Eh? What? Yes? yes? yes?

NORA. I think you might understand that though I might choose to be an old maid, I could never marry anybody but you now.

BROADBENT [*clasping her violently to his breast, with a crow of immense relief and triumph*] Ah, thats right, thats right: thats magnificent. I knew you would see what a first-rate thing this will be for both of us.

NORA [*incommoded and not at all enraptured by his ardor*] Youre dreadfully strong, an a gradle too free with your strength. An I never thought o whether it'd be a good thing for us or not. But when you found me here that time, I let you be kind to me, and cried in your arms, because I was too wretched to think of anything but the comfort of it. And how could I let any other man touch me after that?

BROADBENT [*moved*] Now thats very nice of you, Nora: thats really most delicately womanly [*he kisses her hand chivalrously*].

NORA [*looking earnestly and a little doubtfully at him*] Surely if you let one woman cry on you like that youd never let another touch you.

BROADBENT [*conscientiously*] One should not. One ought not, my dear girl. But the honest truth is, if a chap is at all a pleasant sort of chap, his chest becomes a fortification that has to stand many assaults: at least it is so in England.

NORA [*curtly, much disgusted*] Then youd better marry an Englishwoman.

BROADBENT [*making a wry face*] No, no: the Englishwoman is too prosaic for my taste, too material, too much of the animated beefsteak about her. The ideal is what I like. Now Larry's taste is just the opposite: he likes em solid and bouncing and rather keen about him. It's a very convenient difference; for weve never been in love with the same woman.

NORA. An d'ye mean to tell me to me face that youve ever been in love before?

BROADBENT. Lord! yes.

NORA. I'm not your first love!

BROADBENT. First love is only a little foolishness and a lot of curiosity: no really self-respecting woman would take advantage of it. No, my dear Nora: Ive done with all that long ago. Love affairs always end in rows. We're not going to have any rows: we're going to have a solid four-square home: man and wife: comfort and common sense. And plenty of affection, eh [*he puts his arm round her with confident proprietorship*]?

NORA [*coldly, trying to get away*] I dont want any other woman's leavings.

BROADBENT [*holding her*] Nobody asked you to, maam. I never asked any woman to marry me before.

NORA [*severely*] Then why didnt you if youre an honorable man?

BROADBENT. Well, to tell you the truth, they were mostly married already. But never mind! there was nothing wrong. Come! dont take a mean advantage of me. After all, you must have had a fancy or two yourself, eh?

NORA [*conscience-stricken*] Yes. I suppose Ive no right to be particular.

BROADBENT [*humbly*] I know I'm not good enough for you, Nora. But no man is, you know, when the woman is a really nice woman.

NORA. Oh, I'm no better than yourself. I may as well tell you about it.

BROADBENT. No, no: lets have no telling: much better not. *I* shant tell you anything: dont you tell me anything. Perfect confidence in one another and no tellings: thats the way to avoid rows.

NORA. Dont think it was anything I need be ashamed of.

BROADBENT. I dont.

NORA. It was only that I'd never known anybody else that I could care for; and I was foolish enough once to think that Larry –

BROADBENT [*disposing of the idea at once*] Larry! Oh, that wouldnt have done at all, not at all. You dont know Larry as I do, my dear. He has absolutely no capacity for enjoyment: he couldnt make any woman happy. He's as clever as be-blowed; but life's too earthly for him: he doesnt really care for anything or anybody.

NORA. I've found that out.

BROADBENT. Of course you have. No, my dear: take my word for it, youre jolly well out of that. There! [*swinging her round against his breast*] thats much more comfortable for you.

NORA [*with Irish peevishness*] Ah, you mustnt go on like that. I dont like it.

BROADBENT [*unabashed*] Youll acquire the taste by degrees. You mustnt mind me: it's an absolute necessity of my nature that I should have somebody to hug occasionally. Besides, it's good for you: itll plump out your muscles and make em elastic and set up your figure.

NORA. Well, I'm sure! if this is English manners! Arnt you ashamed to talk about such things?

BROADBENT [*in the highest feather*] Not a bit. By George, Nora, it's a tremendous thing to be able to enjoy oneself. Lets go off for a walk out of this stuffy little room. I want the open air to expand in. Come along. Co-o-ome along. [*He puts her arm into his and sweeps her out into the garden as an equinoctial gale might sweep a dry leaf*].

Later in the evening, the grasshopper is again enjoying the sunset by the great stone on the hill; but this time he enjoys neither the stimulus of Keegan's conversation nor the pleasure of terrifying Patsy Farrell. He is alone until Nora and Broadbent come up the hill arm in arm. Broadbent is still breezy and confident; but she has her head averted from him and is almost in tears.

BROADBENT [*stopping to snuff up the hillside air*] Ah! I like this spot.

I like this view. This would be a jolly good place for a hotel and a golf links. Friday to Tuesday, railway ticket and hotel all inclusive. I tell you, Nora, I'm going to develop this place. [*Looking at her*] Hallo! Whats the matter? Tired?

NORA [*unable to restrain her tears*] I'm ashamed out o me life.

BROADBENT [*astonished*] Ashamed! What of?

NORA. Oh, how could you drag me all round the place like that, telling everybody that we're going to be married, and introjoocing me to the lowest of the low, and letting them shake hans with me, and encouraging them to make free with us? I little thought I should live to be shaken hans with be Doolan in broad daylight in the public street of Rosscullen.

BROADBENT. But, my dear, Doolan's a publican: a most influential man. By the way, I asked him if his wife would be at home tomorrow. He said she would; so you must take the motor car round and call on her.

NORA [*aghast*] Is it me call on Doolan's wife!

BROADBENT. Yes, of course: call on all their wives. We must get a copy of the register and a supply of canvassing cards. No use calling on people who havnt votes. Youll be a great success as a canvasser, Nora: they call you the heiress; and theyll be flattered no end by your calling, especially as youve never cheapened yourself by speaking to them before – have you?

NORA [*indignantly*] Not likely, indeed.

BROADBENT. Well, we mustnt be stiff and stand-off, you know. We must be thoroughly democratic, and patronize everybody without distinction of class. I tell you I'm a jolly lucky man, Nora Cryna. I get engaged to the most delightful woman in Ireland; and it turns out that I couldnt have done a smarter stroke of electioneering.

NORA. An would you let me demean meself like that, just to get yourself into parliament?

BROADBENT [*buoyantly*] Aha! Wait till you find out what an exciting game electioneering is: youll be mad to get me in. Besides, youd like people to say that Tom Broadbent's wife had been the making of him? that she got him into parliament? into the Cabinet, perhaps, eh?

NORA. God knows I dont grudge you me money! But to lower meself to the level of common people –

BROADBENT. To a member's wife, Nora, nobody is common provided he's on the register. Come, my dear! it's all right: do you think I'd let you do it if it wasnt? The best people do it. Everybody does it.

NORA [*who has been biting her lip and looking over the hill, disconsolate and unconvinced*] Well, praps you know best what they do in England. They must have very little respect for themselves. I think I'll go in now. I see Larry and Mr Keegan coming up the hill; and I'm not fit to talk to them.

BROADBENT. Just wait and say something nice to Keegan. They tell me he controls nearly as many votes as Father Dempsey himself.

NORA. You little know Peter Keegan. He'd see through me as if I was a pane o glass.

BROADBENT. Oh, he wont like it any the less for that. What really flatters a man is that you think him worth flattering. Not that I would flatter any man: dont think that. I'll just go and meet him. [*He goes down the hill with the eager forward look of a man about to greet a valued acquaintance. Nora dries her eyes, and turns to go as Larry strolls up the hill to her*].

LARRY. Nora. [*She turns and looks at him hardly, without a word. He continues anxiously, in his most conciliatory tone*]. When I left you that time, I was just as wretched as you. I didnt rightly know what I wanted to say; and my tongue kept clacking to cover the loss I was at. Well, Ive been thinking ever since; and now I know what I ought to have said. Ive come back to say it.

NORA. Youve come too late, then. You thought eighteen years was not long enough, and that you might keep me waiting a day longer. Well, you were mistaken. I'm engaged to your friend Mr Broadbent; and I'm done with you.

LARRY [*naïvely*] But that was the very thing I was going to advise you to do.

NORA [*involuntarily*] Oh you brute! to tell me that to me face!

LARRY [*nervously relapsing into his most Irish manner*] Nora, dear, dont you understand that I'm an Irishman, and he's an Englishman. He wants you; and he grabs you. *I* want you; and I quarrel with you and have to go on wanting you.

NORA. So you may. Youd better go back to England to the animated beefsteaks youre so fond of.

LARRY [*amazed*] Nora! [*Guessing where she got the metaphor*] He's been talking of me, I see. Well, never mind: we must be friends, you and I. I dont want his marriage to you to be his divorce from me.

NORA. You care more for him than you ever did for me.

LARRY [*with curt sincerity*] Yes of course I do: why should I tell you lies about it? Nora Reilly was a person of very little consequence to me or anyone else outside this miserable little hole. But Mrs Tom Broadbent will be a person of very considerable consequence indeed. Play your new part well, and there will be no more neglect, no more loneliness, no more idle regrettings and vain-hopings in the evenings by the Round Tower, but real life and real work and real cares and real joys among real people: solid English life in London, the very centre of the world. You will find your work cut out for you keeping Tom's house and entertaining Tom's friends and getting Tom into parliament; but it will be worth the effort.

NORA. You talk as if I was under obligation to him for marrying me.

LARRY. I talk as I think. Youve made a very good match, let me tell you.

NORA. Indeed! Well, some people might say he's not done so badly himself.

LARRY. If you mean that you will be a treasure to him, he thinks so now; and you can keep him thinking so if you like.

NORA. I wasnt thinking o meself at all.

LARRY. Were you thinking of your money, Nora?

NORA. I didnt say so.

LARRY. Your money will not pay your cook's wages in London.

NORA [*flaming up*] If thats true – and the more shame for you to throw it in me face if it is true – at all events itll make us independent; for if the worst comes to the worst, we can always come back here and live on it. An if I have to keep his house for him, at all events I can keep you out of it; for Ive done with you; and I wish I'd never seen you. So goodbye to you, Mister Larry Doyle. [*She turns her back on him and goes home*].

LARRY [*watching her as she goes*] Goodbye. Goodbye. Oh, thats so Irish! Irish both of us to the backbone: Irish! Irish! Iri—

Broadbent arrives, conversing energetically with Keegan.

BROADBENT. Nothing pays like a golfing hotel, if you hold the land instead of the shares, and if the furniture people stand in with you, and if you are a good man of business.

LARRY. Nora's gone home.

BROADBENT [*with conviction*] You were right this morning, Larry. I must feed up Nora. She's weak; and it makes her fanciful. Oh, by the way, did I tell you that we're engaged?

LARRY. She told me herself.

BROADBENT [*complacently*] She's rather full of it, as you may imagine. Poor Nora! Well, Mr Keegan, as I said, I begin to see my way here. I begin to see my way.

KEEGAN [*with a courteous inclination*] The conquering Englishman, sir. Within 24 hours of your arrival you have carried off our only heiress, and practically secured the parliamentary seat. And you have promised me that when I come here in the evenings to meditate on my madness; to watch the shadow of the Round Tower lengthening in the sunset; to break my heart uselessly in the curtained gloaming over the dead heart and blinded soul of the island of the saints, you will comfort me with the bustle of a great hotel, and the sight of the little children carrying the golf clubs of your tourists as a preparation for the life to come.

BROADBENT [*quite touched, mutely offering him a cigar to console him, at which he smiles and shakes his head*] Yes, Mr Keegan: youre quite right. Theres poetry in everything, even [*looking absently into the cigar case*] in the most modern prosaic things, if you know how to extract it [*he extracts a cigar for himself and offers one to Larry, who takes it*]. If I was to be shot for it I couldnt extract it myself; but thats where you come in, you see. [*Roguishly, waking up from his reverie and bustling Keegan goodhumoredly*] And then *I* shall wake you up a bit. Thats where *I* come in: eh? d'ye see? Eh? eh? [*He pats him very pleasantly on the shoulder, half admiringly, half pityingly*]. Just so, just so. [*Coming back to business*] By the way, I believe I can do better than a light railway here. There seems to be no question now that the motor boat has come to stay. Well, look at your magnificent river there, going to waste.

KEEGAN [*closing his eyes*]
    'Silent, O Moyle, be the roar of thy waters.'

BROADBENT. You know, the roar of a motor boat is quite pretty.

KEEGAN. Provided it does not drown the Angelus.

BROADBENT [*reassuringly*] Oh no: it wont do that: not the least danger. You know, a church bell can make a devil of a noise when it likes.

KEEGAN. You have an answer for everything, sir. But your plans leave one question still unanswered: how to get butter out of a dog's throat.

BROADBENT. Eh?

KEEGAN. You cannot build your golf links and hotels in the air. For that you must own our land. And how will you drag our acres from the ferret's grip of Matthew Haffigan? How will you persuade Cornelius Doyle to forgo the pride of being a small landowner? How will Barney Doran's millrace agree with your motor boats? Will Doolan help you to get a licence for your hotel?

BROADBENT. My dear sir: to all intents and purposes the syndicate I represent already owns half Rosscullen. Doolan's is a tied house; and the brewers are in the syndicate. As to Haffigan's farm and Doran's mill and Mr Doyle's place and half a dozen others, they will be mortgaged to me before a month is out.

KEEGAN. But pardon me, you will not lend them more on their land than the land is worth; so they will be able to pay you the interest.

BROADBENT. Ah, you are a poet, Mr Keegan, not a man of business.

LARRY. We will lend every one of these men half as much again on their land as it is worth, or ever can be worth, to them.

BROADBENT. You forget, sir, that we, with our capital, our knowledge, our organization, and may I say our English business habits, can make or lose ten pounds out of land that Haffigan, with all his industry, could not make or lose ten shillings out of. Doran's mill is a super-annuated folly: I shall want it for electric lighting.

LARRY. What is the use of giving land to such men? they are too small, too poor, too ignorant, too simpleminded to hold it against us: you might as well give a dukedom to a crossing sweeper.

BROADBENT. Yes, Mr Keegan: this place may have an industrial future, or it may have a residential future: I cant tell yet; but it's not going to be a future in the hands of your Dorans and Haffigans, poor devils!

KEEGAN. It may have no future at all. Have you thought of that?

BROADBENT. Oh, I'm not afraid of that. I have faith in Ireland. Great faith, Mr Keegan.

KEEGAN. And we have none: only empty enthusiasms and patriotisms, and emptier memories and regrets. Ah yes: you have some excuse for believing that if there be any future, it will be yours; for our faith seems dead, and our hearts cold and cowed. An island of dreamers who wake up in your jails, of critics and cowards whom you buy and tame for your own service, of bold rogues who help you to plunder us that they may plunder you afterwards.

BROADBENT [*a little impatient of this unbusinesslike view*] Yes, yes; but you know you might say that of any country. The fact is, there are only two qualities in the world: efficiency and inefficiency, and only two sorts of people: the efficient and the inefficient. It dont matter whether theyre English or Irish. I shall collar this place, not because I'm an Englishman and Haffigan and Co are Irishmen, but because theyre duffers, and I know my way about.

KEEGAN. Have you considered what is to become of Haffigan?

LARRY. Oh, we'll employ him in some capacity or other, and probably pay him more than he makes for himself now.

BROADBENT [*dubiously*] Do you think so? No no: Haffigan's too old. It really doesnt pay now to take on men over forty even for unskilled labor, which I suppose is all Haffigan would be good for. No: Haffigan had better go to America, or into the Union, poor old chap! He's worked out, you know: you can see it.

KEEGAN. Poor lost soul, so cunningly fenced in with invisible bars!

LARRY. Haffigan doesnt matter much. He'll die presently.

BROADBENT [*shocked*] Oh come, Larry! Dont be unfeeling. It's hard on Haffigan. It's always hard on the inefficient.

LARRY. Pah! what does it matter where an old and broken man spends his last days, or whether he has a million at the bank or only the work-house dole? It's the young men, the able men, that matter. The real tragedy of Haffigan is the tragedy of his wasted youth, his stunted mind, his drudging over his clods and pigs until he has become a clod and a pig himself – until the soul within him has smouldered into nothing but a dull temper that hurts himself and all around him. I say let him die, and let us have no more of his like. And let young Ireland take care that it doesnt share his fate, instead of making another empty grievance of it. Let your syndicate come –

BROADBENT. Your syndicate too, old chap. You have your bit of the stock.

LARRY. Yes: mine if you like. Well, our syndicate has no conscience:

it has no more regard for your Haffigans and Doolans and Dorans than it has for a gang of Chinese coolies. It will use your patriotic blatherskite and balderdash to get parliamentary powers over you as cynically as it would bait a mousetrap with toasted cheese. It will plan, and organize, and find capital while you slave like bees for it and revenge yourselves by paying politicians and penny newspapers out of your small wages to write articles and report speeches against its wickedness and tyranny, and to crack up your own Irish heroism, just as Haffigan once paid a witch a penny to put a spell on Billy Byrne's cow. In the end it will grind the nonsense out of you, and grind strength and sense into you.

BROADBENT [*out of patience*] Why cant you say a simple thing simply, Larry, without all that Irish exaggeration and talky-talky? The syndicate is a perfectly respectable body of responsible men of good position. We'll take Ireland in hand, and by straightforward business habits teach it efficiency and self-help on sound Liberal principles. You agree with me, Mr Keegan, dont you?

KEEGAN. Sir: I may even vote for you.

BROADBENT [*sincerely moved, shaking his hand warmly*] You shall never regret it, Mr Keegan: I give you my word for that. I shall bring money here: I shall raise wages: I shall found public institutions: a library, a Polytechnic (undenominational, of course), a gymnasium, a cricket club, perhaps an art school. I shall make a Garden City of Rosscullen: the Round Tower shall be thoroughly repaired and restored.

KEEGAN. And our place of torment shall be as clean and orderly as the cleanest and most orderly place I know in Ireland, which is our poetically named Mountjoy prison. Well, perhaps I had better vote for an efficient devil that knows his own mind and his own business than for a foolish patriot who has no mind and no business.

BROADBENT [*stiffly*] Devil is rather a strong expression in that connection, Mr Keegan.

KEEGAN. Not from a man who knows that this world is hell. But since the word offends you, let me soften it, and compare you simply to an ass. [*Larry whitens with anger*].

BROADBENT [*reddening*] An ass!

KEEGAN [*gently*] You may take it without offence from a madman who calls the ass his brother—and a very honest, useful and faithful brother, too. The ass, sir, is the most efficient of beasts, matter-of-fact, hardy, friendly when you treat him as a fellow-creature, stubborn when you abuse him, ridiculous only in love, which sets him braying, and in politics, which move him to roll about in the public road and raise a dust about nothing. Can you deny these qualities and habits in yourself, sir?

BROADBENT [*goodhumoredly*] Well, yes, I'm afraid I do, you know.

KEEGAN. Then perhaps you will confess to the ass's one fault.

BROADBENT. Perhaps so: what is it?

KEEGAN. That he wastes all his virtues – his efficiency, as you call it – in doing the will of his greedy masters instead of doing the will of Heaven that is in himself. He is efficient in the service of Mammon, mighty in mischief, skilful in ruin, heroic in destruction. But he comes to browse here without knowing that the soil his hoof touches is holy ground. Ireland, sir, for good or evil, is like no other place under heaven; and no man can touch its sod or breathe its air without becoming better or worse. It produces two kinds of men in strange perfection: saints and traitors. It is called the island of the saints; but indeed in these later years it might be more fitly called the island of the traitors; for our harvest of these is the fine flower of the world's crop of infamy. But the day may come when these islands shall live by the quality of their men rather than by the abundance of their minerals; and then we shall see.

LARRY. Mr Keegan: if you are going to be sentimental about Ireland, I shall bid you good evening. We have had enough of that, and more than enough of cleverly proving that everybody who is not an Irishman is an ass. It is neither good sense nor good manners. It will not stop the syndicate; and it will not interest young Ireland so much as my friend's gospel of efficiency.

BROADBENT. Ah, yes, yes: efficiency is the thing. I dont in the least mind your chaff, Mr Keegan; but Larry's right on the main point. The world belongs to the efficient.

KEEGAN [*with polished irony*] I stand rebuked, gentlemen. But believe me, I do every justice to the efficiency of you and your syndicate. You are both, I am told, thoroughly efficient civil engineers; and I have no doubt the golf links will be a triumph of your art. Mr Broadbent will get into parliament most efficiently, which is more than St Patrick could do if he were alive now. You may even build the hotel efficiently if you can find enough efficient masons, carpenters, and plumbers, which I rather doubt. [*Dropping his irony, and beginning to fall into the attitude of the priest rebuking sin*] When the hotel becomes insolvent [*Broadbent takes his cigar out of his mouth, a little taken aback*] your English business habits will secure the thorough efficiency of the liquidation. You will reorganize the scheme efficiently; you will liquidate its second bankruptcy efficiently [*Broadbent and Larry look quickly at one another; for this, unless the priest is an old financial hand, must be inspiration*]; you will get rid of its original shareholders efficiently after efficiently ruining them; and you will finally profit very efficiently by getting that hotel for a few shillings in the pound. [*More and more sternly*] Besides these efficient operations, you will foreclose your mortgages most efficiently [*his rebuking forefinger goes up in spite of himself*]; you will drive Haffigan to America very efficiently; you will find a use for Barney Doran's foul mouth and bullying temper by employing him to slave-drive your laborers very efficiently; and [*low and bitter*] when at last this poor desolate country-side becomes a busy mint in which we shall all slave to make money for you, with our Polytechnic to teach us how to do it efficiently, and our library to fuddle the few imaginations your distilleries will spare, and our repaired Round Tower with admission sixpence, and refreshments and penny-in-the-slot mutoscopes to make it interesting, then no doubt your English and American shareholders will spend all the money we make for them very efficiently in shooting and hunting, in operations for cancer and appendicitis, in gluttony and gambling; and you will devote what they save to fresh land development schemes. For four wicked centuries the world has dreamed this foolish dream of efficiency; and the end is not yet. But the end will come.

BROADBENT [*seriously*] Too true, Mr Keegan, only too true. And most eloquently put. It reminds me of poor Ruskin: a great man, you know. I sympathize. Believe me, I'm on your side. Dont sneer, Larry: I used to read a lot of Shelley years ago. Let us be faithful to the dreams of our youth [*he wafts a wreath of cigar smoke at large across the hill*].

KEEGAN. Come, Mr Doyle! is this English sentiment so much more efficient than our Irish sentiment, after all? Mr Broadbent spends his life inefficiently admiring the thoughts of great men, and efficiently serving the cupidity of base money hunters. We spend our lives efficiently sneering at him and doing nothing. Which of us has any right to reproach the other?

BROADBENT [*coming down the hill again to Keegan's right hand*] But you know, something must be done.

KEEGAN. Yes: when we cease to do, we cease to live. Well, what shall we do?

BROADBENT. Why, what lies to our hand.

KEEGAN. Which is the making of golf links and hotels to bring idlers to a country which workers have left in millions because it is a hungry land, a naked land, an ignorant and oppressed land.

BROADBENT. But, hang it all, the idlers will bring money from England to Ireland!

KEEGAN. Just as our idlers have for so many generations taken money from Ireland to England. Has that saved England from poverty and degradation more horrible than we have ever dreamed of? When I went to England, sir, I hated England. Now I pity it. [*Broadbent can hardly conceive an Irishman pitying England; but as Larry intervenes angrily, he gives it up and takes to the hill and his cigar again*].

LARRY. Much good your pity will do it!

KEEGAN. In the accounts kept in heaven, Mr Doyle, a heart purified of hatred may be worth more than even a Land Development Syndicate of Anglicized Irishmen and Gladstonized Englishmen.

LARRY. Oh, in heaven, no doubt. I have never been there. Can you tell me where it is?

KEEGAN. Could you have told me this morning where hell is? Yet you know now that it is here. Do not despair of finding heaven: it may be no farther off.

LARRY [*ironically*] On this holy ground, as you call it, eh?

KEEGAN [*with fierce intensity*] Yes, perhaps, even on this holy ground which such Irishmen as you have turned into a Land of Derision.

BROADBENT [*coming between them*] Take care! you will be quarrelling presently. Oh, you Irishmen, you Irishmen! Toujours Ballyhooly, eh? [*Larry, with a shrug, half comic, half impatient, turns away up the hill, but presently strolls back on Keegan's right. Broadbent adds, confidentially to Keegan*] Stick to the Englishman, Mr Keegan: he has a bad name here; but at least he can forgive you for being an Irishman.

KEEGAN. Sir: when you speak to me of English and Irish you forget that I am a Catholic. My country is not Ireland nor England, but the whole mighty realm of my Church. For me there are but two countries: heaven and hell; but two conditions of men: salvation and damnation. Standing here between you the Englishman, so clever in your foolishness, and this Irishman, so foolish in his cleverness, I cannot in my ignorance be sure which of you is the more deeply damned; but I should be unfaithful to my calling if I opened the gates of my heart less widely to one than to the other.

LARRY. In either case it would be an impertinence, Mr Keegan, as your approval is not of the slightest consequence to us. What use do you suppose all this drivel is to men with serious practical business in hand?

BROADBENT. I dont agree with that, Larry. I think these things cannot be said too often: they keep up the moral tone of the community. As you know, I claim the right to think for myself in religious matters: in fact, I am ready to avow myself a bit of a – of a – well, I dont care who knows it – a bit of a Unitarian; but if the Church of England contained a few men like Mr Keegan, I should certainly join it.

KEEGAN. You do me too much honor, sir. [*With priestly humility to Larry*] Mr Doyle: I am to blame for having unintentionally set your mind somewhat on edge against me. I beg your pardon.

LARRY [*unimpressed and hostile*] I didnt stand on ceremony with you; you neednt stand on it with me. Fine manners and fine words are cheap in Ireland: you can keep both for my friend here, who is still imposed on by them. *I* know their value.

KEEGAN. You mean you dont know their value.

LARRY [*angrily*] I mean what I say.

KEEGAN [*turning quietly to the Englishman*] You see, Mr Broadbent, I only make the hearts of my countrymen harder when I preach to them: the gates of hell still prevail against me. I shall wish you good evening. I am better alone, at the Round Tower, dreaming of heaven. [*He goes up the hill*].

LARRY. Aye, thats it! there you are! dreaming! dreaming! dreaming! dreaming!

KEEGAN [*halting and turning to them for the last time*] Every dream is a prophecy: every jest is an earnest in the womb of Time.

BROADBENT [*reflectively*] Once, when I was a small kid, I dreamt I was in heaven. [*They both stare at him*]. It was a sort of pale blue satin place, with all the pious old ladies in our congregation sitting as if they were at a service; and there was some awful person in the study at the other side of the hall. I didnt enjoy it, you know. What is it like in your dreams?

KEEGAN. In my dreams it is a country where the State is the Church and the Church the people: three in one and one in three. It is a commonwealth in which work is play and play is life: three in one and one in three. It is a temple in which the priest is the worshipper and the worshipper the worshipped: three in one and one in three. It is a godhead in which all life is human and all humanity divine: three in one and one in three. It is, in short, the dream of a madman. [*He goes away across the hill*].

BROADBENT [*looking after him affectionately*] What a regular old Church and State Tory he is! He's a character: he'll be an attraction here. Really almost equal to Ruskin and Carlyle.

LARRY. Yes; and much good they did with all their talk!

BROADBENT. Oh tut, tut, Larry! They improved my mind: they raised my tone enormously. I feel sincerely obliged to Keegan: he has made me feel a better man: distinctly better. [*With sincere elevation*] I feel now as I never did before that I am right in devoting my life to the cause of Ireland. Come along and help me to choose the site for the hotel.

To the Audience
at the Kingsway Theatre

A Personal Appeal from the Author of
John Bull's Other Island

Dear Sir or Madam,

It is your custom to receive my plays with the most generous and unrestrained applause. You sometimes compel the performers to pause at the end of every line until your laughter has quieted down. I am not ungrateful; but may I ask you a few questions?

Are you aware that you would get out of the Theatre half an hour earlier if you listened to the play in silence and did not applaud until the fall of the curtain?

Do you really consider that a performance is improved by continual interruptions, however complimentary they may be to the actors and the author?

Do you not think that the naturalness of the pre-presentation must be destroyed, and therefore your own pleasure greatly diminished, when the audience insists on taking part in it by shouts of applause and laughter, and the actors have repeatedly to stop acting until the noise is over?

Have you considered that in all good plays tears and laughter lie very close together, and that it must be very distressing to an actress who is trying to keep her imagination fixed on pathetic emotions to hear bursts of laughter breaking out at something she is supposed to be unconscious of?

Do you know that even when there is no such conflict of comic and tragic on the stage, the strain of performing is greatly increased if the performers have to attend to the audience as well as to their parts at the same time?

Can you not imagine how a play which has been rehearsed to perfection in dead silence without an audience must be upset, disjointed, and spun out to a wearisome length by an audience which refuses to enjoy it silently?

Have you noticed that if you laugh loudly and repeatedly for two hours, you get tired and cross, and are sorry next morning that you did not stay at home?

Will you think me very ungrateful and unkind if I tell you that though you cannot possibly applaud my plays too much at each fall of the curtain to please me, yet the more applause there is during the performance the angrier I feel with you for spoiling your enjoyment and my own?

Would you dream of stopping the performance of a piece of music to applaud every bar that happened to please you? and do you not know that an act of a play is intended, just like a piece of music, to be heard without interruption from beginning to end?

Have you ever told your sons and daughters that little children should be seen and not heard? And have you ever thought how nice theatrical performances would be, and how much sooner you would get away to supper, if parents in the theatre would follow the precepts they give to their children at home?

Have you noticed that people look very nice when they smile or look pleased, but look shockingly ugly when they roar with laughter or shout excitedly or sob loudly? Smiles make no noise.

Do you know that what pleases actors and authors most is not your applauding them but your coming to see the play again and again, and that if you tire yourselves out and spoil the play with interruptions you are very unlikely to come again?

Do you know that my plays, as rehearsed, are just the right length: that is, quite as long as you can bear; and that if you delay the performances by loud laughter you will make them half an hour too long?

Can I persuade you to let the performance proceed in perfect silence just this once to see how you like it. The intervals will give you no less than five opportunities of expressing your approval or disapproval, as the case may be.

And finally, will you believe me to be acting sincerely in your own interests in this matter as

your faithful servant,

THE AUTHOR.

New Year, 1913

Author's Note

(From the programme of the production at the
Regent Theatre, London, 15 February 1926)

John Bull's Other-Island was written in 1904, when the Irish Free State
was unborn and undreamt of, and when Liberals like Mr Thomas Broadbent, still smarting from their recent unpopularity as pro-Boers, were
ardent advocates of Home Rule for Ireland, the emancipation of
Macedonia from the Turkish yoke, and, generally, an implacable resistance to oppression everywhere except at home. They believed that freedom would come to Ireland from the Gladstonian tradition; and if an
enchanter had shown them in a magic mirror the Easter rebellion, the
ruins of bombarded Dublin, the sanguinary campaign in which the Black-
and-Tans and Sinn Fein tried which could burn most houses until
Michael Collins won, and the armistice which established the Irish Free
State only to inaugurate a purely Irish civil war in which every bridge
in Ireland was broken, they would have regarded that enchanter as the
most ridiculous romancer that ever showed the grossest ignorance of the
modern, sensible, matter-of-fact, parliamentary world he was living in.
As to these events passing almost unnoticed in England because England
was fighting hard for her own life, and Broadbent's and several other
London houses had been blown to bits by the bombs of a foreign enemy,
that would have seemed too silly to be even funny.

The play you are about to see takes you back to that state of innocence
and false security. As no attempt has been made to bring it up to date,
the younger members of the audience must listen as patiently as they
can to Mr Broadbent delivering a few speeches which will make them
wonder what on earth he is talking about. But, in the main, human nature,
though it has changed its catchwords a little, is very much what it was
then. There are still Rosscullens in Ireland and still Broadbents in
England. I do not believe there is a single character in the play that you
may not find today not perceptibly different from what he or she was
then. The Macdona Players therefore present the play just as it was,
feeling confident that its few discrepancies with the world just as it is

will not prevent you from enjoying it, and may even add to your amusement.

G. B. S.